Praise for

Breaking the Rock

"In suspenseful detail, Babyak describes the course of events leading up to the fateful telephone call received by her father on the morning of June 12. . . . essential for all crime collections."

—*Library Journal*

"In Breaking the Rock, the actual escape is a thrilling, chilling crescendo after the chicanery and intrigue leading up to it."

—Anneli Rufus, *East Bay Express*

"Numerous interviews with inmates and guards who knew the escapees, extensive investigation and Babyak's personal interest in and access to the events distinguish this account."

—*Publisher's Weekly*

"Jolene Babyak has created a riveting historical account of one of the world's greatest escapes that reads like the best hard-boiled crime fiction. She takes us inside the minds of the criminals and jailers and reveals intimate details never before disclosed. Absolutely fascinating."

—Sarah Kass, Producer/Director, "Beneath Alcatraz" & "Public Enemies on The Rock," Michael Hoff Productions

"Babyak is an astute observer and a tireless researcher. . . . Her account of the Great Escape is fresh and insightful, a portrait of a time and place that are part of our national psyche."

—Jay Wurts, coauthor of *Honored and Betrayed, Irangate, Covet Affairs and the Secret War in Laos*

"Jolene Babyak gives her readers a blow-by-blow account of the 'escape of the century.' Nobody knows the heart and soul of Alcatraz like Babyak."

—*Philip Carlo, author of The Night Stalker, The Life and Crimes of Richard Ramirez*

BREAKING THE ROCK

The Great Escape
from Alcatraz

Other Books by
Jolene Babyak

Eyewitness on Alcatraz

Birdman:
The Many Faces of Robert Stroud

Alcatraz Most Wanted:
*Profiles of the Most Famous
Prisoners on the Rock*

BREAKING
THE
ROCK

The Great Escape
from Alcatraz

Jolene Babyak

Ariel Vamp Press
Berkeley, California

Library of Congress Catalog Card Number: 00-192457
Cataloging-in-Publication Data
1. Alcatraz Federal Penitentiary 1934-1963. 2. Prisons-United States-
Federal-Alcatraz. 3. Escape attempts, Federal prisons, Alcatraz.

Babyak, Jolene
Breaking the Rock: The Great Escape from Alcatraz
Includes photographs, bibliographical references and index.

ISBN: 0-9618752-3-2

Cover design by George Mattingly,
Front cover photograph by Ira Bowden,
courtesy of Don Bowden.
Back cover photograph courtesy of the
National Maritime Museum Library.
The author is grateful for permission to quote lines from
"Jailhouse Rock"
© 1957 (Renewed) Words and Music by JERRY LEIBER MUSIC
and MIKE STOLLER MUSIC, All Rights Reserved.

Printed in the United States of America.

Ariel Vamp Press
P.O. Box 3496
Berkeley, CA 94703

To
the L.T.M.

CONTENTS

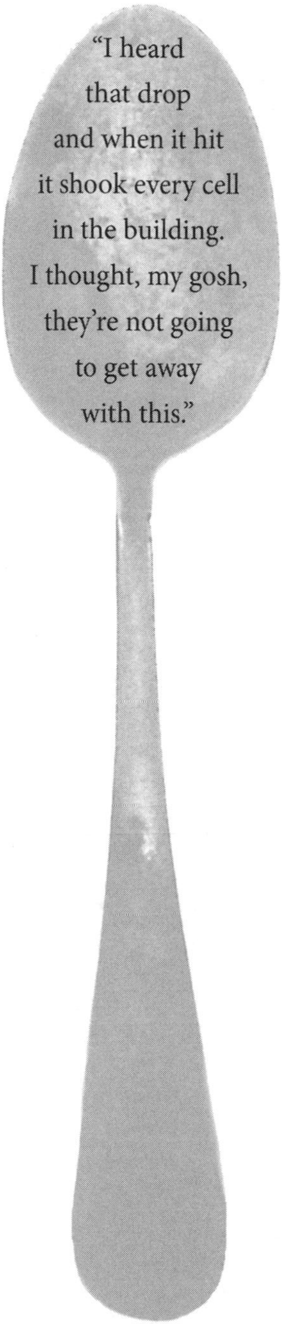

"I heard
that drop
and when it hit
it shook every cell
in the building.
I thought, my gosh,
they're not going
to get away
with this."

Introduction

DID THEY MAKE IT?

Sure—*off Alcatraz Island.* That much we know.

The rest of it—the facts, the evasions and the cover-ups that made up the initial investigation; the telephone calls, postcards and letters, which masqueraded as evidence; the sightings of men on a raft, of men resembling the escapees in New Orleans, Washington D.C., Rio de Janeiro and Canada; the alleged appearance of mysteriously veiled, heavily made-up women, or bearded men, who showed up at family funerals; the movie myths, the urban myths, and the rumors of boat pickups based on little but a con's nod—have all made the 1962 escape from Alcatraz one of the most enduring mysteries of the twentieth century.

And it all began for me at my house on Alcatraz Island at 7:15 A.M. on June 12 when the telephone rang with a shrill, angry summons.

The institution's phone was one of those old, stand-up, cradled black phones hardwired into the wall with a heavy, nappy cord. My father, Arthur M. Dollison, eight months into his new job as associate warden, had been "acting warden" for almost two weeks while Warden Olin G. Blackwell was away on vacation. Dad stepped to the desk and reached for the phone with dread. He knew it couldn't be good news. He listened as the control room officer said that three dummy masks had been found in the cell house. Uttering a profanity I had never heard fall from his lips, he stormed out of the house, and put into motion one of the largest manhunts since the 1932 Charles Lindbergh baby kidnapping.

I was fifteen that summer and upstairs still asleep. Within seconds of my father's departure from our house, a loud, piercing siren woke me. I tumbled down the stairs as my mother met me, telling me to get dressed—there had been an escape. I was thrilled; I was going to be late for school but I had a terrific excuse.

VIEWED FROM A Landsat camera, San Francisco Bay barely shows up. But forty percent of California's waterways drain into it—mostly snow runoff from the Sierra Mountains gushing down fourteen tributaries into the Sacramento and San Joaquin Rivers. These rivers in turn drain into the bay and eventually mix with the tides flowing under the Golden Gate Bridge and out into the Pacific Ocean.

If you place your left hand in front of your face, fingers together, palm away, your thumb becomes the peninsula of the city of San Francisco. Alcatraz Island would only be a millimeter from your thumbnail. Most people wonder how the most maximum-security federal prison in the United States gained its "escape proof" reputation when it's so close to San Francisco you could almost reach out and touch it. In fact, it's only a mile and a quarter from the city. But if your thumb is San Francisco, then your index finger would be the Golden Gate Bridge, three miles from Alcatraz, and the rest of your hand would be the Pacific Ocean. Someone standing ninety-seven feet from you with his right hand in front of his face would represent the next piece of land. That would be Hawaii.

Alcatraz is a twenty-two acre, battleship-shaped rock, made out of sandstone. Tides flow across its port and starboard sides on their way to and from the Pacific Ocean.

Continuing with our hand geography, if you take your right hand, palm away, and form a loose triangle with your thumbs and index fingers, your right hand becomes the East Bay—Oakland, Berkeley and beyond. The bridge that connects San Francisco to the East Bay— The San Francisco–Oakland Bay Bridge—is three miles from Alcatraz, but land on that side can be as far as eight miles away.

Meaning that if you swim from Alcatraz to San Francisco you'd better pick slack tide—the quiet time between the tides when the sea is neither rushing into the bay for high tide nor cascading out resulting in low tide. That's the moment when the ferocious currents, the speed and the angle are the most beneficial for swimming to land. And if it's your first time swimming San Francisco Bay you'd better wear a cap, and maybe a wet suit, because the bay's temperature runs a close second in risk factor behind the tides. It's a cold, cold bay—about forty-eight to fifty-four degrees Fahrenheit, or nine to twelve degrees Celsius, year around. Some good swimmers cannot tolerate being in the bay more than forty-five minutes before they are so chilled they must get out, their body temperature so low they begin to feel the affects of hypothermia. Yet despite that, every year hundreds of people swim from Alcatraz to San Francisco in two large, friendly meets. Those prisoners *could* have made it. That much we also know.

And between those two possibilities lies a story that I felt compelled to examine.

"Did they make it?" is the most commonly asked question at the National Park on Alcatraz today. And there are strong arguments for both answers. But that's never been the most compelling question for me. How did they do it? How did they amass all the tools and keep them hidden for months? How did they dig through concrete without the holes being discovered? How did they turn common prison clothing into life jackets and a raft? The 1962 escape from Alcatraz remains one of the most well-planned and elaborate escape attempts in U.S. history. How did my father; the captain who lived next door to us; the lieutenants, whose children were friends of mine; and the officers, whose lives and the lives of their families depended on their vigilance, not see this escape coming?

In researching this book I discovered that two parallel stories existed. There was the escape, of course, with all its fascinating, cunning details, but there was another story as equally determined. And like railroad tracks moving toward a vanishing point, the two stories converged in an almost fated way that broke "the Rock."

THE READER WILL see that I have taken some liberties in telling this story. Although I have been interviewing Alcatraz officers and prisoners since 1978, by the time I began to research this book all the principals were dead or missing. And because other men who were close to the escapees or worked inside the prison didn't participate in the attempt, nor see the work being done, nor view some of the handmade products, nor always tell the truth, I had to distinguish between facts, rumors, lies, and myths. One of my first challenges, for example, was translating the common words used by the informants, and the original investigators, to describe the tools used and the methods incorporated to break out of the building. In the end, I not only relied on the investigative reports, prisoner files, original photographs and interviews with men who were there, but also the expert advice of hardware store owners, glue manufacturers, float makers, crime scene investigators, coast guard officers, museum ethnographic conservators, vacuum cleaner engineers and thread manufacturers.

It was not possible to know which of the four men proposed each idea during the course of their planning stage, nor even, to know the sequence of their decisions. But once I became familiar with the plan and its inevitable outcome, as well as the physical evidence, a logical sequence began to emerge.

The reader will see that italics are used to suggest what the principals might have said in furthering their plan. Quotes, however, are only used when derived from interviews or files. Although facts and dates are culled from files, the reader may also see that conjecture is sometimes a part of the story, ideas based not on hope, but analysis of information from many sources.

Ultimately, I wanted to treat this escape attempt like an archeological discovery, pulling the facts out of the slag heap of myths to tell an age-old exciting tale. But mostly, I wanted to satisfy my own curiosity about a spectacular event that came at the tail end of my father's career and was the very kernel of mine.

~~~~~

U. S. PENITENTIARY
ALCATRAZ
1335

Part 1

The Man

"WOULD YOU BE interested in leaving this place?" Allen West asked the library orderly as he stopped in front of West's cell. The prisoner pulled a magazine from his stack and slipped it between the bars.

"Szh—," he replied. "You have to ask me that?"

West tossed the magazine onto his cot. *I got an idea*, he said.

"And right away I got leery," the orderly said years later, "because I know West and too many people know his business." But he patiently listened as West began divulging his latest scheme.

They were standing on the third tier of "C" block near the prison's library in the nation's most maximum-security federal prison. If the orderly's memory is accurate, it was a sliver of time in which West was housed in one of the main cell blocks during his last years on the Rock, rather than in "D" block—the high-security wing known as the "Treatment Unit," or "TU," to officers and "seg," "solitary" or "the hole" to cons.

D block was the punishment wing for men who had racked up assaults, knifings, murders or escape attempts. D block men remained in their cells almost twenty-four hours a day; they ate in their cells. Some went to the yard, but on opposite days of men in the main population. West's behavior in 1960 had earned him a lot of seg time. But just now he was out of D and, as yet, unassigned to a job. The main blocks were not as noisy as D, especially this morning when most guys were out working. But you could hear cons calling out chess plays, or others talking sports. It was "like living in a drum," the orderly said. He and West kept their voices low.

West was always looking for an escape, always talking about escape. He didn't differ from anyone else on Alcatraz in that respect, but he had told so many escape stories—such fantastic tales—that it was hard to believe he was anything but talk. A man of such low self-esteem, perhaps, that he needed to keep the focus on himself. Or—a man in search of the perfect idea.

A hot-wired, self-absorbed enfant terrible, Allen West was short, wiry, with flared nostrils, sneering lips and a hard Georgia drawl. He was thirty-one years old. According to his file, he had an eighth-grade education, had survived mostly on car theft and breaking and entering and was arrested twenty times over the course of his life. Convicted of eight felonies and involved in multiple escape attempts, self-mutilation, stabbings and eventually, a prison killing, he was doing, as they say, life on the installment plan.

Inside, he was a racist and an agitator, often found whipping up anger in the middle of loan sharking schemes, racial tension and prison power struggles. "He was a bullshit artist," Thomas A. Kent, AZ 1443, said. "Quick to start an argument over nothin'." West was so explosive, in fact, that out of fifteen hundred and seventy-six registered prisoners who eventually served time on Alcatraz, he was one of about thirty-five who was there twice.

Although he was on a ten-year sentence for transporting stolen vehicles across state lines, that doesn't begin to describe his treachery. According to the Alcatraz warden's file card, West had escaped from a Florida state prison by aiming a gun at the associate warden's head. *Then* he stole the AW's car.

"Go-convict all the way," Officer William "Bill" Rogers, a five-year Alcatraz veteran, described him.

West was so boastful about his exploits, however, that it was difficult to ferret out the truth. He told one examiner that he had once injected sour cream into his hand to make it swell so that he could get into the hospital where the chances of escape were better. He told another officer that after swiping the associate warden's car he drove into Georgia, where "according to the FBI report" he and the Georgia state police shot it out in a gun battle. But he added that he didn't know *nothin' about that.*

He once bragged to the library orderly that he'd escaped from a jail cell by enticing sparrows with food to fly up to his window. After days of training the birds to come to his window, he tied a long thread he had unraveled from a bed sheet to a morsel of food, and when a bird scooped up the morsel, it pulled the thread to a nearby tree. West had already talked an outside worker into attaching a key to the thread for West to haul in.

Big story. *Good* story. But if he was so good, why was Allen West still behind bars?

"West was a big talker," said former prisoner, Herb "Lucky" Juelich, AZ 1190. "Con this, con that. He tried to maintain his life there by trying to con everybody."

Juelich killed a U.S. Marshal and had been on Alcatraz since July 1955, long enough to spot the big mouths. Everyone talked about escape—it was the number one topic on Alcatraz. Even Juelich dreamed of constructing a hot-air balloon and floating up to the sky—the only free space anyone could see. Somehow taking his chances in a rather large, slow-moving target seemed more appealing than diving into the San Francisco Bay. Because it was the bay that was the ultimate obstacle. Although security on Alcatraz was notoriously high—about one officer to every three prisoners—it was the turbulent, moody, fifty-degree bay with its unforgiving tides that gave the prison its "escape proof" description. It looked to some like an easy swim. But you couldn't spend more than three days on the Rock before realizing that you probably didn't have what it took to swim it.

Most cons were not serious about escaping; it was just an academic pursuit. The difference was that Allen West was constantly recruiting men to his wild schemes like he really meant it. One of his ideas involved overpowering a yard wall officer, obtaining guns and taking over the prison yard. After weeks of talking it up, he abandoned it as too risky. Now he was on to a new game plan. As he whispered through the bars, the orderly saw that he was becoming more animated, gripping the bars, *selling* his idea.

He outlined a plan that involved escaping from a ceiling vent.

The library orderly wasn't surprised at the idea; he'd always thought a vent over in "A" block was the best one to go out of. *Fact, I have a diagram of a key to an A block door,* he said. Block A was seldom used to house prisoners, and now mostly used for storage. West argued with him. *B's the vent,* he said. The orderly didn't want to stand there arguing the point. He shrugged and moved on, but he glanced sideways back at West. Although he

Carnes as he appeared about 1961.

didn't dismiss West's idea out of hand, he knew he didn't stand a chance if he got involved. Still, he'd heard enough to think it might be an intoxicating idea.

The library orderly, Clarence Carnes, was a thirty-three-year-old, full-blooded Choctaw Indian from Oklahoma who had been behind bars every day since he was fifteen. Convicted of kidnapping and transferred to Alcatraz because of a couple of escape attempts (one involving hijacking a car and taking its occupant across state lines), Carnes had arrived on Alcatraz in 1945, at age eighteen, as number AZ 714. He had a ninety-nine year sentence, complicated with other offenses and wouldn't parole out until the year 2049.

He promptly got involved in the bloody 1946 "Battle of Alcatraz," a spectacularly stupid escape attempt involving officers and hostages in which two guards and three cons were killed. Two other cons were later executed. Only Carnes' life was spared because of his age. But he paid dearly for that lucky break; rumors circulated for years that he had ratted his way out of the gas chamber, and cons and even guards hated him for it. Some cons wouldn't speak to him. But West would approach anybody who could advance his ideas. And Carnes was a man with access. As the library orderly, he pushed a little cart around the cell house; he could move things around without officers knowing it.

But that Carnes got even a little involved with West and his escape attempt was both fortunate and lamentable; Carnes told stories and over the years some of those stories moved from fanciful to "fact," making it difficult to untangle the strands of truth and myth. Carnes was initially intrigued by West's idea, and would come to call West a remarkable man in his own devious way. And it was true.

"I don't think you could find anybody in that institution that would have attempted what West did," Carnes told me years later, "because they could see a dozen ways it was going to fail."

Guys like Allen West, and even Clarence Carnes, seldom left the cell house except to go to the yard. They never sat in the back of a pickup truck on their way to and from the dock detail or an outside maintenance crew, waving to the staff kids who lived on Alcatraz. I never saw West. Nor did our fathers talk about him and his foolish tricks. When the staff meandered down the hill after work they wanted to forget guys like West. Even cons were wary of him. It was difficult for anyone to defend himself against West because he could stoop lower than anyone wanted to go. He didn't walk, cons had said, he slithered.

No one would have even remembered Allen West. He would have been just another anonymous Alcatraz thug if it hadn't been for what he would do—orchestrate one of the most fantastic escape attempts in U.S. history. But how he got that far by 1960— thinking about breaking out of the nation's most secure prison— was a story in of itself.

2

ART DOLLISON ALSO looked around, wondering if there was anything else he could change. By 1960, he'd been superintendent of Alcatraz industries for a year, and a year before that, acting superintendent. The industries shops, located in a long building down the hill from the prison's yard, were where the majority of prisoners worked. Dollison had made significant changes in industries which had improved working conditions for cons and boosted production and profits. Now he was asking himself if this was going to be the peak of his career.

Quiet, remote, principled and modest, Dollison was the exact opposite of Allen West, a fact that began with their very ages. At fifty-one, he was old enough to be West's father, a difference that was amplified in any prison setting. The older men thought cons acted like seven year olds. Cons thought men like Dollison tried to be their father, a relationship that was flawed from the git-go.

There were other differences. The prison administrator had

Art Dollison had been superintendent of industries.

thinning white hair, a ruddy complexion, cobalt blue eyes and ham-sized hands. He usually wore gray or dark suits—never blue or pinstripe suits, which he would have considered too flashy. In fact his only nod to frivolity seemed to be the bow ties he frequently wore, which gave the industires superintendent a gleeful look. Moreover, unlike West and the other cons, he had done everything right in life, even when things had gone badly for him.

The only child of a small town Ohio newspaper editor, Arthur M. Dollison graduated from Ohio Weslyan University in business administration in 1933, a bad year. A series of poorly paying jobs during the depression eventually led him to apply for a position in 1938 as a guard at the U.S. Penitentiary at Leavenworth, Kansas. Leavenworth was a large prison housing more than three thousand men. But the job was a permanent government position, and he had a wife and two kids to support. Unfortunately, at five-feet-ten inches tall, he weighed only a hundred and thirty-eight pounds and didn't satisfy the weight requirement. They gave him a week to gain it, but he didn't gain an ounce. On the day of the physical, desperate and determined, he sat in front of the penitentiary and stuffed down pounds and pounds of bananas. He walked out the gate with the job, green in more ways than one.

Later, after serving in the army during World War II, he transferred into Federal Prison Industries and worked in prisons in Ashland, Kentucky, where I was born, and Terre Haute, Indiana, until he arrived on the Rock in December 1953.

Although Dad was apprehensive about working in the infamous penitentiary, our family was ecstatic about moving to San Francisco. After my mother sold our house in Indiana, my sister, brother and I flew to California in April 1954. I was seven years old, a tiny, big-haired, gun-totin' tomboy. For now, because toy guns and even water pistols were forbidden on Alcatraz, my guns and my prized Annie Oakley cowgirl getup would remain in storage.

San Francisco was not like Terre Haute. It was a big, bustling port city with stunning views, a colorful, glamorous and eccentric population, huge hotels with costumed doormen who whistled up yellow cabs with their high-pitched pipes, and two magnificent bridges, one of which, the Golden Gate, was perhaps the most famous bridge in the world.

Not only did I get my first airplane ride to a world-class city, but then we got on a boat that bucked and kicked its way to Alcatraz Island, a mile and a quarter away. I stepped off the boat and ran up a short gangplank, landing on the dock of the most famous prison island in the world.

Surprisingly, about sixty-five families already lived there. Although our apartment in the old army barracks known as "Sixty-four building" which rose from the dock, was dark and depressingly ugly, and just down the hill from the prison, I was thrilled to be living in a neighborhood with seventy-five other kids, on an island with a sweeping view of San Francisco and her lovely bridges. Nearly everyone had come from dingy prison towns in the midwest and the south. Alcatraz felt, as one woman put it, like a "poor man's Hawaii." I soon made friends, hopped on the boat to go to school in San Francisco and made myself right at home. Although the "no guns" rule was difficult during the Roy Rogers–Dale Evans era we learned to fashion popsicle sticks and rubber bands into implements for playing "guards and cons."

Half the staff lived in buildings around the parade ground at right. The prison is at the top, its yard, center, and the industries building is the long structure at the left.

I soon grew to understand a little about my father's job. Prison industries was a separate department within the federal Bureau of Prisons (BOP). It paid prisoners to make products, such as gloves, brushes and clothing, sold to the institution and to other government agencies. Its outside-of-security status, especially at Alcatraz, was blatantly obvious; the industries' supervisor was often left out of the decision-making loop. And on Alcatraz, industries was ignored as a financial tool as well.

When the island was converted from a U.S. Army prison into a federal prison in 1934, the moribund, inefficient army industries was simply folded into the federal. Many of the employees also transferred over, thus insuring that things remained the same. When Dollison arrived in 1953 as assistant office manager, prisoners had little incentive; the shops operated below capacity and the laundry, the biggest shop which required a huge supply of water to be imported, insured that little profits were made. Even the weather could affect profits; if the fog was too thick, cons remained in their cells. Thus, industries often couldn't fulfill its government contracts on time.

When Dollison became superintendent in 1957–58, he persuaded the prison to take over the laundry and reduce its service to the island. Then he had the building remodeled and enlarged the more profitable glove, brush and clothing factories. He placed more prisoners on a piece-rate pay scale (the more pieces, the more pay), and began awarding prisoners meritorious "good time," or time off their sentence, as added incentive. To get more military contracts, he invited army officers to tour Alcatraz (until a plot involving hostages was uncovered). He hired inmate barbers to cut hair in the shops, so he wouldn't lose productivity. He had drinking fountains installed, and was even considering background music. That he'd even been permitted to make such radical changes on Alcatraz was a testimony to his idealism and pragmatism, as well as a measure of how modern the prison had become. According to the island newsletter, the *Foghorn,* industries went from a net profit of $3,500 in 1958 to a whopping $69,500 the next year.

Yet, years later, Warden Olin G. Blackwell referred to him as a "a reasonably good business manager," a comment which would have left my father bewildered and a little chagrined.

A listener, with an even-handed analytical sense, my father's initial reaction to con tricks was bemused detachment. But he could quickly harden into dogmatic finger-tapping when he felt people had stepped over a moral line. He was skeptical of people's stated good intentions, a result perhaps of the job, but he could also be a touch naïve, a quality that led to a lifelong, almost childlike sense of curiosity. He'd been the only child of stern parents and his ability to relate on a deeply personal level, like many men of his generation, was limited. He seemed most tender with dogs or cats whom he treated with patience and wonder—traits my brother, sister and I felt were sometimes lacking when it came to his relationships with us. He was surprised by the violence he sometimes saw at work, but he didn't bring it home with him.

"Your father never smiled—he grinned," said Benjamin Rayborn, AZ 1028, a con who worked closely with him in industries for many years. "But when he grinned, you knew you'd done good."

OUR FAMILY LIVED on Alcatraz for the first two years after my father began working there. By late 1955, my parents felt financially able to move into San Francisco, where they bought a house in a nearby suburb. Five years later, by 1960, I was in the eighth grade, a kid who moved from cap pistols to burning softballs into my dad's baseball mitt. I cared little about his job on Alcatraz and he never talked much about it. Instead, we talked about baseball, and frequently went to San Francisco Giants games. One of my fondest memories was of a day we spent together in the backyard, just before we moved back to Alcatraz, listening to a San Francisco–Milwaukee game in which Willie Mays hit four home runs.

I had never thought about his safety on Alcatraz. Maybe I inherited some of his naïveté because it never crossed my mind that he could be beaten or stabbed. Nor did it occur to me in 1960 that we would soon be living on the island again. But Dad was restless for new challenges. When a Washington auditor visited Alcatraz, my father had asked if his current position was as high as he could go. Never did I imagine that events were to transpire so much that he would become a bit player in one of the world's most spectacular escape attempts. Or that his story could illustrate how bad things happen when men of integrity remain silent.

3

ALLEN WEST, ON the other hand, arrived on the dreaded island prison by doing everything wrong.

He was sadly typical of men confined there whose files were replete with parental abuse, alcoholism and abandonment. Born in New York City on March 25, 1929, he was the third of four children of Roland and Marie West. His father had lost a leg in World War I, and was said to be an embittered alcoholic. During the depression the family moved to the less genteel side of Savannah, Georgia, where he worked periodically as a mechanic, an electrician and a machinist, mostly whittling away his paychecks on liquor. According to West, the family often had to flee for their safety or suffer beatings.

Maybe it was true that West broke into his first car for a place to sleep. Maybe when they hauled him into the police station one of the cops tried to counsel the eleven year old. Tried to warn him away from a life of crime; give him a second chance. After all, even cops had alcoholic fathers. But within a year he became known as a cocky, manipulative kid who never tired of trying to lie his way out of jams, and they lost interest in helping him. From their viewpoint he had turned from hooligan into thug.

By age fourteen, in 1943, he was serving time in the Georgia State Farm for Boys for car theft. He escaped three times.

The next year, for stealing another car, he received six months in Georgia state prison at Reidsville, an adult state prison. Burglary and auto theft that fall got him two-to-five years again at Reidsville. He remained three. West was a tiny, tough punk about five feet seven inches. He fit right in. At Reidsville, he picked up a morphine habit, and frequently scored Nembutal and phenobarbital tablets.

West eventually got out and took what may have been the only job in his life, working as an electrician's helper for four months in the Savannah, Georgia shipyards. Then at nineteen, in December 1948, he enlisted in the army. But he couldn't maintain. Soon after basic training he was arrested and charged with sodomy and absent without leave (AWOL). Court-martialed, he was given four years, dishonorably discharged in June 1949, and transferred to the federal prison at Lewisburg, Pennsylvania. After several racial incidents there, the associate warden described him as "one of our most aggressive racial agitators," and he was transferred to the U.S. Penitentiary at Atlanta, Georgia.

Atlanta was a maximum security federal joint. Known among cons as the "Big Top," it was, along with the U.S. Penitentiary at Leavenworth, Kansas, the last stop before Alcatraz. In January 1951, officers found a diagram of the prison's roof in his possession. West denied it was his, then claimed it was a diagram of an apartment roof. To other accusations, he responded with a barrage of bragging defenses. "I don't know nothin' about those explosives," he said, his leg bobbing with nervous excitement. But then, he couldn't resist: "I know they're made out of sulfur and pressed in nuts. You can use celluloid shavings, scratch 'em off with a razor blade. You got to throw it real hard to make it go off." Punishment never altered his behavior, a checkpoint characteristic of a psychopathic personality.

West was released in October 1951, and nailed again the following March in St. Petersburg, Florida, for breaking and

USPA ▬ 70385 ▬ 7 26 50

West in Atlanta the first time.

entering and grand larceny. He was sentenced in May for four years at Florida State Prison in Raiford, a tough chain-gang prison, which West described as his "first rough, raw deal."

He bragged to a federal examiner that he killed a prisoner at Raiford and later regretted it. "I never completely recovered from this," he claimed. "I guess I decided then to join the tide—not to fight it—and let the chips fall." But there was no record of his killing anyone at Raiford at this time.

West escaped from Raiford the day after Christmas in 1952. A month later, he was picked up in Vicksburg, Mississippi for crossing state lines in a stolen vehicle. Records show he was packing a machine gun and a sawed-off shotgun. That got him five years on a federal charge. He escaped from Mississippi authorities and was arrested a month later on a burglary beef in Meridian, Texas. By now he had racked up an auto theft charge, crossing state lines with stolen goods, two escapes and a state burglary charge. He got five years on a federal charge and a second trip to Atlanta. It was June 1953 and he was barely twenty-five years old.

At Atlanta that year, he had to be segregated four times, once for strong arm activities, once for assaulting a Puerto Rican prisoner. The staff had had enough. They requested that he be transferred to Alcatraz. The BOP in Washington D.C. approved his transfer.

West arrived on the Rock the same month as I did as a seven year old in April 1954.

He hobbled up the gangplank with twenty-six other cons from Atlanta and Leavenworth. Among them was an already well-known black prisoner named Ellsworth "Bumpy" Johnson, AZ 1117, an infamous narcotics wholesaler from Harlem, and Larry Trumblay, AZ 1129, on a twenty-five-year jolt for bank robbery. "Trump," as he would become known, smoked three packs of cigarettes a day, had six bullet wounds in his body, and would one day be caught sticking shards of glass in a bowl of cooked carrots. Both men would become involved with West.

Having traveled by train across the nation handcuffed with waist chains, and leg irons chained to each other, they would have appeared a deflated,

On Alcatraz at age twenty-five.

weary bunch when they arrived, missing the usual tough-con strut. None of them said much as they waited on the dock. A few shivered in the cold, wet fog that enveloped the island. Above them, on the balcony of the looming apartment building, two housewives leaned over the railing, smoking cigarettes and watching the cons being loaded onto a small bus. Soon the women would hear the gears grinding on the old bus as it managed each hairpin turn up the steep incline to the top of the island.

Once at the prison, the men hobbled off the bus one by one and were escorted into the basement shower and clothing room. Officers were cordial but perfunctory; no one wanted any trouble. After West's wrists were uncuffed, he rubbed them to ease the soreness. They stripped, showered, were examined and given a set of freshly laundered clothing—nickel gray chambray work shirts, navy dungarees, shoes and socks—and cell supplies. After they put on their clothing, officers began escorting them up the stairs. West was twenty-five. His dark hair was beginning to recede. He'd been behind bars for nine years and he was now Alcatraz number 1130.

HE SAW RIGHT away what he'd always heard: Alcatraz was not like other joints. It was tiny and a lot cleaner. While both Atlanta and Leavenworth held two to three thousand men, Alcatraz averaged only about two hundred and sixty—or about *one percent* of the twenty-five thousand men then in federal prisons. The Bureau had skimmed off the worst one percent—not because of their crimes but because of their behavior in other prisons.

As West stood by the west end desk getting his cell assignment, he looked down the main corridor known as "Broadway," on either side of which were the two main cell blocks, B and C, which were three tiers high. To his right was a wall behind which was the D segregation block, an area with which he would eventually become very familiar. Above and behind him was an armed guard locked inside the west gun gallery, which extended the width of the building. That man was stone faced and watchful, protecting the officers on the floor. All the way down Broadway, near the main gate, was another gun cage high on the wall, known as the east gun gallery. West thought he could see a man there, his rifle in hand. Being a seasoned con, West betrayed no feeling. His gaze dropped to the floor, a high polished concrete so spit shined he could lick ice cream off it and never scratch his trongue.

West was taken up the stairs to the second tier. A cell overlooking Broadway was cocked open and then closed behind him with a loud, rolling thunder. These were the least desirable cells because everyone across the aisle could see what you were doing. This is where they put the new "fish." His cell was bare except for a cot, a sink with one cold faucet, a toilet and a small folding metal table and bench riveted into the wall.

He had nothing to do that first night. He didn't even have a cell mate. On Alcatraz, although the mattresses stank like urine and he could touch both walls with his arms outstretched, it was what West would have called a *friggin' luxury apartment:* one man to a cell.

He dumped his stuff on his cot, turned and looked out his bars. His whole world now consisted of a foreshortened view of stacked cells across an aisle. Each man was illuminated by a single bulb in the middle of his ceiling. Some were calling out to each other. Some were sitting on their cots, writing or reading. One con flushed his toilet. It was a familiar, other-worldly scene. His cockines began to return.

Gripping the bars he spoke to the man in the cell next to him. *Got a cigarette?*

Nope, the voice called out, *don't smoke. And don't do no favors neither.*

Then a bell rang, and what was laughingly called the "music hour" began. Men snapped open their musical instrument cases. West heard guitars beginning to strum. Then an accordion wheezed open. Somewhere a violin started screeching out a children's ditty, painful and awkward, the notes coming hesitatingly and flat. "Mary Had a Little Lamb."West fell onto his cot and buried his head under a pillow.

ONE OF MY earliest memories on Alcatraz at age seven, as my mother was tucking me into bed, was a roar that came from the cell house. Sixty-four building was a stone's throw from the prison, just down the hill, and the roar sounded like that from a distant sports stadium when the home team scores. Men were raking their bars with their shaving cups, bouncing their bed frames, grabbing the bars and yelling out. It was a steady uproar and it seemed to last a long time.

My friends and me (in the hat) on Alcatraz in about 1954.

"What's that noise?" I asked, crinkling my nose.

Years later, Officer Bill Long told me that sometimes when a new group of cons arrived—say twenty-seven guys—all the others would put on a display, a sort of "welcoming party."

"Oh nothing," my mother said, "Just the prisoners letting off steam."

I can imagine now that West, or even my mother, slept little that night. I slept like a baby.

WITHIN A DAY Officer Jack Mitchell dropped by West's cell and slipped a rule book through the bars. West took it and looked back at him. Given to every con upon arrival, the regulations outlined expected conduct, disciplinary action, good time awards, the inmates' trust fund accounts, the clothing and dining room rules. But more importantly, it contained a drawing of a cell along with a diagram which detailed where every item was to be placed—shoes under the bed; cleaning powder and toilet paper on the tiny ledge in front of the air vent; sink stopper on the right of the sink; soap on the left. Musical instrument cases were stored under the bed. West would soon figure, and rightly so, that guards were fanatic about neat, orderly cells.

Read it, Mitchell said, *there'll be a test everyday.* He left.

So that was the famous Mitchell, West thought, his eyes narrowing. Known among cons as "Blue Boy," after a fat comic strip character, James T. "Jack" Mitchell was a gruff, at times overbearing, man who tipped the scales at two-fifty, sometimes ballooning to three hundred pounds. He was a coarse, fearless, unsentimental guard, with a voice that thundered like a bulldozer.

Mitchell's background, in some ways, was similar to the cons he guarded. In fact, Carnes once deadpanned, "People sensed—given a different set of clothes, 'Mitch' could be one of us."

Mitchell dropped out of school when he was about sixteen, "got the wanderlust," hopped a railroad car and began working as a "gandy dancer," repairing railroad ties for sixty cents a day. He quickly learned the difference between hobos and predators, and how to brawl his way in or out of trouble. While still underage, Mitchell joined the U.S. Marine Corps, eventually becoming a sergeant. Mitchell was a fearless Marine. In one incident in Saipan during World War II, in which he was overrun by enemy soldiers and wounded twice by a saber, he resorted to hand-to-hand combat and eventually choked his victim to death. Then, for more than five hours while under fire, he rescued six other wounded soldiers. He was decorated with the Navy Cross for this, the second highest medal in military service.

After the war ended, Mitchell quit the Marine Corps and landed in San Francisco where took a job in 1947 as a guard on Alcatraz. He moved his wife and three children onto the island, and also became known as "Jungle Jim." The only article ever written about children who lived on Alcatraz was a 1954 *Collier's* magazine issue with one of Mitchell's children on the cover.

Mitchell worked the periphery for only a few months before he was moved into the cell house. In 1955 he became a lieutenant and worked almost exclusively in the cell house.

"Alcatraz was run by *one* man," Juelich said, "and that was Lieutenant Mitchell. And he *ran* Alcatraz when I was there."

He ran it, in fact, like a Marine Corps drill sergeant, following the rules to the letter. Every man's cell was sparse with limited items all placed exactly where the rule book required. In those years, the cells were painted mint green, but the wall behind the faucet, sink, pipes and vent were painted a forest green; everything in front of them stood out in high relief.

Mitchell kept a little notebook in his pocket with every man's name, number, cell number and often his crime and sentence. He also kept track of everyone's property. "I knew everything every man had in his cell," he said with pride years later, " 'Cause I *looked* in his cell all the time. When anything was bought, they'd give it to me and I'd give it to the convict. We put it down on a property card. I had a card and the convict had a card. And, if he had something in his cell that wasn't supposed to be there—and it wasn't on my card—I knew it."

To him, it was simple: it was not what you gave cons or took away from them, it was controlling everything they did, and letting them know exactly who was in charge.

You got no trouble from Mitchell if you were a good boy. But if you hurled fists, obscenities or feces at him—or went off on him in any other violent way—you got trouble. He was big and tough, and part of the "goon squad," a loosely defined team that existed in all maximum security penitentiaries in those days to deal with emotionally immature, strong, violent males, feral catlike psychopaths and even the occasional hyper-vigilant schizophrenic.

"The biggest balls of any guy I ever met," said Juelich flatly. He saw Mitchell walk onto the prison yard one day during a race riot and roar to armed officers on the wall to shoot anyone who moved. The cons were so stunned they stopped dead in their tracks and the riot was done. Others talked of seeing "Mitch" jump between two fighting cons and spreading them. That impresses cons.

"Best prison officer that ever entered Alcatraz," a former captain of the guards, Philip R. Bergen, called him, "Never cheated, never lied, never took advantage, never brutalized anybody and never backed up from anybody."

But there was a rumor that Mitchell had once kicked a con down the stairs. In fact his other, more colorful name was "Ass Kicking Fats."

"He got a little rough in there," my father said.

When I first moved onto Alcatraz, Mitchell was the resident boogeyman. He was big, gruff, unsmiling—the guard, the kids all said, to avoid. Few of us knew that it was men like Mitchell who kept men like West under tight screws. But unfortunately, he would become known more for his rough tactics than his cell house supervision. Years later as an adult, I traveled several hundred miles to interview him, still feeling like a little kid. He was a little thuggish, and his diction was gangster tough. But he was direct, unabridged and perceptive.

Today, prison officers receive psychological training to handle violent men. In those days, it was left to men like Mitchell. But even then he was controversial. He had to take a prisoner out of his cell once, a man who had smeared himself with excrement. His cell was filthy, he was dirty and they had to "extract" him and take him down to the shower to clean him up. Mitchell didn't bat an eye. "There was never a time when I went in and beat a guy up 'cause I didn't like him. We had to control him. And there was only one way to control him and that was to knock him out." I blinked; it was the first time an officer had ever said anything so stark to me. "Boxer don't get hurt when he gets knocked out," Mitchell explained. And then he added ruefully, "But—ah—they frown on that."

By the time Mitchell rolled the rule book and slipped it through the bars to West, he had no doubt already seen West's file, noting wearily the military court-martial. Just another reason to hold this con in contempt.

WEST GOT A job down in industries in the laundry and the clothing factory, and he kept his nose clean.

And like everyone, he quickly learned to hate Alcatraz. It wasn't the alleged brutality—everyone had spent years in worse prisons. It wasn't the fact that he could only have one visitor a month. He'd long ago given up on having any; his family was too poor and practically disowned him anyway. It was the boredom, the restrictions and the regimentation. He could never get away from men like Mitchell, or like Maurice Ordway, another curt taskmaster better known as "Double Tough," who at the time was the industries lieutenant, or men like Captain Philip R. Bergen, who ran the custodial staff like a tough, battle-tested general. In fact, West arrived on Alcatraz during a period of its tightest security, a ten year stint after 1946 when there was not a single escape attempt.

The guards made everything move like clockwork. And they were poised like hawks to strike at anything that was out of place. Opportunities to escape the infamous prison island were nonexistent. That was the thing: you could never get away. And even if you got "out of pocket," as they called it, the San Francisco Bay was a wall. The food was good, the treatment was fair, but it was that "escape proof" label. Most cons believed it, although they were always thinking up angles to fool themselves and each other.

On Saturdays and Sundays West got to the yard—as cold as it was—and that's when he got his fill of Alcatraz lore and how escape proof it really was.

He heard about all the attempts. How Joe Bowers was "murdered" by a tower guard in 1936 when he wouldn't stop climbing a fence. How Roe and Cole were still missing after a '37 attempt. Guys on the yard were still debating whether or not they made it. He heard about 1938, when Lucas, Limerick and "Whitey" Franklin killed an officer and tried to storm a tower. Limerick got killed and they threw Franklin in solitary for years. After an incident in which Lucas was found naked with another con in a walk-in refrigeration unit, he became more famous as "Ice Box Annie."

West snorted.

He heard about the ill-fated "Doc" Barker–Henri Young attempt in January 1939. Although this was the fourth escape attempt in Alcatraz history, it was the first from the cell house— the most difficult place in any prison from which to escape. Barker, Young and three others sawed through the bars in their five D block cells, then spread window bars and escaped down the hill. Barker was fatally shot, the others were returned alive. They got caught simply because their cells were empty.

West smirked, *he'd never make that mistake.*

The other cons looked away with hooded eyes.

He urged them to tell him the other stories. In May 1941, four convicts were stopped before getting to the beach. That September, John Richard Bayless, known as "Jack Rabbit," tried to swim but turned around and swam back. He told everyone the bay was just too cold to swim. *Yeah, sure.*

In '43, four more guys tried. One of them was fatally shot while bobbing up and down in the bay. Another, Floyd Hamilton, reportedly a buddy of Bonnie and Clyde, eventually swam back to Alcatraz after officers thought he too had been fatally shot. He climbed back up the cliff and crawled through the same industries window he had climbed out of the night before. He was the only con known to have escaped *into* Alcatraz. West snickered as his eyes scanned the armed tower guards.

Another con in August '43 tied tin cans to his waist for buoyancy—West must have thought, *Now that was a new idea*— but the escapee was caught before he could even jump in.

Then in July '45, dockworker John Giles tried to escape on an a military launch in an army uniform he'd been collecting for months. Even the officers were impressed with that scheme. When they brought him back, they photographed him in his crinkled G.I. uniform and tried to cajole him. Giles wasn't laughing.

Every con could recite the escapes by heart. West sat on the concrete steps at yard, hunkered down in his pea coat, tugged at his cap, and jammed his hands into his pockets to ward off the

Pacific Ocean winds. He gazed out at the beautiful San Francisco skyline—which didn't look that far. *Nobody had come up with a good plan,* he said.

Tell me about '46, he asked Carnes one day, and Carnes shook his head. *Five dead guys,* he said, *that's all it amounted to.* The 1946 "battle" was the most notorious to date, and only the second attempt from the cell house. It was over almost the minute it started, but it took two days and five fatalities to regain the cell house. After that there were no more escape attempts.

In ten years? West asked.

Ten years, he was told, *too tight.*

West kept his cell in perfect order and shied away from Lieutenant Mitchell. But it was a challenge, wasn't it? To break the Rock.

Everyone hated the place. Even the nice days mocked you. From Alcatraz, San Francisco and the bridges looked liked the colorful ornaments, tinsel and ribbons on a Victorian Christmas tree. But sometimes the fog was so thick and wet, it felt like the prison was sitting in a toilet of tissue paper. That was worse. West gazed at the cons on the yard, playing ball in their raincoats, or walking around in tight groups wearing navy pea coats. *It was summer, for Christ' sake. 'Supposed to be 'sunny California' and it was fifty-nine degrees with gale force winds that could knock you off your feet.* Even the guards were decked out in heavy woolen overcoats, wool uniforms, big fur-lined gloves and their hats hitched low. It didn't matter. The damp winds beat right through your clothes. It seemed like everybody was trapped on a cold, wet, blustery rock in the middle of a raging bay and not one of them could escape.

If you were a philosophical guy, you could figure that the guards were just as trapped as you.

For them, at times, it was even spookier. Officers patrolled the island at night with only their flashlight. Sometimes is was so foggy your light just bounced right back from a gray wall. And the fog felt like an eerie presence, like at any minute something alive would jump out at you. One foggy night, officer William "Bill" Long, Jr., who'd been on Alcatraz since 1954, stumbled over a two hundred pound sea lion at the beach; he nearly had a heart attack. Sometimes it was so thick, the dock tower officer couldn't

Alcatraz and the prison yard were often covered in fog.

see the boat until just before it pulled into the slip right below him. Residents walking across the parade ground appeared out of nowhere, scared you half to death and disappeared again.Then came the foghorns.

There were ninety-one around the bay in those days—two on Alcatraz—and buoys with bells and clappers that rang when they dipped and bowed on the waves. For the islanders it was magical. The Alcatraz horns sounded out two tones—a long moan followed by a short blast. *Beeeeeeeee-Oh.* If you were a teenager on the Rock, lucky enough to sit on lovers' bench on the east side of the parade ground with San Francisco appearing like a soft, impressionistic painting and fog horns calling out to each other all over the bay, you couldn't ask for more.

But if you were a con stuck in a little five-by-eight-and-three-quarters-foot cell with the blanket pulled up around you, or a guard standing on a tower from midnight to 8:00 A.M., the fog soaking into your woolen uniform, those foghorns only made your feel colder.

Beeeeeeeeeeeee-ohh.

A reminder of a life you'd never lived.

Ding-ding.

Little guards ready to rat you out.

Of holidays you'd never celebrate.

Ships sometimes cruised into the bay, greeting San Franciscans with deep, breathy blasts of their airhorns. No doubt the cons felt taunted: no cruise for them. It would remind you of all the chain gangs you ever worked, swinging a scythe along county roads while sleek, black, air-conditioned cars flew by, leaving you in a cloud of dust.

And the loud, crazy, dirty seagulls. From February to September hundreds of them nested all over the island, gliding overhead with their chorus of ear-splitting screams, strafing the yard with their poop. Everyone felt like a target. No wonder guys wore raincoats on the yard. And when you surprised them, or got too near their nests, they flushed in a panic, flailing into the air and scaring all the others until it seemed like hundreds were circling overhead, screaming, barking—*ratting you out*. Then you were in trouble.

Cons felt like the gulls were better shots than the guards.

It was the whole place. It wasn't just a prison; it was a curse. A brooding, bitter, gusty, fog-bound trap. Cons—and officers—were stuck in little concrete boxes or steel cages, each there because of the other. West snorted. Mitchell was the boss, sure, but *he* was Mitchell's employer. Each man forced to remain on this miserable island because of the other. West thought someone should break the "escape proof" myth. He winced as he looked around the yard. Even the cons had bought into it.

And he had just enough ego to think he could break it.

But two years flew by and no opportunity arose. Then in June 1956, West was transferred back to Atlanta and the heat and humidty made him feel like he was living in a cow's mouth.

Less than a month after he departed, in the Rock's eleventh escape attempt, a con slipped away from the dock and hid in a crevice for several hours. He was unable to put together a driftwood float and was caught, but he broke the ten-year record.

West didn't hear about that for a while. His federal sentence ended in December 1956, and he was shackled back to Raiford to serve out his Florida state escape time. Raiford was a worse prison than Alcatraz. But it was easier too. That's when he put a gun to the associate warden's head and escaped on July 16, 1957.

He remained at large for four months, stacking up charges in Maryland, Pennsylvania, Georgia and North Carolina. They caught him in November in Baltimore, Maryland and he was sentenced to ten years and sent to Atlanta for the third time. He arrived in February 1958. That's when he heard about the latest escape. He laughed when he heard it. *They broke the ten year record!* He rolled on his cot and kicked his legs and cackled like a hyena.

4

ALCATRAZ WAS AN ill-fated, infamous prison island almost from the beginning. It started as a U.S. Army fort in 1859 to protect the port of San Francisco from foreign invasion. All forts have guardhouses for drunks, thieves and deserters. But because the Rock looked so cold and forbidding, other forts in the western territories began sending their army prisoners there. By the 1900s as many as two to three hundred army convicts were imprisoned on Alcatraz in wooden, ramshackle fire traps. Even for the army it was an expensive post, requiring tons of water to be imported. Then, from 1909 until 1912, army convicts built the cell house that can be seen on top of the island today. A good grade of Portland cement was used, but the aggregate consisted of too many irregularly sized rocks, coarse sand and even salvaged brick. To save money, the army flushed the toilets with salt water from the bay. Salt water coursed through the entire cell house plumbing system into every toilet in every cell, corroding the pipes over time and even flooding the utility corridors. Thus, a design decision that had been made as early as 1908 would have a direct affect on West's scheme in 1962.

In 1933–34, during the Great Depression, the army unloaded Alcatraz as an expensive albatross. The U.S. Attorney General and the federal Bureau of Prisons, in the throes of one of the most violent decades of the century, snapped it up and Alcatraz became the most maximum-security penitentiary in the nation—and instantly notorious. And ever-lastingly expensive.

The island eventually housed more than five hundred people—two hundred and eighty cons and about two hundred and fifty civilians—all of whom needed imported fresh water in one of the most expensive states in the nation. It was also the most criticized prison in the nation. Rumors fed by infamous murder trials and ex-cons' exaggerated claims throughout the 1930s, '40s and '50s, led people to believe that it was a brutal institution. As a result, in congressional budget hearings every year, the BOP was pressured to justify its existence and the prison's financial support remained tenuous at best. Thus, Alcatraz wardens often sought to curry Washington's favor by trimming its own budget. In prison, that means compromising security.

When Warden James A. Johnston took over as the first federal prison warden in 1934, for example, he had six guard towers built—the dock and road towers, which were manned twenty-four hours a day, and the hill, model roof, powerhouse and main towers, which operated during the day when cons were out working.

When Edwin B. Swope became warden in 1948, he abandoned two of them—the powerhouse and the main tower. Although abandoned, the main tower on the prison's roof was still visible when I moved onto to the island in 1954. But within a few years it would be dismantled, ending any pretense that it might still be manned. When West returned to Alcatraz on his second stretch, he would become aware that there was no line-of-sight view from the cell house roof to the north shore.

Then Swope abandoned the east gun gallery—a night time post that left the east side of the cell house vulnerable.

As the 1950s rolled into the early '60s, the changes accelerated—largely because of staff cutbacks. When Jack Mitchell began working there in 1947, ten lieutenants were in charge of officers. By '62, there were only six—with senior officers like Bill Long, Dick Barnett or George Gregory pulling duty as "acting" lieutenants for months at a time. The cutbacks and temporary assignments made officers feel as if security was being compromised. "One more cutback," said Officer John Hernan, who worked there from 1953 to 1956, "and they'd have to shut down."

And shutting it down was a constant rumor.

When Carnes arrived in 1945 he was told that it would close. Three years later, Officer Ben Blount quit because he heard it was closing and he didn't want to leave San Francisco. In 1949, an Alcatraz engineer named Thomas Butterworth warned the BOP that, "We are skating on extremely thin ice with respect to the power plant." The director of the BOP had recently toured Alcatraz and "intimated" that the island would be abandoned. Butterworth wrote, "If we are to evacuate within a year, I will try to keep the utilities operating for that length of time." Alcatraz, of course did not close, and the engineer kept the power plant patched together. When my father arrived in 1953, an officer told him to leave his furniture in storage because the place would soon close.

Bergen, who worked on Alcatraz from 1939 until 1955, eventually becoming the Captain of the Guards, called it "Alcatraz as Damocles"—the fabled member of the court of Dionysius who sat at the banquet table under a sword suspended by a single hair to demonstrate the precarious nature of the King's whims.

All prisons have high turnovers, especially among new officers. But Alcatraz almost always operated below its officer authorization, in some months as many as six or eight positions short. In one famous story, an officer put on his uniform for his first day, was unlocked into the cell house, took one look, turned around and quit. Passing the control room, he said, "Would you tell 'em I showed up?"

Rumors, budget tightening and staff shortfall created other vulnerabilities. Sometime in the late 1950s or '60s, the mail censor position was eliminated. That post called for a man to review all incoming or outgoing inmate mail. Throughout many of the years the mail censor also retyped letters to prohibit secret messages or drug-soaked paper from entering or exiting the prison. He also scanned magazines cons subscribed to, tearing out articles about crime, criminals or anything that might aid in the conception of escapes. That position was eliminated as a separate job and the duties were shunted to another, overworked officer.

Every shutdown, every cutback—the powerhouse tower, the main tower, the fewer number of lieutenants, the east gun gallery and the mail censor—would all play directly into the hands of Allen West.

THROUGHOUT THE YEARS, Alcatraz changed in other ways as well. The "rule of silence," the few "dungeon cells" in the basement from the U.S. Army era and the hated coveralls that cons wore to work and the mess hall, had all disappeared within the first few years.

Since 1946 no guards or cons had killed one another. Then in the mid-1950s, after Paul J. Madigan became the third warden, the first modernization was instituted when cells were wired with radio headsets. Now cons could listen to two radio stations at night. Magazine subscription and letter writing policies became more liberal as time wore on, and more amenities were allowed— like the purchase of tennis shoes for playing ball on the yard and new recreational equipment. It was still the most strict federal prison in the country, but it was no longer the draconian prison of the 1930s.

But nobody was prepared for the changes that would take place when Olin Guye Blackwell arrived in April 1959. He was the new associate warden under Warden Madigan. Even cons noticed the difference. Alvin "Ol' Creepy" Karpis, AZ 325, who had been on Alcatraz since 1936—almost longer than any of the staff—wrote that with "Blackwell and Warden Madigan working as a team the prison becomes as congenial as a prison can get."

Jack Mitchell sounded far more defeated. "I could feel the changes coming," he said.

Nearly six feet tall, Blackwell had a high forehead, a red-veined hawk nose and close-set, crinkly eyes. His clothes hung haphazardly from his frame, cigarette smoke wafted around him and he had the hacker's cough. Not sophisticated, he was, nonetheless, as wily as a coyote. Early in his prison career, his slow, sly Texas drawl earned him the name "Lagartija" from the Mexican-American prisoners, which means the "wall lizard." Friends, including James V. Bennett, the director of the BOP, called him "Blackie." On Alcatraz, where his gold bracelets, turquoise rings and string neckties seemed out of place, cons called him "Gypsy."

At age forty-four, Blackwell was the youngest associate warden in Alcatraz history and temperamentally quite different. He was neither as aloof nor as maniacal as other associates had been. Instead, he was casual, and promoted a relaxed, friendly alertness, something new at Alcatraz.

"People who are jumpy," he explained years later, "—every time they see the associate warden coming, 'Good God, here comes the associate! You better straighten up!'—now those people are worrying about something that isn't security. They're worrying about their own well-being."

But with his breezy style, Blackwell ran smack into Alcatraz hard liners who'd been doing things the same way for years: Lieutenant Maurice Ordway had been on Alcatraz since October 1934; Lieutenant Fred Mahan had worked there for more than fifteen years. Mitchell had been there since 1947. Lieutenant A.O. Severson had been almost ten years on Alcatraz. The new associate warden thought they were all too rigid.

"Nearly every time you wanted to do something [new]," he complained years later, "They'd say, 'Oh, you can't do that; this is *Alcatraz.*' "

Mitchell agreed but from another vantage point. Most officers in other prisons never knew how tightly Alcatraz operated, "and consequently they came and thought they could do it like other places," he said, shaking his head. "You had a different type of inmate [there]."

The new associate warden sat in on prisoner disciplinary hearings, where Mitchell, the cell house lieutenant, presented cases. Blackwell didn't like Mitchell's reputation or his controversial Marine Corps methods. He reassigned him to the dock, where the lieutenant had control of only six or seven prisoners. The dick on the dock. It was usually a sixth-

Olin G. Blackwell

month rotation. Mitchell might as well have been in Russia.

But there was more than just a style difference between the two men. Their careers had taken different turns.

Blackwell was born in the Texas hill country on February 15, 1915. He grew up "choppin' cotton, shuckin' oats, shearin' sheep and goats," on his daddy's stock farm near Lampasas. He never lost his hick cowpoke twang, his twinkly sarcasm and his shrewd and deflecting self-mockery, which tended to make you lose sight of his lack of intellectual sophistication. "They talk about the deprived in their youth and that makes them muggers and so forth," he said, for example. "That's a bunch of crap! There's nobody had it a damn bit rougher than I had when I was a youngster. Nobody ever spent a dime on my summer vacation."

He quit college after a semester and eventually took a job as a guard in 1941 at a minimum-security institution at La Tuna, Texas. Twenty miles north of El Paso, La Tuna looked like a big walled hacienda. Tom White was warden then. A colorful, former Texas Ranger and an early FBI agent, White liked to have target shooting matches between other government agencies, but he didn't have a showcase team until Blackwell showed up. And "Blackie" it turned out, was "a ringer."

"I seen him so drunk he couldn't walk," said Bergen later, "and he'd sink six bullets into the target."

Blackwell was a target shooter all of his life, even sauntering down to target practice on Alcatraz years later. Officer Ron Battles remembered him stepping up to the range one night and begin firing two guns—from the hips. Battles was a little embarrassed. "He wanted to be a good ol' boy. He should have been above that sort of thing," he said. But "Blackie" was a "pistolero" from the old Warden White tradition.

Even back in the La Tuna days, he was charming, cagey, a colorful ad-libber, a ladies' man and a big drinker. He'd often tour Washington bureaucrats to nearby Juarez, Mexico, and consequently, from there, he moved up the ladder quickly. In 1951, he was bumped to federal jail inspector, a rather heady promotion counseling the jail staffs in five western states. But Blackwell represented the shift that was taking place in the BOP from burly, blackjack-toting guards to more enlightened correctional officers. This shift wouldn't be completed until after Alcatraz closed in 1963, but it had its beginnings in men like Blackwell.

Six months later, he was sent to Washington, D.C. to become the director of custody, another ego boost. Blackwell was thirty-six.

He became captain of the guards at Lewisburg, Pennsylvania in May 1953. Two and a half years later, he was associate warden there. Then, in April 1959, he became the associate warden of Alcatraz. Into the most austere, hidebound prison in the nation walked one of the most progressive, controversial associate wardens— a Texas gambler—who would turn the institution on its ear.

5

WEST LEFT ALCTRAZ before Blackwell arrived, and he was too self-centered to care what changes might be taking place. And too busy renewing acquaintances back at Atlanta. One of his friends—an old buddy from his Raiford state prison days—would have an enormous impact along with West on the future of Alcatraz—John William Anglin.

John Anglin, known among his prison friends as "J.W." or, invariably "J-Dub," was a charming, goofy twenty-eight-year-old

Clarence, left, and John, at Atlanta in 1958.

cornpone from the rural south serving ten years for bank robbery. Five foot ten, one hundred and forty pounds, blond and buffed, J-Dub was talkative, mostly unemployable, slow and the needy half of his partner and brother, Clarence Anglin, who was also serving time at Atlanta for the same offense.

The Anglin brothers were the middle of fourteen children born during the Great Depression to a hapless, itinerant farm couple who eventually settled in Ruskin, Florida. Ruskin was famous for being tomato country, and every year the family migrated north to Michigan to pick cherries and other crops.

Years later on Alcatraz, I met an insurance agent who traveled the back roads near Ruskin, collecting weekly twenty-five cent premiums on two-hundred-and-fifty-dollar policies that parents took out on their children. The boys' mother, Rachel Anglin, had at least one such policy. He described the Anglins as living the typically hardscrabble existence of sharecropper families in those days. Most lived in "shotgun" shacks on concrete blocks with lean-to porches. The locals fished in the nearby pits of abandoned phosphate mines and hunted raccoons and possums for a living. A rough, wooded area adjacent to the Little Manatee River near

Tampa Bay, it was filled with water moccasins, coral snakes and alligators. The Anglin boys were said to have been daring swimmers, who broke ice to swim the cold waters of Lake Michigan. They were cute, mischievous and foolhardy, and not afraid *a nothin'*. They weren't too interested in school either; in prison intelligence tests, J-Dub scored at a third grade level, Clarence topped off at the fifth grade.

"They had all the marbles," said Officer Bill Long, "but some of them were kinda small."

Another older brother, Alfred Anglin, led them into a life of petty crime while all three were still in their teens. None of them wanted to pick fruit all their lives. Not surprisingly, prison was a step up.

Clarence, at twenty-seven, the youngest of all three and exactly a year younger than John, was smarter, louder, greedier, more puffed up and hostile, and because of it, he had served harder time all of his life. One childhood friend told the FBI that Clarence was a thief even at a young age. He said that both brothers "seemed to feel that the world owes them a living and they intend to have things without working for them." Clarence first went to reform school at age fourteen, getting into trouble in 1941 after he "began taking girls to the moving pictures," his mother said. Both John and Clarence served time in Mariana, Florida, then to the Georgia Work State Camp for burglary until they ended up in Raiford working on a chain gang. While John only served about three years at Raiford state prison, Clarence escaped twice, and was still there in 1957. By then, he was almost six feet, a hundred and sixty pounds and had brown hair.

West lost sight of them along the way, and John paroled out of Raiford in 1953 and went home where he had a series of poorly paying jobs from which he invariably quit or got fired. John was photographed in 1955 in a white sports coat and two-toned shoes, leaning against a flashy car. Casual, somewhat sweet and dreamy, he attracted the girls. But he seemed plagued by minor health problems: frequent boils, stomachaches, dizziness, weakness, month-long sore throats, minor accidents—ailments that reflected boredom, stress or need for attention. His teeth were rotten; by his midtwenties, J-Dub had a full set of upper dentures and two partials on the lower jaw, prison dental work which in photographs made him look uncomfortable. He stated on record that he brushed his teeth once a week.

In 1957, Clarence again escaped from Raiford. He got back with John and Alfred, and in early 1957 they began planning a bank job.

Prisons are full of incompetent bank robbers, but the Anglin boys stood out like fleas on a Mexican Hairless dog.

The three drove into Columbia, Alabama—a small town with a tiny mom-and-pop national bank—in what witnesses said was a late-model, two-toned, out-of-state Cadillac. The FBI later identified it as a '55 Ford Thunderbird. They drove up and down the main street of town in the fancy car, cased the bank, and planned their getaway. One can almost hear the loud music thumping out of a turquoise and white dashboard. Everybody in town saw the car. "I paid particular attention to it," one woman said, who worked across from the bank, "because it was such a beautiful car."

That evening they stole a black Chevy in Georgia, returned the next day and parked both cars in front of the Alabama bank. After sticking up the bank president with what the family later claimed was a toy gun (which scared the man so much he fainted) they roared out of town, dumping the stolen Chevy—with their finger prints all over it—and hightailed it to Ohio.

Gubmint agents caught up with them within four days, and poked them awake with the butt of their guns.

The money was recovered. Even more unfortunate, the Anglins had picked a bank in a bad state. In Alabama in 1958, you could get the death penalty for armed robbery. There was no trial. Sheepish, hostile, poor and flummoxed, they pled guilty. J-Dub and Alfred got ten years each, Clarence, fifteen. Alabama gave them each twenty-five more years. They hobbled into "Ad-Lanna," in February, almost the same month as West. It was like a grade school reunion.

WEST ALSO BECAME acquainted at Atlanta with another Raiford prison graduate—Frank Lee Morris.

Morris, known as "Frankie" or "Ace" to his prison friends, was a short, tough, tightly wound, thirty-two year old who had been behind

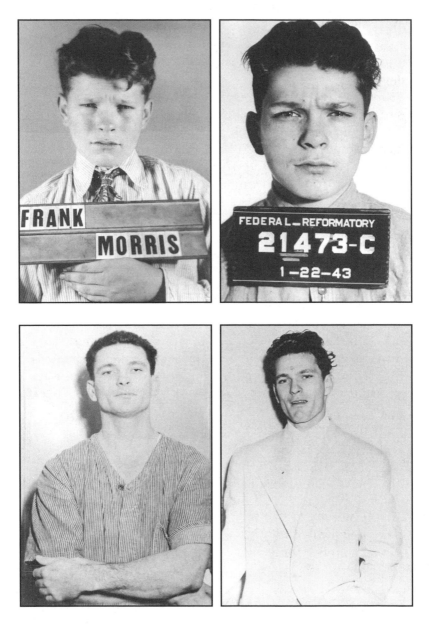

Morris, from top left, at age fourteen and seventeen in reform schools,
at Angola state penitentiary about 1955 and out of prison
briefly in New Orleans.

bars since the age of thirteen. Abandoned at birth, unsuccessfully fostered out, a runaway, a petty thief and a social waif, Morris was extremely bright, a master at escaping, but a lousy criminal. He'd already served three times in state and federal reform schools, twice in Louisiana's hardcore Angola State Penitentiary, as well as Raiford, from all of which he had made multiple escape attempts. Had you met him on the outside, you would have avoided him: gaunt, with a haunted look and a star tattooed on his forehead, he

In Atlanta his second time.

was thin and as mean looking as a snake. But he cleaned up real nice in federal prisons.

Legend had it that in 1955, Morris had been bank-rolled by a well-known Kansas City hood named Junior Bradley. Ace and his accomplices went south and bored into the back wall of a bank in Slidell, Louisiana. Using an acetylene torch, they burned through two stand-up vaults, setting off tear gas canisters. What they found inside must have made them cry even harder: $6,500 *in coins*—bags of nickels, dimes, quarters, and half dollars—which the FBI said collectively weighed about twelve hundred pounds. They returned to Kansas City where they hid the coins in the bottom of strawberry tins, placing strawberries on top, filling the tins with water and freezing them. The bank robbers remained at large for about nine months.

Criminals don't always make best friends. One of their accomplices was caught throwing counterfeit money around and flipped Junior Bradley and Morris. Ace was arrested in 1956 in possession of burglary tools, acetylene torches, gas masks, a revolver, two automatic guns, a .16 gauge double-barrel shotgun, a long record of burglaries and more than eleven escapes. The coins were hustled into coke dispensers and washing machines.

Morris was already serving a fourteen-year sentence when West and the Anglins arrived in Atlanta. All lousy criminals, most of them experienced at escaping, they gravitated towards each other like gnats on a hot summer day. West liked the diminutive, quiet Morris; he was cool, calm, calculating, a solid con. Morris may have initially been wary of West's hot-blooded ruthlessness, but he would have been impressed with his rap sheet, which included a stint at the infamous Alcatraz. West, no doubt, bragged about it, a cocky grin sliding across his lips.

West didn't remain at Atlanta long enough, however, to make plans with Morris or the Anglin brothers. In June 1958, his escape history, his coiled temper and unpredictability earned him a second trip to Alcatraz.

He couldn't imagine then that one day he would lead all of them into the most well-planned escape attempt in U.S. history.

BUT WEST WAS a different man when he returned to Alcatraz in 1958. For one thing, he now had detainers filed in Maryland for larceny and breaking and entering, in Florida for escape and grand larceny and in Pennsylvania, Georgia and North Carolina for robbery. That meant that after his ten-year federal sentence ended, he could serve time in each of those states. Now registered as AZ 1335, he was twenty-nine, his hair had receded even further and he'd been behind bars for fifteen years. But he was looking at many more prison years in the future. His demeanor had hardened because he had nothing to lose.

Written up by Alcatraz officers as "sneaky," "demanding" and "belligerent," one report described him as "one of the most bitter, vicious and criminally inclined person[s]" ever interviewed.

"West was prone to have mouth," said Officer Bill Long.

"He could turn on the tears and act crazy and do anything," said Alcatraz lieutenant, Fred Mahan.

It was as if he had given up any pretense at cooperating. In the eighteen months from December 1960 until May 1961, West was in segregation all but forty-six days for nine different disciplinary reports. Four involved assaulting prisoners; one involved assaulting an officer.

West joined a crowd of thugs who stood out even on Alcatraz: guys like Jimmy Grove, AZ 158, a black con, who, in his nineteen years on Alcatraz, went to seg more than forty times, once for killing a con, other times for attempts to stab, strangle or beat cons to death, and Walter Sawyers, AZ 1326, a powerfully built white man of low intelligence and psycho-sexual pathology who was on Alcatraz twice, taunted officers for sexual favors, waved his penis at them or tried to knock them in their groins, and Homer Clinton, AZ 1294, a childlike screamer, serving life for kidnapping, who used a sharpened spoon handle in 1958 to slice his Achilles tendons, and dangerous cons, like Roland Simcox, AZ 1131, who was hated by many for stabbing two Alcatraz cons, killing one of them.

Much of West's bounce back and forth to segregation had to do with a racial incident that shocked even Alcatraz cons. In early 1960, a black bank robber named James Gilliam, AZ 1361, had refused to honor a prison work strike. Enraged, West and several of his buddies held a contest to determine who would kill him. Carnes called it, "one of the most vicious things I ever witnessed on Alcatraz."

"West was devoid of honor and respected no human being," said Officer Victor Mills. "He hated blacks. He worked for me in the kitchen and his baiting of black inmates was a source of irritation."

Gilliam, a two-timer on Alcatraz, was reportedly six feet and two hundred pounds. Jerry Clymore, AZ 1339, drew the short straw. He was a little white guy, Officer Rogers said, who "might have weighed a hundred and thirty if he had his pockets full of change."

Two attempts were made to separate Gilliam and stab him. In one, West and Billy Boggs, AZ 1415, a bitter, aggressive, twenty-two-year-old narcotic addict, who acted like a hipster, staged a fight to divert guards' attention. Gilliam escaped unharmed, and both Boggs and West went to seg.

Then on August 27, 1960, Clymore stabbed Gilliam in the back with a "shank"—a handmade knife—in the prison showers. Nearby cons heard what was described as a "pop" then saw blood seeping down the drain. The knife stuck in Gilliam's vertebra and Clymore couldn't pull it out to finish him off. Gilliam lived, but

Billy Boggs, a good friend of West.

was paralyzed. Clymore was indicted for attempted murder.

West returned to seg on yet another assault. He shot off his mouth about Gilliam, the blacks in general, the officers, the lieutenants and the upcoming Clymore trial, ratcheting up the pitch until he, Boggs, Clymore, Homer Clinton and six others staged a protest by slicing their Achilles tendons with a smuggled razor blade. Heel string slicing is an old trick often employed to protest cruel working conditions. Men would cripple themselves and become useless in the sugarcane fields or on the chain gangs. But this was a phony protest. The island medical technical assistants and consultant doctors from the U.S. Public Health Service Marine Hospital in San Francisco found that Homer Clinton and three others had only skin lacerations; another had cut only an eighth of a tendon on one leg; and three, including West, had cut only a fifth of a tendon on one leg. Later, West claimed he had been "harassed into doing it." Only two men, one of them Clymore, had cut one half of their tendons, each on one leg.

Officials were at a loss to understand their motives. But it had everything to do with the upcoming trial. Frank De Ford, AZ 1318, ratted them out in a long letter to officials, reporting that it was going to be a "dirty trial." Clymore was going to plead self-defense, De Ford wrote. He would state that Gilliam had *fallen* on his own knife. West, Boggs and others were going to testify that Gilliam was a homosexual who was after Clymore. As an added attraction, all nine would limp to and from the witness stand, DeFord wrote, and accuse prison guards of brutality. The ruse worked. The January 1961 trial in San Francisco proved to be dirty and Clymore was acquitted on attempted murder charges.

On Alcatraz, animosity deepened between West and the blacks, but there was more seething than snarling.

6

NOT ONLY HAD West changed significantly from his first stretch there, but Alcatraz had also changed. So much so that the fog would lift and West would begin to see his way out.

The removal of Lieutenant Mitchell from the cell house to the dock was just the first of the changes in the modernization.

Blackwell, who was acting warden during parts of 1960–61 while Warden Madigan was at another prison, began making sweeping changes. He led, generally, by cajoling people into his way of thinking and by removing others who got in his way. Documents show him to be an able, progressive administrator; he constantly addressed security concerns at monthly custodial meetings and urged everyone to keep on their toes; he brought lieutenants into budget meetings so they could see how the money was allocated and he pushed newer, younger officers into responsible positions to widen their experience.

But his nonchalant style communicated far more than his administrative acumen. He liked to leave his office, "delegate some of that junk," and wander down to the maintenance building near the power house, where Hank Casey was chief of mechanical service (CMS). Casey was a good ol' boy, loaded with charm and good prison stories. Much of the time Blackwell, the CMS and Bill Bones, the business manager, were in meetings discussing the large remodeling projects then in the works. But the fact that the meetings were held in the CMS's office rather than Blackwell's office in the prison building, gave people the wrong impression. And he may have been having too much fun. "Blackwell used to come down and we'd talk by the hour sometimes," said one maintenance officer who worked there from 1938 until 1962. At times Blackwell invited others to join him. Lieutenant Mitchell was supervising a group of prisoners on the dock on several occasions when Blackwell sauntered down. "He'd want me to go up to the mechanical services building and have coffee and talk," Mitchell said. Mitchell declined, and his refusal to join Blackwell's coterie may have been his undoing.

Mitchell was savvy enough to realize that he had often been used by supervisors who wanted him to be a threat to dangerous cons, but who would discard him when his reputation as Ass Kicking Fats got too big. And the tactics that gained him medals in World War II became too controversial for the 1960s.

Lucky Juelich had another explanation. "When Blackwell came out here," he said, "there was a lot of friction between them— kind of a power struggle—and Blackwell did have the power to send Mitchell back to Leavenworth. And back he went."

Mitchell was transferred in December 1960, and was replaced by a new lieutenant from McNeil Island, Robert K. Weir. Weir would play a tiny, but crucial, role in the 1962 escape attempt.

Because when Blackwell got Mitchell transferred, Alcatraz lost its drill sergeant, spit-shine, cell house discipline. That's one thing West noticed between stints in seg. After Blackwell gained power and Mitchell departed, there were going to be two escape attempts in 1962—*both* from the cell house.

7

IN FACT, ALTHOUGH he didn't know it, things were falling into place for Allen West. Frank Morris turned up on January 18, 1960, becoming AZ 1441.

He arrived on a train with Tom Kent, AZ 1443, a tenacious, fast-talking, bull terrier from Boston who at age thirty-three, had a record of burglaries, assaults, weapons charges and bank robberies dating back to his teens. Kent was being yanked to Alcatraz because of a bitter work strike at Leavenworth. It would have a profound effect on his life.

Morris, now thirty-three, had been transferred to Alcatraz after an escape attempt from Atlanta. Although his mandatory release date was 1967, he had detainers from Louisiana for escape and burglary, from Kansas for robbery, from Texas for burglary and from Florida for escape. He was looking at a lot of years.

Morris was well liked, but had few friends and almost no one with whom he corresponded with on the outside. Inside he was a chameleon. "Part of the wall," Juelich called him. "He was there

Kent, left, and Morris arrived on the same chain.

but you didn't see him."

Morris was also hard to figure. "He was a shy, neat, nice looking young man," said Officer Mills. "If I had been asked to pick any inmate at Alcatraz who was likely to make a run for it, Morris would have been my last choice."

But that was a profound misreading of the man. Morris had made escape his life, departing from nearly every prison in which he'd served time—including the infamous Angola State Penitentiary on his second stint there. But although he was an ace at escaping, he was a joker outside of prison; from the age of thirteen until thirty-three, Morris had never been free more than two years accumulatively. Often, he had been caught the same day he had escaped. Put another way, when Morris arrived on Alcatraz at age thirty-three, he had been behind bars nearly every day for twenty years.

He was five foot seven, weighed a hundred and thirty-five pounds, had dark wavy hair and a determined jaw. Not surprisingly, when photographed at Alcatraz, he actually looked better than in photos taken while he was outside. He had scored one hundred and thirty-three on his IQ tests. Although the five-pointed star on his forehead was now gone, he had several small prison tattoos—

a devil's head on his upper right arm, a star at the base of his left thumb and the number "13" on his left index finger. He had a molasses "Loosiana" drawl, and an ease in prison, which comes from growing up there.

And the tattooed number "13" was prophetic. Morris' escape attempt from Alcatraz would become the prison's thirteenth, and undoubtedly, its most amazing.

Kent said years later that before they even set one chained foot on the Rock, they talked about escaping.

RECORDS SHOW THAT within eleven days, Morris was assigned to the library with Clarence Carnes, and days later, Kent also worked in the library. That's when West, who was temporarily out of segregation and working at a job in the cell house, had approached the three of them, Kent later said.

Maybe up until now, no one had taken West's escape ideas seriously. Maybe he wanted to impress the new guys. He started talking about the ceiling vents.

They're weak sisters, he said.

He told them that originally there had been about eight air exhaust blowers sitting on top of the cell blocks. They were attached by ducts through the ceiling to large vent hoods on the prison's roof. Some of them had never worked properly, others had been damaged during the '46 shoot out. Eventually most of the air exhaust blowers were dismantled and tossed into the bay, the motors deactivated and the vent openings reinforced with bars and sealed with concrete. But West had heard that one blower unit over B block still existed and still had the ductwork up to a ceiling vent. That might mean that the vent was not sealed with concrete.

If we could get up there, we could rip out the ductwork and get out on the roof, he told them.

It would have been a quick conversation—cons talking without moving their lips—watching for guards with eyes in the back of their heads.

West departed, Kent said, and the three of them discussed his idea. Carnes knew about the ceiling vents. In '46, cons had also wanted to exit from one, but someone who was assigned to get scaffolding over to it chickened out. Carnes also remembered that

"Red" Winhoven, AZ 772, had tried to cut his way out of a ceiling vent in the late 1950s. Indeed, "Red" been an inmate electrician in '57, and had removed a motor from one blower unit. But he could never get away from the guard long enough to work on it. Nonetheless, he had spread the word of an open vent to the roof.

Morris wondered if West could be trusted.

Carnes equivocated.

WEST RETURNED TO segregation like a bowling ball down a gutter, and no one heard from him in awhile.

But Morris was not idle. He had his own ideas, and he quietly questioned other cons about the prison's security and the routine. The basement particularly interested him. He went down there for showers, but he couldn't see the layout of the other rooms. Kitchen workers who sometimes went down there filled him in on the layout. Eventually Morris drew a little diagram of the basement that was found later in his cell. It was remarkably accurate, noting exits, the position of a security phone, a nearby tower, even the foundation of the old fort, "where the 'Spanish tunnels' were rumored to exist!" he exclaimed, adding, "No exterior exits in this area."

Clearly the diagram was an early escape plan.

Nor did he ignore West's ceiling vent idea. On October 15, 1960, while West was in seg recovering from his superficial heel string wounds—and more than a year before he would began to dig out of his cell—Morris politely requested to relocate to B-356.

That cell, on the top tier of the back side of B block, just happened to be directly *under* the ceiling vent from which Morris and West would try to escape. He could now keep it in his sights everyday.

NINE DAYS LATER, on October 24, 1960, probably scared and copping a tough guy smirk, J-Dub arrived. He was con number AZ 1476.

From Atlanta in 1958, John Anglin had transferred to Lewisburg, Pennsylvania, where a poorly planned escape attempt had earned him harder time at Leavenworth, where his brother, Clarence, had been transferred. Together, at last, in the culinary department, they tried to escape in one of the more hapless

J-Dub and Clarence, small timers who finally hit the big time.

attempts in Leavenworth history.

Clarence hid in a large bread box bound for the outside. When John and another con struggled to lift an otherwise lightweight box, one of the guards, Arthur Davidson, took notice, opened the box, and out tumbled a sheepish, but armed, Clarence Anglin. John "emphatically denied that he was aware that his brother had intended to escape," records stated, "and did not know that he was concealed in the box." It was J-Dub's version of, *I ain't never did it.*

Guards and cons grinned and waved good-bye. Clarence arrived on Alcatraz three months after John, in January 1961, as AZ 1485.

Like in all social settings, some reign at the top by virtue of their personality, prowess or reputation. Others are bottom-feeders. The Anglins suffered mightily as small-time, primitive hustlers. Cons called them "morons."

"I stayed away from them," Juelich said, "They were phonies and bad news."

A Leavenworth con had scoffed to the FBI that they weren't dangerous, "just adventurous."

They were also loud. "Dry snitchers," cons sometimes call

them—guys who talk loud to bolster their egos.

"Clarence couldn't take a bite out of a tuna fish sandwich," Juelich said, "without telling everybody at the table about it." Later he said they were both braggarts, claiming that the cops would "have to smack" John "to shut him up."

John was still whining about his numerous health problems. His boils, stomachaches, dizzy spells, sore throats and minor accidents continued while he was at Alcatraz.

Clarence was defensive, hostile and a smart-ass. "A spoiled brat," Officer Mills called him. But Clarence must have imagined he and his brother had arrived in the big time. When they hit the Rock, the twenty-nine-year-old, dark-haired Clarence had spent nine years behind bars; John, blond, and thirty, had spent four. The real question was: which one was dumber?

Like J-Dub and Frankie, the Ace, Clarence had a prison name: "Larry." Larry was initially placed in a B block cell. Five days later, J-Dub rolled over to C-219. A month later, Larry joined him in C-217—the next cell. Despite warning notes in their files to keep them separated, Clarence and John Anglin were in cells right next to each other.

8

YOU WILL SEE that breaking the Rock was not just a matter of determined and whip smart cons—or lucky, incompetent ones— who outfoxed guards, but also a mix of building deterioration, random personnel changes, modernization, risky staffing and lame decisions by lazy individuals that aided the escapees in ways in which they could never anticipate, resulting in an outcome which would make the entire staff feel foolish.

In April 1961, just one month before West finally got out of D block, for example, Thomas D. Bradley, Jr., arrived as captain of the guards. Bradley was to become the fall guy in the escapes of 1962. And for good reason.

Alcatraz was his first assignment as captain—the departmental head of security. In prior years, lieutenants who were promoted to captain were sent away from Alcatraz for experience, then returned to command the post. With Bradley, the opposite was happening.

He moved into the associate warden's–captain's duplex next to Blackwell and quickly adopted Blackie's laid-back style.

Bradley was a bundle of contradictions, some of which could be read on his face. He had kind eyes, but a strong, stubborn chin, which he held high as if he had pulled himself up by his bootstraps. Friendly, ingratiating, at times brusque and arrogant, the fifty-year old captain was just under six feet and two hundred and thirty-five pounds—what one of his friends called a "heavy-set Georgia peach."

The youngest of four children of a train conductor and his wife, Thomas D. Bradley, Jr. was born in Georgia on January 17, 1911. He quit high school at fifteen, was running his own gas station at twenty-six, and by 1942, at age thirty-one, had become a prison guard at Atlanta. Serving in the U.S. Navy during World War II, he returned to Atlanta for eight more years where he consistently got high marks as an officer.

Fiercely ambitious, Bradley attended night classes at Atlanta's John Marshall Law School, where he received a law degree in 1950. He was admitted to the Georgia Bar the next year. And it paid off; in '54, he was promoted to lieutenant and transferred to Leavenworth. Then in April '61, he was promoted to captain and sent to Alcatraz.

Southerners, country boys and self-made men, Bradley and Blackwell quickly became friends. They shared the same dislike for the cold, foggy San Francisco summers, and the stubborn, immutable older lieutenants. As powerful outsiders, they both wanted to modernize the Alcatraz culture.

Everyone on the island knew the captain had a law degree. "Bragged about it," said Officer Lewis Meushaw. But what wasn't known was that his degree was from an American Bar Association nonapproved school, meaning that admission standards were lower and he could never practice law outside of Georgia. Yet when he died in 1976, one of his obituaries called him a "retired U.S. Justice Department attorney."

There were other things. The captain was the department head of security—what the cons call the "screwdriver." He set the tone. His word was law. If he was a tough prison man who set high standards for inmate and officer discipline, fair treatment, by-the-book searches, his lieutenants followed suit, and therefore, so did the officers. Generally not popular, the best the captain could hope for was respect. But Bradley deeply wanted to be liked.

"Hail fellow well met," Don Martin called him.

"He gave the impression of a happy-go-lucky, everybody's friend, type of guy," said Lieutenant Lloyd Miller.

"He would have been a good captain at a minimum-security institution," my father allowed, "but he was much too concerned with being well liked at Alcatraz."

Thomas D. Bradley, Jr.

Even prisoners noticed. "He wanted everyone to like him," Juelich said.

Others were less flattering, calling him a "backslapper" and a "grab ass."

"Bradley's big fault was that he wanted to be a good guy, " said Jack Mitchell, who worked with Bradley at Leavenworth. A maximum security prison, Leavenworth nonetheless was more open than Alcatraz. Cell fronts remained unlocked until lights out, men had more items in their cells, and more privileges (Leavenworth, after all, was where the "Birdman," Robert Stroud, had maintained an aviary and an amateur lab from 1920 until 1942). Mitchell gave Bradley his file on Alcatraz regulations, but he felt later that he hadn't paid much attention. "I think that Bradley never spent enough time inside the institution to know what was going on," Mitchell said. "It was Bradley, the ol' good guy buddy. He'd come in, wave at everybody—'Hi, Hello'—talk a bit, then go. He probably spent most of his time talking to Blackwell."

"Things kind of eased up with Bradley and Blackwell," said Officer Fred Freeman, who'd been there since 1958.

"With Bradley, anything went," said Charles Herman.

Not only was the captain following Blackwell's casual lead, but he talked Alcatraz down. Pat Mahoney, an officer and a boat pilot on Alcatraz, heard Bradley say several times that he couldn't wait to return to Leavenworth as a captain, what Officer Bill Rogers called "a more prestigious post." Bradley was openly critical of Alcatraz' notoriety and vocal about the idea that Leavenworth was a much tougher joint. He liked to say that he could match any prisoner on Alcatraz with any at Leavenworth.

It was an understandable attitude. Leavenworth had ten times the number of cons as Alcatraz, many of them arguably as dangerous. But Bradley was acting like a big city kid who transfers to a small town high school thinking that because of where he's been he's now got it made. It never works that way. Denigrating Alcatraz and its small, but tough, prison population set a careless tone. The captain was head of security. His derisive attitude, along with Blackwell's casual air, and eventually, the new associate warden's lack of cell house experience, would be the prison's undoing.

But more than that, Bradley represented what happens when authorities make shortsighted decisions based only on their immediate needs.

Bradley recognized that Blackwell was a comer; despite rumors and controversy most of his career, Blackwell seemed untouchable. And Bradley courted success; he was the loyal follower seeking approval to his own detriment. Blackwell, at the same time, loved and protected his friends. The two men formed an alliance that would last the rest of their careers, in part perhaps, fueled by what each of them knew about the other.

9

BY THAT SPRING, West had been talking up escape for more than a year. He had talked to Carnes, Kent, Morris, Boggs, Clinton and anybody else who would listen. Men were beginning to see that it was his supreme desire to escape from Alcatraz. Some of them even dubbed him "The Brain."

But his biggest problem was that it was tough to escape from seg. Records show that he sometimes talked late into the night to his neighbors, or into the toilet with the water removed—the "telephone" by which cons could talk or listen on a conference call without guards hearing. A lot of times he was talking escape—taking hostages, grabbing guns, getting out on the roof via the ceiling vents, commandeering the boat, lashing planks together and drifting to shore, blowing up surgical gloves to make "water wings," swimming. Guys tossed out ideas like playing cards. Alcatraz cons even had an expression that betrayed their obsession about escaping. "We got the boat," they'd say. It wasn't meant literally of course. It just meant that all the loose ends were tied up. But currently, West's "boat" was snagged. He had to get out of seg.

By April 20, 1961, he was making conflicting noises about wanting out. He was described in reports at times as "sullen," and "uncommunicative," at other times he was "cooperative" and "anxious to get back into the population again."

West began focusing on Lieutenant A.O. Severson as his ticket out. Severson was a ten-year veteran on Alcatraz. At one point the lieutenant offered West the chance to come out and take a job on the cell house paint crew, but West shot back that he'd rather stay in seg.

Others in segregation, however, made West think about that. Boggs who had worked in cell house maintenance before, told West it was a job with a lot of access. Could even get him into A block where paint, mattresses, clothing and other supplies were kept.

West's ears pricked up. But he had to wait until the big lieutenant circled back before asking for that job.

※ ※ ※

Part 2
The Plan

TU-23, IN SEGREGATION, was racked open with a loud crack and a rolling thunder. Out strutted a grinning Allen West. *You'll be back,* one of his friends shouted, laughing. I can hear West peppering the tier with profanity. Then TU-20 slid open and out popped Billy Boggs. *You'll both be back!* the voice taunted.

The cell house officer unlocked the D block segregation door and both men coolly sauntered over to the west-end desk. They would now be accorded full privileges, including eating in the dining room and going to the yard with the main population. It was Friday, May 5, 1961, a good day to be back in the main pop.

West requested a cell along the floor on the outside of B block, and was assigned B-152. Boggs was assigned B-140.

Although it had three hundred and thirty-six cells, Alcatraz seldom held more than two hundred and sixty men, thus approximately seventy-five cells were always empty. And while sometimes men moved for security reasons, often they moved because they wanted to. Morris, in his two and a half years on Alcatraz, for example, lived in six different cells. West, because of his behavior, was housed in twenty-nine cells during his last four years on the Rock.

After getting cell supplies in the basement, West and an officer ambled down Broadway. Boggs followed later. Although most cons were out working, some were in their cells, reading, laying down, some were out on furlough—the Alcatraz equivalent of a week off work for a year's good record. As West slinked by, he could see the arms of men sticking out of their bars; he may have felt others watching him from above. He saw a black con glare at him, then felt his eyes bore into the back of his head as he passed by.

They strolled past the "cut-off," a fenced-in empty space that

Looking down Broadway toward the main gate.

cut each block in half. Continuing to the end of the block, they turned left.

To West's right was the main gate, the prison's double-gated entrance. The main gate officer stood inside the sally-port on his eight-hour shift, controlling who came and went from the cell house. He handled keys to the bar front, which opened onto the cell house, as well as a steel door behind him. But it took the officer in the fortress known as the control center—just outside the main gate—to electronically activate a metal plate over the key hole, for the main gate officer to unlock it. Thus, two men were required to allow anyone in or out of the cell house. Beyond main gate and the control center were the offices of the warden, associate warden, captain and records clerk, the officers' break room and the armory, where guns and ammunition were kept. Cons seldom got to that side of the main gate.

Above the main gate was the east gun gallery, which was no longer manned, a good reason why West wanted to cell near here.

They passed the locked, steel door, on their left, which opened into the utility corridor, a three-foot wide dead space running between the two rows of cells in B. The utility corridor was filled with water, waste and electrical pipes feeding into each cell.

B block "outside" with the target vent above the third tier.

The guard waved West on while he stopped at the locked box which housed the cell door gears. Unlocking it, he dialed in B-152. West turned left again and walked to the third cell from the end. The gears clicked in and the cell gate slid open with a rolling, metal-to-metal rumble that echoed throughout the cell house. West stepped in as the gate roared shut, locking him inside. He tossed his clothes and bedding on his cot. He pulled out a pack of cigarettes, realized he didn't have a match, turned and thrust his arms out the bars, clapping to get the guard's attention. *I need a light,* he shouted into the void.

West was now exactly three tiers below the target ceiling vent. He may have casually told the officer that it was quiet on the outside of B. But there were obvious advantages. Those cells were across the aisle from A—an unused housing block that still had the old easy-to-saw flat bars from the army days. Thus no one could see what he was doing and snitch him out. His cell was also the farthest from the west-end desk near the dining room—the most active post. And, of course, the east gun gallery was empty. That meant that no officer patrolled near the target vent. It was also darker over there. But more importantly, every time West walked from the dining room to his cell he could look up and see the target ceiling vent.

WEST TOOK THAT job on the cell house maintenance crew and during the day he performed odd jobs. That summer, he painted cells. Eventually, he began painting the building's interior walls.

While painting alone in locked cells, West soon discovered that the concrete walls were actually smoothed over with an eighth-inch skim coat of plaster, cement paint and layers of green wall paint which made them look impregnable. He could prick the skim coat and see that the concrete beneath it, in some cases, had lost its integrity.

Each morning his officer escort unlocked West into the unused A housing block, which over the years had become a storage area. It was stacked with cans of mint green and eggshell paint, turpentine, pails of brushes, bags of cement powder, ladders, paint rags and other maintenance supplies. For a man like West, the A block supply area was a gold mine.

Boggs worked in the utility corridor, as a plumber's assistant.

The cell house in 1961 still reflected the army's draconian accommodations. The toilets were still flushed with salt water and fresh cold water ran into the cell faucets. Thus, cons shaved and washed daily in cold water. In 1960, however, the BOP had authorized funds to modernize the cells with hot water faucets. A plumber and two convict assistants had been fitting pipes cell by cell, block by block, from the utility corridor. The entire project took two and a half years to complete. Boggs helped drill holes into the back of each cell and fit pipes into new faucets inside the cells.

Even before 1960, the saltwater plumbing in the cell house was the single biggest nightmare. The pipes in the utility corridor

The utility corridor with corrosive saltwater pipes.

were old, corroded, leaked and were jury-rigged. In fact, the 1949 Butterworth memo recommended that the entire plumbing system be replaced then, meaning, of course, the saltwater sewage system. Nothing was done, and by 1961–62, the corrosion had reached catastrophic proportions. There is considerable evidence, in fact, that the B block utility corridor was awash in broken water pipes. On July 22, 1961, near where West celled, a water pipe burst and flooded the utility corridor. Five days later another one popped at 3:30 A.M. In October and again in January 1962, other pipes broke. The leaks, mixed with human waste, made for a permanent stench back there. But a bigger disaster is that the fifty years of flooding salt water weakened the concrete, and although the concrete on the exterior walls had been sealed, perhaps in 1959, no one had thought of resealing the inside walls.

Boggs didn't stay at his plumbing job long, but he got a good look at the pipes and the condition of the concrete and he probably told West that the pipe chase, as some called it, was his best route to the roof.

Something persuaded the day-watch cell house officer that

West should clean up behind the plumbers. He got into the utility corridor one day and immediately saw what he had been hearing: heavy cast-iron waste pipes, small electrical conduit and hot and cold water pipes snaking three stories high to the top of the block. He must have come to a smirking realization that the pipes were his ladder to the ceiling.

West later claimed to have found drill bits wrapped in oilcloth; he told others he found bullet casings left over from the '46 escape attempt. He may have spotted a bag of portland cement the plumbers were using. But his genius was in finding that the concrete was riddled with rocks and so porous in places that he could scrape it off with his fingernails. The boys in seg were right, he thought, cell house maintenance was exactly where he needed to be.

2

AS SOON AS he hit the chow line, West saw his old friend, J-Dub, from Raiford and signaled him with a grin. By Saturday, they were on the yard, punching each other playfully in the shoulders, *You look damn grow'd up,* West said. John was thirty-one and neat as a pin.

Your hair's thinnin', J-Dub replied.

West knew a sucker when he saw one; within minutes, he was outlining his escape plan. And just like that, J-Dub was in. By July, he rolled into B-150, right next to West. It was the cell from which he would eventually dig out.

It's not clear who thought of making dummy masks for the beds, but it is obvious that once West decided that they would escape from their cells, dummy masks would have to be made to conceal their escape.

West repeated the 1939 "Doc" Barker escape attempt to John one night telling about the five cons who had sawed their cell bars. *Seg didn't look like it does now,* West said, *those bars were like the ones over yonder, in A block; they were flat bars.* J-Dub looked across the aisle. *Oh, shit,* he thought, *easy as cuttin' through pie.* The five men left their cells, spread window bars, escaped and scattered down the cliff.

It didn't take a genius to reckin' those five cells were empty, West whispered icily.

No dummies, J-Dub retorted.

That was the beginning of their plan. Each night, they talked through the bars. Whispering back and forth, their knuckles gripping the bars, they were unable to see each other, but their excitement was palpable.

On weekends they hit the prison's recreation yard, gravitating to the concrete seats that buttressed the building, discussing methods of getting down from the roof. Morris often played softball along the west wall. From his position at bat, he could see a long pipe that extended from the roof to the ground—the bakery exhaust pipe. It vented the large industrial, kitchen ovens. West and John casually walked up the concrete seats to get a better look at the pipe.

For Morris, the plan was still theory; he hadn't committed to it yet. But he agreed—it was a possible route down.

West wasn't taking any chances, however. He figured he'd need a hundred feet of rope, or electrical wire, just in case the pipe couldn't hold a hundred and fifty pound man three stories high. *Rope would be better, but no problem,* West thought. He knew where he could get the wire.

WEST AND JOHN continued to run through ideas. Sawing bars was not possible. Sticking a "hack" and forcing him to unlock the utility corridor was too tricky; it'd be like '46, with hostages and killings. They were talking through the music hour. No one could hear them because of the cacophony echoing through the house.

Finally, when every other idea was found wanting, they began focusing on the little air vent at the back of their cells—a five-by-nine-and-a-half-inch diamond-patterned metal grill that was recessed into the wall and ventilated into the utility corridor. Maybe they could get through that.

The next night West told John he had studied the vent opening that day while inside a cell. The back wall wasn't more than about five and a half inches thick. But they'd need to expand the entire opening to about ten by fifteen inches to crawl through.

A whistle blew and an officer rounded the corner, counting heads. When he passed, West began whispering again.

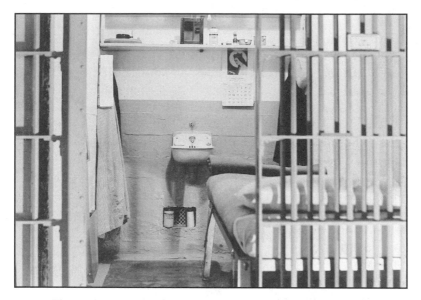

The grill, under the sink, vented air from the utility corridor.

*We need to get about three and a half inches just to get to the vent,
then another one to two inches to get through the entire wall,* West
told John. *I figure we'kin crack through that.* He took a drag off his
cigarette and blew smoke out his cell. *I read a book once, 'bout how
you can melt concrete by heating it to five to nine hundred degrees.* J-
Dub was impressed and urged him to try it.

Within a day or two, West got Glenn May, the inmate
electrician, to rig up some wire.

Like West, Glenn May, AZ 1392, moved around the cell house,
sometimes working with a minimum of supervision. He was often
called out early in the morning to repair toasters, bakery ovens
or the dishwashers. Seemed like things in the kitchen were always
breaking down.

At age forty-two, Glenn May was an odd character. Six feet
tall, stooped and emaciated at one hundred and twenty-nine
pounds, he ate little, refused meat, and often munched only on
peanuts or crackers. Passive and withdrawn, he avoided conflict.
He was a chess player, a cell house intellectual—buying books on
poetry, Russian grammar and philosophy. He was also one of the
best artists in the cell house.

The cell house electrician had racked up years behind bars for larceny, bad checks, postal burglary, forgery, and was now serving fifteen years for counterfeiting. Of him, my father had written: "Is electrician, and good. Also expert lock picker." Glenn May was on Alcatraz for possession of a key diagram and participating in a Leavenworth escape plot. West persuaded him to help out, and May agreed to it. But it would have a devastating effect on him later.

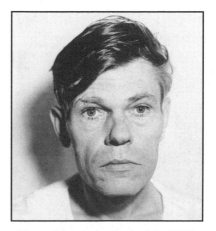

Glenn May, as he looked in 1962.

May liberated a heavy black electrical cord, stripping both ends to bare wire, and obtained some element wire, like in a toaster. When West finally got it, he attempted to rig it to the electrodes in his ceiling light socket while John covered for him. Jumpy after shocking himself, he finally got the two wires taped. But then in stretching it down to the wall, he inadvertently ripped it off, and had to retape it. Painstakingly, he reattached the wires, then carefully stretched it down to the back wall, pressing the element wires together against the concrete. Nothing. He pushed harder against the wall, generating a couple of sparks. Nothing. After an agonizing amount of time, West jerked the wire out of the socket and threw it aside.

Defeated, frustrated, he could have easily flown into a rage, slamming down on his cot, a slur of profanities hurling from his mouth. It was obvious. They'd have to dig.

IN THE MEANTIME, unknown to West, John had been sharing West's idea with his brother. John and Clarence were inseparable. That summer Clarence "Larry" Anglin came in on it and by July, Clarence had moved from a job in the culinary department to the cell house barbershop.

West was ticked off when he heard John had told Clarence. *It's my plan*, he said that night in his cell, *I do the inviting*. West dropped his cigarette butt on the floor and ground it up with his shoe.

'Course my brother's goin', John replied through his cell bars, *what'd you expect? 'Sides, he's working in the barbershop, cuttin' hair. We're gonna need some of that.*

West walked to the back of his cell. He didn't trust Clarence Anglin. He thought he was a loud screw up. He lit another cigarette and toss the pack onto his table. He decided to focus on Morris, and within a couple of days, he forgot about John's little indiscretion.

3

BY JULY 1961, the biggest modernization since the radio headsets were installed came to Alcatraz. It reflected what was happening in prisons nationwide since President John F. Kennedy had been elected.

Well, lookie here, West exclaimed when he walked into the dining room. Instead of the old ten-man dining tables in use since the army days, now there were new four-man tables. He noticed also that the old metal dishware had been replaced by new plastic dishware. *Tryin' to make us believe we're in some 'Frisco joint,* he

The old ten-man tables were in use until the summer of 1961.

said while standing in the food line. Couple of guys grinned back at him. But right away he knew that this was going to be an advantage: three times a day, he could sit with his buddies. Three times a day, they could plot out ideas and nobody—*nobody*—could hear them.

Regulations called for cons to fill up tables in sequence as each man got his tray and food. You sat with the men who celled near you. At first West sat with Billy Boggs and J-Dub, but sometimes Morris, who lived on B block third tier, arranged to sit with them.

On weekends in the yard, West was joined not only by the Anglin brothers, Boggs and Morris, but sometimes Kent and Carnes. They huddled on the concrete steps where it was warm, continuing the conversations they had at mealtimes.

"The whole plan was to swim," Kent said years later. "When 'Larry' came, he said, 'Why don't we build a raft?' "

Everyone was stunned into silence.

Then they started talking at once.

We could use raincoats, one of them said.

It'd have to be big enough for six, said another, *that's a lot of raincoats.*

West perked up, *Raincoats been used before.* Three months after

The new tables were tough to monitor but a boon to the foursome.

West had arrived in 1958, Aaron Burgett and Clyde Johnson had tried to escape in the twelfth attempt in the prison's history. They made plywood fins as paddles and "water wings" out of raincoats. The full-length, navy-issue, water-repellent raincoats, made of rubber-backed cotton, were long considered as "boat" material.

After overpowering a guard on a garbage detail, the two escapees jumped in. But Johnson turned around and climbed back up the sea wall. "Johnson claimed he got about sixty yards when his 'wings' failed," my father said. "The prisoners had a different version."

It weren't no wings that failed, West scoffed.

Burgett got a little further out and found himself in trouble almost immediately. With his clothes on, his heavy shoes lashed with plywood, and his "water wings," he fought to stay afloat. The tower officer heard him shouting for help but didn't know an escape attempt had occurred and couldn't locate the voice on the bay. Burgett sank, drowned and floated up days later, as decomposed and as soggy as a piece of bread.

'Gator bait, Clarence taunted, and they all snickered.

IN THE DINING room one Friday, West and the Anglins picked up their trays and got in the food line. Alcatraz "cuisine" was considered the best in the federal prison system. None of those sliced cold cuts, a staple in other pens that cons called "Donkey Dick." Instead, they regularly got grilled beef and pork sausage, baked Swiss steak, stuffed bell peppers, "Bob-que" spare ribs, chili con carne—what the southerners called "a good lube job." Soup was served at every lunch—split pea, beef barley, Yankee bean.

"We ate like a first-class hotel there," said Juelich, "Food was a big thing."

Today, they were served grilled fillet of perch, with tartar sauce and lemon, baked Idaho potatoes, buttered green beans, coleslaw, corn muffins and chocolate cream pie. West put his tray down and walked to the coffee urn. Morris and the Anglins sat at his table.

If we had 'nuff raincoats, we could make pontoons, Clarence said when they sat down, *blow 'em up 'n' float away.*

Hell, it don't take nothin, J-Dub said, *I seen logs float.*

Cain't depend on a log being out there, West agreed, *We got to plan to get across.*

John mentioned a November 1960 issue of *Popular Mechanics.* There was an article in it about making duck decoys out of rubber inner tubes. *Showed how you could vulcanize the seams by heating them.*

Morris listened, but even he began to fidget. Finally, he spoke up, telling them that he could fly a helicopter. They all looked at him. West swallowed a fork full of food and picked up his coffee cup. Everybody knew Morris was a brainy guy. Some thought he was a genius. Busted out of every pen he'd ever been in. Much later, a prisoner actually came forward and told officials that's what he'd told the Anglins.

You 'kin fly a helicopter? J-Dub said, buttering his corn muffin.

I read a couple of books, Morris said evenly, looking at each of them. *It don't look that hard.*

Man! Clarence said. *They'd never catch us!*

I studied it one summer, Morris told them, *got everything I could read on it. Trust me, it ain't that hard.*

West said nothing, but he was in his glory. Animated, alert, his men talking about his idea—everyone else out of hearing range—he must have felt like the entire dining room was out of focus except for his table. And the food was great, the tartar sauce and the lemon juice just burst in his mouth. No one knew much about helicopters. They just believed him. Like he believed it.

Reckon we can steal one, John said, chortling, shoving the corn bread in his mouth.

I been thinkin', Morris said. *I figure I can fly us into the desert, hole up there for a while.*

Shit! Clarence exclaimed. *We could git us a coupl'a trailers, hang it up 'til the heat's off.* He looked around for approval.

By early that fall, it appears that Morris had decided to join. West and he had already discussed how to hide the holes they would dig, because on September 7, 1961, Morris turned in a purchase order for oil paints, art brushes and a roll of canvas about eight to nine feet in length. Although he had some experience as a draftsman, he had never shown interest in art before.

4

WEST REMAINED ON his job into the fall, among a small group

West painted the cell house that summer, sometimes up on scaffolding.

of semi-skilled and unskilled men who worked in cell house maintenance. Usually guys cycled in and out after serving time in segregation and before being assigned a more permanent job elsewhere. Sometimes simple cell house jobs were used to humiliate the big boys. Al Capone, AZ 85, the Italian-American mobster—and the most famous gangster in history—had been cell house sweep in the mid-1930s. Cons called him, "the wop with the mop."

West liked his job, he told the lieutenant.

He was observed all day long by the officer-in-charge (OIC), two or three floor officers, the west-end guard, the main gate officer, even the lieutenant who strolled in and out of the cell house. Moreover, every section of the house was locked, so West needed an officer to access any area—D block, the hospital, the kitchen, A block, the basement.

But no one observed his every move. And it's clear he could steal things and move them around without officers knowing it.

That fall, West was proving to be such an eager worker that he was now painting the cell house ceiling—starting at the west end near the gun gallery. To do that, he happily wheeled over a three–story scaffolding and climbed to the top of the platform.

Cons had a game of using paper clips and rubber bands to shoot out the ceiling light bulbs. Glenn May later said that sometimes West changed light bulbs for him while up on the scaffolding.

Three stories up on the scaffolding gave West a commanding view of the top of the cell house. He saw that enough space existed between the top of the cell blocks and the ceiling that a man could walk around comfortably. On the outside of B block, he could actually see the target ceiling vent with the exhaust blower still intact.

Sometime in September, West convinced the cell house officer that he needed to see if he could paint, standing, on top of the block. The two men walked up to the third tier, West carrying a ladder. Talking casually, West set up the ladder on the third tier landing, the guard climbed up and unlocked a gate so West could get up on top of the block. They walked around up there, deciding that West could paint the ceiling using a step ladder. West stole a look at the exhaust fan and its egress into the ceiling.

More importantly, he had broken a barrier: He now knew how easy it was to get an officer to let him up there.

In fact, they were all precisely positioned by then.

Morris worked in industries. He was racked out each morning with the biggest group. They lined up in the yard for the clothing, glove, brush, furniture refinishing, laundry or dry-cleaning shops and walked down a long flight of stairs to the industries building along the southwest side of the island.

"It was his idea of going down to industries," Kent had said, "where he could get tools and materials." Kent had arranged for Morris to get in touch with Trump, Larry Trumblay, the handsome, wavy-haired bank robber with a torso filled with bullet holes and a penchant for broken glass, and Teddy Green, AZ 1180, doing twenty-six years on a bank charge who thought of himself as a big shot. Kent said they "vouched for him" and Morris worked in the brush shop as a "puller." He assembled the wire-drawn floor sweeps used to clean long hallways. Using a crochet hook, he pulled horsehair and synthetic fiber through a hundred little holes in a long wooden board. After tying off the fibers, he tossed the finished board into a box and picked up another blank. A good

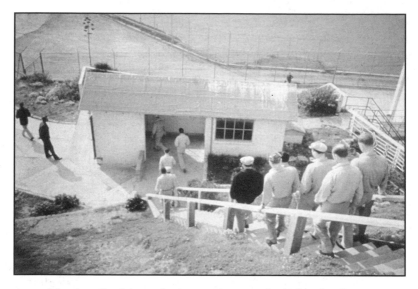

Morris walked down the long stairway to the industries shops.

steady worker could finish twenty boards a day. Some men found
the brush shop boring, quickly tranferring to other shops. Morris
worked there for sixteen months, the drone of the work like a
mantra to him.

The industrial shops were chock full of sewing machines, drill
presses and special cutting tools; industrial-size mangles and
washers and dryers; boxes of raw materials, old file records; bins
of clothing; spools of wire; scales; saws and hammers; cleaning
solvents, varnishes and paints; and old discarded machinery used
for parts. To a new officer it could look chaotic and dangerous.
To a seasoned con like Morris the shops were an endless supply
of potential contraband. Hence the reason why cons walked
through two metal detectors before returning to the cell house.

John worked in the clothing room in the prison's basement.
Boggs also worked here for several months. So did, for a time,
Los Angeles mobster Mickey Cohen, AZ 1518. They bagged clothes
to be sent to the laundry and sorted into bins the freshly laundered
socks, pants, and shirts. J-Dub also arranged stacks of army
blankets, bins of toilet paper, soap, shoes, canvas belts, caps, navy
pea coats and a ready supply of old navy raincoats. Every con
stopped in the clothing room first when he was transferred to the

John worked in the clothing room in the prison's basement.

island. And twice a week, every con got a shower and a fresh set of clothes.

Years later, when an old con who had transferred off before the escape attempt, wondered how the four men could get so many supplies, I told him where John worked. "Oh!" he said, laughing, "That explains it!"

The clothing room was a freeway for contraband.

It wasn't a demanding job and therefore was reserved for the castoffs like J-Dub who were not skilled or motivated enough to work in the better paying industries jobs. Worse, John's 1962 annual review reported that he did "just enough to get by and must be constantly supervised." He liked to fool around, doing push-ups on the floor and chin-ups on the pipes. He was cool. And remarkably well placed.

One of his coworkers was a guy who'd grown up in the San Francisco Bay Area. J-Dub's eyebrows shot up. He questioned him about the currents and tides. He was also interested in the nearest point of land from Alcatraz. His friend told him, "Angel Island."

John was really into it. On November 8, 1961, he purchased artist paint brushes and nine twelve-by-sixteen canvas drawing boards, although he had seldom shown any interest in painting before.

Clarence worked in the barbershop in the A block alcove. He was described as a "fair barber," who cut the white inmates' hair. He was also a yakker, constantly whispering in guys ears. Sometimes he got a little too full of himself, bragging about their plan, and asking questions about the tides and the currents like he was a big shot planner. While sweeping up one day, he picked up a lock of black hair, looking at how each strand of hair hung together like a curved ribbon. He may have even remarked about it to the guard—like his own private joke. The guard glanced back, uninterested, as Clarence dropped it into the dustpan and tossed it into the waste basket.

And West. Although among guards he had always been considered "sullen" and "uncommunicative," during the fall of 1961, he turned into one of the best employees on the Rock. He was commended for his "improved conduct and work record," and the "conscientious manner in which he performed his duties." It was, in fact, considered a "remarkable change." Chirpy and animated, West returned to painting on his scaffolding. He dipped his brush into the white paint, tapped it lightly, then stroked the ceiling like a drummer marching toward his goal.

"THEY ALL WANTED out," Carnes said about them years later. "*Bad.* They would have slept with a rattlesnake to get out."

Building a raft was an astounding challenge, however. It would require more material and take more time. The chance of discovery was much greater. Yet once proposed, the idea stuck.

But Kent began to fret about it. He couldn't swim, especially in fifty-degree water, maybe with sharks in it. And he worried about a handmade raft for six people. He was also leery of the Anglins. After days of agonizing, he told them he was out.

Carnes was scared too. "Suddenly the Anglins were in on it," he wrote later, "and Morris, and there were other people who were approached. And the thing was just too complicated. You had to have too much material. And there was no way you were going to get that material without The Man becoming aware. And they'd zero in on certain people. And they'd watch 'em, shake their cell down and sooner or later they'd catch you." He dropped out, telling West, "I don't think I can be involved in this."

But both men would stay in touch. In the library, they too, were well placed for passing contraband items to West and the others.

On Sunday, September 10, 1961, Morris moved down from the third tier into B-138—ten cells from the east end. West rolled over next to him in Boggs' old cell, B-140. On Monday, Clarence moved into West's old cell, B-152, next to J-Dub.

Thus, by September 11, 1961, all four were in the cells from which they would escape: Clarence and John Anglin were in cells B-152 and 150, and four cells down the line Allen West and Frank Morris were in B-140 and 138.

5

NINETEEN SIXTY-ONE was a big year. On, May 5, the same day West got out of seg, the entire nation celebrated when Astronaut Alan B. Sheppard, Jr., became the first American to make a fifteen minute suborbital flight aboard the *Mercury 3*. In August, the Soviet Union erected a barrier for hundreds of miles dividing East and West Germany. The Cold War was felt thousands of miles away, even on Alcatraz; when men took out their garbage from Sixty-four building they could see the stenciled arrows on the old casemate walls printed with the words, "Air Raid Shelter."

Fishing on the island was pretty good that year—a particularly favorite pastime for staff who needed no license and had no limit. The striped bass were running so fast that twice on September 11 and 12, officers Gene Jones and Darrel Pickens brought up "wheelbarrows" of fish for the cell house culinary department.

The film *West Side Story* was released in October that year, and Henry Miller's sexually explicit 1934 novel, *Tropic of Cancer*, was published in the U.S. for the first time. Ray Charles topped the charts with "Hit the Road Jack." The smooth Sam Cooke was crooning a song called "Cupid," and an unknown group, The Tokens, became famous with "The Lion Sleeps Tonight." Actor Gary Cooper, who had always reminded me of my father, died that year. Then on October 1, Roger Maris of the New York Yankees hit his sixty-first home run, shattering Babe Ruth's old record. It seemed like a new era had dawned.

That same month, Olin Blackwell became warden of Alcatraz.

After being acting warden for more than a year, Blackwell and his wife moved into the warden's mansion up next to the prison.

Although "warden of Alcatraz" was a distinguished position in the Bureau, "Blackie" had inherited a crumbling facility, which now required financial gymnastics to keep afloat. The powerhouse, the guard towers, the prison catwalks, the saltwater and sewage pipes, the cell house intercoms, the boat engines and the water barge all broke down at various times, and competed for funds in a restricted operating budget. There were continual comments in monthly budget meetings about deferring repairs and about requesting emergency funds from Washington, not all of which were granted.

Storms and high winds that winter wrecked havoc on the island boats and fences, and leaked water onto the floor of the business office. In November, a large rain gutter flew off one of the apartment buildings. Faulty wiring caused a potentially dangerous fire in one of the prison bakery ovens. A 1961 engineering survey, in fact, stated that the island would need $4 million worth of repairs to continue operating. Everyone could look around and see what was going on.

At the same time, Alcatraz was in the middle of one of the biggest construction booms since it had opened. Beginning in 1959, the BOP had decided that the antiquated control center and armory had to be modernized. The control center was the heart of the prison's security, all population counts, keys and armaments ended up here. Because of its importance, it couldn't be dismantled and rebuilt; a second control center had to be built across the hall. This one would have state-of–the-art paging and telephone systems. Begun in July 1960, the new control center was manned for the first time on August 15, 1961.

Other remodeling projects were also approved—the visitors' room, the staff dining room upstairs, and finally the offices of the warden, associate warden, captain and records clerk. For the last three or four years that Alcatraz operated, the administration section of the prison building was crawling with carpenters, plumbers, electricians, and painters—some of whom were civilian contract workers from San Francisco and some of whom had inmate helpers.

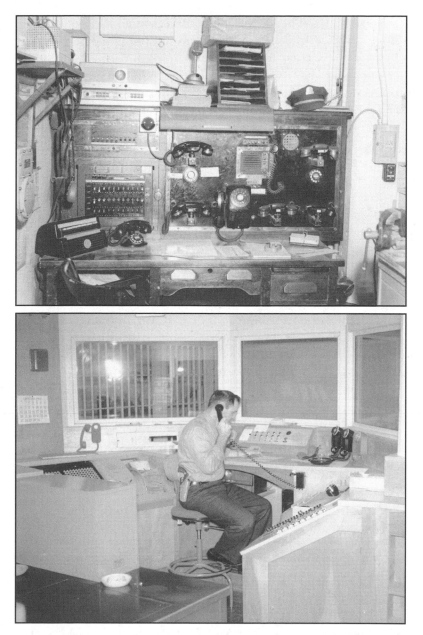

The old control center, top, was in use until August 14, 1961. The new
control center, built across the hall, opened the next day
with state of the art equipment.

Moreover, the cell house plumbing project was a major, long-term operation handled by a civilian employee and two inmate helpers.

In a kind of bipolar frenzy, capital improvements like the hot-water plumbing and a new control center were being authorized up until Alcatraz closed, but the prison's annual budgets almost never took into consideration its mounting operating problems.

Furthermore, new employees sometimes quit unexpectedly, resulting in a high turnover. Budget memos from 1961–62 began showing an "excess of salaries," due sometimes to "the fact that we did not get all the people we had originally anticipated." While Alcatraz was authorized to have ninety-eight officers, it was cut to ninety-five in the spring of 1962. And even then, it often operated between two and eight positions short every month.

Moreover, Blackwell sought to put his own stamp on Alcatraz. Almost immediately he increased the number of boat trips to San Francisco from fourteen to eighteen. It was more convenient for on- and off-island staff and residents, but it put more pressure on the old engines and the maintenance staff. But that was rectified when Captain Bradley announced a new procedure to allow prisoner dock workers to provide simple maintenance on the island's boat. The pilot house and engine room would be locked, of course, and the inmates carefully watched, but it was a risky operation that had never before been authorized on Alcatraz.

Blackwell also decided that the prison's administrative offices were threadbare and wanted them remodeled. In the spring of '62, the budget committee, which he headed, decided rather than requesting additional money from the Bureau for office furniture they'd use the excess salary funds.

Although in hindsight this looks more questionable than it may have at the time, catastrophic events seek out just these kinds of practices.

And as warden, Blackwell's offhand, folksy air became even more instructional. Dick Waszak, a rookie officer living on Alcatraz with his family, recalled an incident when he and the warden were fishing off the island dock past midnight one night. Joe Burlingame was the morning watch lieutenant. He patrolled from midnight to 8:00 A.M., checking posts in the cell house, using his flashlight to signal towers, shaking down industries. It was the top position on the watch and vital to the security.

"The water was just solid with striped bass," Waszak remembered excitedly. "Blackwell broke his rod, and of course we're just trying to hoist these stripers out of the water any way we can. When Burlingame came by, Mr. Blackwell told him, 'Just grab the damn gaff and forget about rounds'. And that's what we did until it was about time to go to work—about seven."

In another incident that blurred the line between warden and his employees, Blackwell drove up to the San Francisco dock one night, close to midnight. Sitting in the car next to him was an officer also waiting for the boat.

The warden rolled down his window. "You sober young man?" he asked.

"Yep," said the officer.

"Well, that's no way to go home," Blackwell quipped. He pulled out a bottle of liquor and handed it to the man.

In fact, hard drinking seemed at the center of stories about Blackwell. Those who disliked him called him an alcoholic. My father, older and more conservative than the warden, felt that he could "hold his liquor," and never saw him drunk. But wild parties at the warden's mansion were not unknown. One officer told me he danced the polka up at the warden's house, and he and his dance partner were so drunk they both fell down.

Stories floated around the island like clucking seagulls.

Blackwell liked kids. He was friendly and easygoing. None of us were afraid of him like kids had been with Warden Swope, whom nearly everyone disliked because he kept a dog on the island when no one else could, or Warden Johnston, whom you spoke to only if he spoke first. Blackwell was just one of the guys. At the annual "Frontier Days," he fit right in as the "wagon master," entertaining kids with rope tricks and regaling officers and wives with colorful prison tales. In one skit in 1962, four teenage girls sang a western song while brandishing toy guns in their holsters, realistic looking guns said to have been provided for the occasion by Blackwell. It seemed to some the iron-fisted rules were being flaunted.

Even the warden's wife, a friendly, garrulous Texan, came under scrutiny. Together, they didn't present the picture of an

The warden entertaining the kids at the annual "Frontier Days" party.

aloof warden and his demur wife.

It was said he played favorites with the staff and even some of their wives. But it was difficult to tell which of the rumors were true and which were rooted in the traces of jealousy and bile that shot through the prison service—especially at Alcatraz. If anything, "Blackie" stood for what we northerners thought of as a loud, steer-wrestling cowpoke. He had succeeded the highly popular, very proper warden, Paul J. Madigan, who was considered a "giant" by some—a top-notch security-minded administrator who had proven the old adage that excellent preparation makes you lucky.

"Let's put it this way," Officer Herman said, "If I hadn't worked with Madigan, then the warden would have been okay."

BUT PERHAPS THE biggest shock in October came when my father was promoted to associate warden. Officers were astonished that an outsider from industries had been promoted to associate warden. "If that wasn't a milestone," said Waszak, for example, "I can still remember all the hushed talk. . . . If you weren't *custody,* if you weren't *treatment*, forget it. . . .We knew the Bureau was falling apart." Such promotions from outside the security bastion were still rare twenty years later.

Arthur M. Dollison

We moved back to the island just before I turned fifteen, settling into the duplex along the east end of the island right next to Captain Bradley and his wife. I had only a vague idea that Dad's promotion was unusual. I was more excited about making new friends and starting a new school in San Francisco.

It was a cold winter that year. It seemed like it started raining in November and never stopped. Gusts blew up to seventy miles an hour; huge waves lashed at the island and stinging, horizontal rain pounded the concrete. I'd look out my bedroom window, while getting dressed for school, and see my father walking up "windy gulch," clutching his hat, holding onto his topcoat to keep it from whirling in the stiff winds, making his way up to the prison where the U.S. flag unfurled and snapped, its lanyard banging and ringing off the hollow, lonely pole.

He had what many considered a glaring weakness: he had never worked in the Alcatraz cell house.

"They done a disservice to him when they made him associate warden," Mitchell said years later. "I don't think Art had an idea in the world what he was getting into."

"Your father wasn't cut out to be associate warden," said Senior Officer Marvin Orr. Orr had worked on Alcatraz since 1939, under all four wardens and numerous associate wardens. "He was not a custodial man. It was a shock all over the service."

"If I'd been captain [then]," Bergen said years later, "I would have taken him under my wing."

The associate warden supervised the administrative, custodial, mechanical, food service, medical and industrial department heads. He spent much of his week in budget and inmate classification meetings, in overseeing remodeling projects, in approving menus, inmate requests and interviews. Dad was well organized and adept. But on Alcatraz, unlike prisons in later years, the associate warden was also responsible for staff and prisoner discipline. He chaired inmate court proceedings, along with a lieutenant and a cell house officer. In past years the associate wardens were men I chose to avoid; tough prison men whose hard-edged speech patterns easily identified them as cops, and whose world views were not tangled up in pleasant ambiguities or moral dilemmas.

I like to think that my father's powers of judgment were fair and unfettered by prejudice. Documents show that he was equally able to eliminate, as well as award, two and three-hundred days' good time allotments to prisoners for their behavior. He made notes in every classification meeting most of which were sketches of prisoners' sentences, ("25 years–Bank," "Death–Life–Treason,") or comments about their behavior, ("has a phony halo he polishes up"). He had the reporter's nose for interesting detail; about Theodore "Blackie" Audett, who was on Alcatraz three times on three different convictions, Dad had written, "20 years bank robbery; one of his codefendants was sentenced to only an hour."

Dad was charmed by Tom Kent. In one of his longest notes, he wrote, "Fifteen years, bank—why all the trouble outside? Greedy, poor and wanted money. Worked a year and earned $4,600; never made that much in all his stealing. Wonderful, Irish, sunny personality." An escape note was found in Kent's cell in 1962, which he denied writing. Dad had the note analyzed by a handwriting expert in San Francisco and, although the results were inconclusive, he backed Kent. Had he known later that Kent was an early, frequent conspirator with West and the others, he would have removed his glasses in bemused disappointment.

Unfortunately, it would turn out that the three top men were the margin of error that West needed to succeed. In all the criticism that came later—especially from officers who had worked on Alcatraz years before—no one noticed that these three administrators had all assumed their positions only months before the escape attempt occurred. Wardens, associates and captains had all come and gone in Alcatraz' history—but *never* at the same time. By November 1961, as the four escapees were debating at every meal about how to get out of their cells, Blackwell and Dollison had been in their positions less than a month. And Bradley, on his first assignment as captain, had been there slightly more than a year. All three men were at the peak of their careers. To varying degrees, they were all seasoned prison men. But they were blind to what was going on around them. "You don't know," said Officer Irving Levinson about the lapse in security, "until after it happens." And they were all hurtling toward a disaster that only Blackwell would survive intact.

Because Alcatraz, in fact, was deconstructing. Not only was its physical plant rotting from the inside, but the poor grade of materials that had been used for years were beginning to show wear at an ever-increasing rate. The years of budget tightening, the elimination of security positions, the officer attrition, the paradoxical modernization in the center of a crumbling facility and the new emphasis on relaxing the atmosphere were all bumping around like loose boulders on land under which a volcano is about to erupt. And that volcano was Allen West. He could look around and see for miles that things had changed. Think of him as the geologic equivalent of an igneous intrusion. In the midst of all the weakness, distraction and instability, his plan to break the Rock would heave out of the ground like molten lava—bubbling up and smothering everything in its wake.

Blackwell could never admit his own responsibility in the fracas, however. Unlike Mitchell, who was coarse but intuitive and too blunt to be political, Blackwell, when interviewed, was cagey, darting this way and that, refracting criticism the way looking into water distorts your sight and the catfish slips through your fingers.

Years later, I was to wonder if the cons had taken control of the cell house: if all the files and scrap metal and drill bits and ice picks and sharpened spoon handles that would be relayed to the four men, if the motors that would soon be lifted, the portland cement, the human hair, the dozens of raincoats that would be stockpiled, weren't proof that the inmates had taken control of the asylum. Once in a rambling answer to another question, Blackwell had mused about the futility of allowing prisoners more control. And then as an afterthought he wisecracked, "If they goin' to run the institution, you just as well go fishin'."

Ironically, come June, that's just what he would do.

6

ONE LUNCH, WHILE slurping soup and the others were talking, John suddenly looked at his spoon. It was a large soup spoon, its bowl almost as big as a cupped hand. He looked at its handle, turned it over, noting how it tapered down to a narrow gauge. He tried to bend it. It was a tough, old steel spoon. Grinning, he held it up. *Our little rooter,* he drawled.

He tipped his bowl and scooped up the last of the soup, then casually fingered the spoon into his shirt. That was the number one advantage over the ten-man tables: officers had always checked utensils, especially knives, but it was harder now with more tables, and they hadn't geared up. A guard must have checked their table, but didn't notice the missing spoon. Nor was there a stationary metal detector by the dining room door. Officers could wheel over a portable metal detector if they heard a con was packing a knife. But not that day. John sauntered out with his homey little tool.

That night, during the music hour, he broke off the bowl and began grinding the handle on his concrete cell floor, sharpening it like an ice pick. West was excited by the simplicity of it. Spoons were easier to steal—at least until he could get a concrete drill.

Over the next few weeks several utensils were lifted from the dining room. No one seemed to notice.

"THERE'S A TIME right after supper," Carnes said, "when the guys are talking, yelling—before they settle down." The mail has been passed out. Guys are getting out their oil paints and brushes, others are pulling down their radio earphones, or snapping open their musical instruments cases. It was "happy hour," the period when musicians practiced in their cells. "And that's the best time to work," he said.

Non-musicians hated "happy hour." Few musicians were any good and the chaos was irritating. "They'd ring that bell," said

An early, staged photograph showing an Alcatraz musician.

Juelich, "and for most of us it was agony. All you'd hear was guitars, trumpets, saxophones and accordions. . . . Guys calling chess numbers out. It was nothing but a jangle of noise. . . . By five minutes to seven, those that didn't play were sitting on the edge of our beds, hoping that that bell would sound."

For others, it was the nicest part of the day. Former prisoner Jerie Bremmeyer, AZ 1086, got out his guitar and tuned up nightly with three other guitar players who celled near him.

In the past, horn players went to the basement. In fact, institutional rules stated, "At no time will you play any wind instruments in the cell house." But according to Bremmeyer, there between '53 and '59, cons learned to muffle their horns by stuffing them with clothing and aiming into their toilets. If you were quiet, the cell house officer didn't care. But this change may have also reflected the reduction in the evening watch staff.

For West, who had by now obtained his own spoon and ground down the handle, it was all the cover they needed. *Hell, it wouldn't matter if I had a jack hammer,* "Twinkle, Twinkle, Little Star," and "Moon River," drowned everything out.

West taped his spoon handle for a better grip. While Morris held a tiny mirror between his bars for any signs of a guard, West folded his coat on the floor, knelt down, and began poking around.

Suddenly his whole world narrowed down to a three-centimeter portion of concrete and the sharpened end of a steal spoon handle. He pried off a small layer of paint and began to prod little pieces of concrete loose. Focusing close, he could almost see every grain. He pried and dug, twisting his handle, then drilled again, lost in concentration.

West! West! Morris whispered, audibly. West pocketed his tool, threw a towel around his sink pipes, and jumped on his cot. You could never hear the hacks approach, so cons had to warn one another. Most officers wore what cons called "sneak shoes," made with crepe soles. They were easier on the shins in the concrete palace but they were quiet too. When the officer glided past West's cell, he was lying on his cot, reading.

He quickly resumed working.

By the end of an hour, however, West had succeeded in raising only a little dust. He chipped some soap with his fingernail, layered it over the dent and blended it into the wall.

Morris had told West he'd watch for him, and the next night West was back at it. This time he taped a nail clipper to one end of the spoon handle, making a "T" shaped handle, and resumed grinding on the first hole. He made very little progress.

Frustrated, he gave up and started working on another hole just to the right of the first one. He pried off a little of the skim coat and began twisting the spoon handle around and around. Within a few minutes tiny grains of sand and a fine powder of fifty-year-old cement began tumbling out. Minutes later, he was deeper into the hole. Worn slivers of old dried wood, orange and black particles that that looked like iron ore, and tiny pebbles gave up and fell out. Sometimes a steady stream of sand and old cement powder came pouring out.

Although Hollywood films and numerous television documentaries showed cons chipping away at one big hole, in fact, each dug only one tiny hole at a time, about the length and size of your little finger. When West finished that night, he plugged up the little indentations with moistened toilet paper and smoothed them over with soap chips. The next night, he was at it again, slowly. It took three nights to drill a single hole of just a few millimeters. And by then he had smuggled in some green paint. After he plugged up the hole with toilet paper and soap, he painted over it. You couldn't tell a tiny crack had already been made in the wall.

The next night, West was able to drill two holes right next to the first one, each about three inches deep. With growing excitement he began to feel that it might work. While Morris kept watch, he plugged up the new holes, rubbed the wall with soap, let it dry, then smeared it all with more green paint.

After lights out at 9:30, he talked in hushed tones to Morris long into the night. He was on his bunk now, his head to the bars as was required, his hands above and behind, gripping the bars as he did leg lifts to strengthen his stomach muscles, scheming, bragging, excited as a punk breaking down his first door.

They talked quietly until Morris drifted off to sleep.

But West was wide awake, barely breathing, his thoughts racing. He was ecstatic. Two holes! He figured he could drill forty holes in about six weeks. ("We'll be through the concrete by Christmas!" he later bragged to Carnes.) He would need that many—maybe more. He'd have to get a lot of green paint. *How'll we get the ceiling vent off? What if the screws hear us up there?* He pushed that from his mind.

Digging at night during the music hour was a perfect idea. There was only one officer—the OIC—on the main floor. And he never bothered to come around the outside of B unless it was to count. The lieutenant was in and out all night, but he just wore a path down Broadway.

All around him West could hear noises. Winds buffeting the windows, gulls clucking as they settled into their nests. Far away, a bell rang as its buoy tossed on the bay and the foghorns were in full chorus. Inside the house, men turned on their cots, snoring, or talking in their sleep. Nights on Alcatraz, especially if you couldn't sleep, could be agonizing. "I could hear guys sobbing into their pillows," Juelich once said.

Close to midnight West could hear the main gate officer unlock the front gate with the slide of a key and the click of a latch. He heard an officer greet the main gate officer, then walk down Broadway, his footsteps quickly fading. Seconds later, West may

have heard the muffled sounds of two men talking down at the
west-end desk. Shift change. Either the morning watch lieutenant,
or the cell house OIC, was starting his midnight shift. Then
another officer was let inside the cell house, and West heard him
stroll down Broadway. West may have even heard the gun gallery
officer speak down to the floor officers, the echo of chortling,
the jiggling of keys. A few minutes later, someone—West figured
it was the evening watch lieutenant—was racked out of the cell
house. Waving good night to the control center officer as he
passed by, the lieutenant turned left to the captain's desk, opened
a ledger called the "Lieutenant's Record," also known as the watch
log, and wrote, "Quiet evening—routine watch," and left the
building.

Within minutes, the midnight to 8:00 A.M. morning-watch cell
house OIC began making his prison count. West heard his
footsteps as he drew closer. Had he looked out his cell using his
peripheral vision, West might have seen the darkened silhouette
of a uniformed officer flashing his light on the ceiling of each
man's cell. West held his breath. The guard approached and West
could see his ceiling bathed in light, then darken just as suddenly
as the guard passed, his footsteps disappearing into the darkness.

The evening watch officer departed the cell house and the
joint was quiet once again.

West resumed his obsession. He figured that only about eight
officers were on duty during the evening and morning watches—
the OIC, the main gate officer, the lieutenant, and one officer
each in D block, the hospital, the control center, the dock and
road towers. He knew the lieutenant was let out of the main gate
several times a night. West assumed he patrolled—checking
towers, maybe shaking down industries. And he knew that
sometimes the main gate officer patrolled outside. *Were they
armed?* West wasn't sure. That was it from about 6:00 P.M. until
7:00 A.M. every night. West also knew that cons could keep a cell
house officer down at the other end of the cell house, if they
needed to. An outbreak of stomachaches, bitty requests, someone
tearing up his cell in a male display—it was pretty easy to keep
the lieutenant or the officer distracted.

And although there were fewer noises at night, it was never

quiet. Two hundred men in the main line were at different times turning in their beds, snoring, talking in their sleep, even getting up and flushing their toilets. The endless winds that whipped the cell house caused the ceiling skylights to rattle, the windows to whistle and the building to creak. Radiator pipes sometimes banged and hissed out steam. It could get spooky, but the noises were usually identifiable.

For officers, the midnight-to-8:00 A.M. morning watch was dreary. The cell house OIC counted sleeping prisoners; the lieutenant patrolled the island. In the towers, said Bill Long, you just looked "until your eyeballs hurt." Long, like half the officers, had a personal interest in the security of the island. His wife and two children lived in one of the Alcatraz apartments.

Sleep was the enemy, said Officer Hernan. "I used to hang on the main gate bars just to keep awake." Hernan told of another officer in a tower who had to call the control center every twenty minutes. He used to light a cigarette and wrap it around his fingers with a rubber band. It'd take twenty minutes for the cigarette to burn his fingers and wake him up. Then he called in.

The morning-watch cell house officer made his midnight count, then counted twice more before 7:00 A.M., when the day watch officers began coming on. And so on, everyday. Officers were assigned to a shift for a three-month rotation. If you were the morning watch OIC, you counted sleeping prisoners five nights a week for three months.

West was surprised much later, when the officer began another count. It must be 3:00 A.M., West calculated. He finally fell into a fitful sleep, vaguely aware that morning was approaching and another guard was making his cell checks. At 7:00 A.M. West was jerked awake by the loud clanging prison bell. He hated that bell. But now it tolled with a new excitement.

MINUTES LATER, THE lieutenant blew the count whistle. Cons stood at their bars while guards rounded the tiers counting and shouting the final numbers down to the lieutenant. After the all-clear whistle, another sharp blast signaled breakfast. They drifted casually into the dining room line together, got their trays and food and slid into chairs around their tables.

Cereal and milk were being served, along with fresh or dried fruit, hominy grits or rolled oats, toast and coffee.

As soon as the four of them were seated, West told them that he drilled a hole about four inches above the top left corner of the grill. He worked on a second hole next to it, then a third. His plan was to line them up to the right for about fifteen inches. Then he'd drill down ten inches, then across to the left, and finally, back up to the top. He used moistened toilet paper and soap—a typical con ruse—to plug each hole. And fresh green paint every night. You could stare at it and never notice that underneath the rough exterior were going to be scores of little holes.

It's not known if the Anglins used the same method—lining up little holes first then chipping out between them later—but, clearly, it was the only method to avoid detection for the first months. And later, investigators would uncover convincing evidence that it was *exactly* the method used by everyone.

They debated about how many raincoats they would need for a raft, and when to begin getting them. J-Dub thought it was a good idea to line the inside floor of the raft with denim—the kind the laundry bags were made of. He could get some of that.

One thing that West was not going to do, he said, was get double-crossed by anybody. He must have brought up the '39 Barker–Young escape attempt again. *They made a second mistake,* West told them. They were counting on getting off the island quickly. But one of them, Rufus McCain, neglected to mention until he got to the beach that he couldn't swim. *They had to build Rufus a boat!* he exclaimed. But they got picked off, instead, Barker, shot to death, the others returned. Henri Young was so incensed that he later knifed his buddy McCain to death.

West may have hammered the point to the others because he talked about it to Carnes later. *When it's time to go,* he would have said with an edge that would make everyone stop, *If anybody cain't carry his own weight—nobody's goin' back to help 'im. Know what I mean? He'll have to be stay behind. It ain't goin'be like it was with Barker and them guys.* West looked at each of them dead in the eyes. Morris shrugged and said nothing—he still hadn't joined up. *No problem,* Clarence smirked. J-Dub pushed on his upper dentures, nodding slightly.

"THEY SAID THEY dug out of there with spoons; that's preposterous!" said Officer Bill Rogers. "A star drill is for drilling a hole in concrete. It's made of extremely hard steel and has cutting edges on it. You tap as you turn it."

Carnes agreed. "I know absolutely," he bragged years later about a star drill. "Even know how they got it from industries."

"I think it was a masonry drill bit," Officer Fred Freeman speculated, "The holes were almost in a perfect round circle." He felt they might have gotten a drill off the plumbing officer's tool kit.

Almost no one was willing to believe that eating utensils were the primary drilling tool, and indeed, even today, it's a debated theory.

"That's what the inmates said," Freeman stated, "and they just told the public what the inmates said."

"They didn't want to admit that those guys were clever enough to get things like [star drills] from industries without being detected," said Rogers.

In fact, there are solid reasons why other, more appropriate, tools might have been used. Every maintenance man's tool kit contained an ample supply of tools that could be stolen. And from FBI photographs taken later, that's exactly what may have happened. West and the Anglins accumulated an arsenal that included saw blades, wrenches, files, metal rulers, nuts and bolts, strap steel, pieces of hand-sharpened metal, electrical wire, white and black tape, a small package containing ten drill bits as well as *thirteen* eating utensil handles. But despite that the cons left all these items lying around to be discovered later, no star drill was ever found.

And there are obvious reasons why eating utensil handles may have been the best tools used during this phase of the operation. They were readily available, plentiful and easy to smuggle. They were large, heavy-gauge steel, soup spoons from the 1930s. When the bowl was broken off and the handle ground down, it became the perfect size to drill tiny holes. They were also easy to hide. A handle could be pushed into a mattress or hidden in a book, shoved into the sole of a shoe or casually placed in the pocket of a hanging jacket. Guards shook down the cells, but if a spoon handle were found, it'd look like a shank and not a drill for concrete. You'd go to seg, sure, but you'd be back and you could get another. Spoons were the perfect tools.

A star or concrete drill, on the other hand, would be difficult to smuggle, harder to hide and would arouse suspicion if discovered. A guard would know instantly that someone was digging. Moreover, a star drill would have to be passed from man-to-man, slowing them down. Ultimately, they used several items—ice picks and drill bit among them. But spoon handles were their chief drilling tools. And later, even more evidence would surface to support that contention.

BY THE BEGINNING of December, Morris had joined up, obtained a spoon and had begun digging little holes. The watch log, in fact, contained a note which may have signaled Morris's decision. On Saturday, December 9, the day watch lieutenant had written, "Possible loss of spoon at noon mainline. Some doubt and no trace."

Inexplicably, another note the next Saturday, showed that a ladle handle was discovered by Officer Ed Deatherage in an empty cell on the B block third tier.

These were the first notes in the watch log about missing utensils—but they would not be the last.

West now had to share every other night with his partner. Nonetheless, he was now averaging one or two holes each time he dug.

The drilling, in fact, was becoming routine. The concrete was riddled with pebbles which could be pried out, using the tool to wedge against another pebble. But sometimes the concrete was so porous, you could stick your little finger in the little hole and coax it out. This was concrete from 1912, mixed and poured by military convicts, and compromised by saltwater leaks. By now West had eighteen or nineteen holes lined up like little soldiers.

One night, he stood up, stretched, and cleaned up the sand and powder around his toilet. The pebbles he hid in his pockets to discard later. He moistened more toilet paper and plugged up a new hole. He waited for it to dry, and was brushing his floor with his hands.He must have felt so smug; he was going to break the Rock. His whole life felt like it was falling into place. He'd show those who'd crossed him, the screws, the cons too, many of whom snickered at his plan. Kneeling down, West concentrated on his twentieth hole, boring deeply with a petulance that drove his arm. He moved his eyes away from the concrete for a minute and looked out the vent. It took a second for his eyes to adjust, but then he saw it.

The one thing he hadn't counted on.

In a cell across the pipe chase, a black con was hunkered down, staring out his own vent—watching West.

West's skin must have leaped off his bones. Like a pro, however, he refocused on the hole without flinching, his hands tightening around the spoon handle, propelled by fear and suspicion. Racial slurs spewed up from the depths of his rage. He looked back and, to his shock, the black con's face moved closer to his vent. Shielding his eyes, he squinted to see what West was doing. Then the black man smiled in a calculated moment of reckoning.

The hairs on the back of West's neck stood on end. He jumped up, dropping his tool.

" 'You can't trust them black guys, every one of them's a snitch,' " Carnes said mockingly. "See? That was the attitude. And the first thing's going to happen, when West started digging little holes, all the black guys on the other side knew it. I bet he wasn't working five minutes before those blacks knew it."

"An organized escape is one of the most severe and unforgiving efforts in prison," Kent once said. "Life and death are at stake."

West figured the blacks would turn on him because of the Gilliam stabbing. He must have felt sick to his stomach. I can see him splashing his face with water, wiping it with a towel and suddenly relaxing into exhaustion.

That night, he wouldn't have slept much, fear racing through his mind. He would get hot and whip the blanket off his torso. Then he'd get cold and cover himself. Panic would spike his chest, causing him to toss and turn all night long.

Exhausted, bitter, when the cell fronts were cocked open the next morning, West would have bolted out of his cell like a race horse at the gate.

～～～

Part 3

Breaking Rock

"THOSE BLACK GUYS across from our cells know what we're doing," West told Carnes later, and now, walking in line to breakfast, he was telling Morris. "They even get down on the floor and peer at us through the vent."

Morris gazed at West. The Anglins were dawdling somewhere back of the line.

West and Morris got their trays, their French toast and syrup, passed several tables filled with convicts and climbed into seats around an empty table.

Ron Battles was working the dining room. One of the few African-American working there, Battles was young, polished and intelligent. He came into the federal prison service in 1958, and by February '61, he had made senior officer. "When you ran people to the dining room," he said, "You ran 'em block by block." Cons sometimes got disciplinary reports for not filling a table in sequence. The Anglins arrived minutes later, passing a half-filled table to sit with West and Morris. Battles walked over and told them they'd have to sit at another table. They balked. Battles insisted they move. The Anglins argued, Clarence becoming louder. Battles signaled the lieutenant to come over. The lieutenant, fair-haired, expressionless and pale in his dark uniform, came quickly to their table. He listened to the brothers' complaints, then waved the black guard away. They could stay.

Battles was stung. The lieutenant, a newcomer who had just made lieutenant, had not backed him up. It was the first indication to him that some of the newer supervisors were not observing the old rules.

West, Morris and the Anglins glanced at each other with subtle, contemptuous asides and resumed talking.

West outlined the problem. Every one of them had a black

con in a cell across the pipe chase. They would soon know what was going down. West had no friends there, he nodded to the black table nearby. The Anglins, also poor, white rebels, and little "cell soldiers" to boot, may have wanted to threaten to shank a few, smack 'em around a little. Morris nixed that idea. He worked with a lot of them in the brush shop.

Less than eighteen percent of Alcatraz cons were African-Americans, but the proportions changed over the years. In the 1930s and '40s, fewer than ten percent were black, reflecting the fact that few were involved in bank robbery, income tax evasion or kidnapping charges, which comprised the bulk of the whites' federal offenses. Instead, most were convicted of serious offenses from Washington, D.C., a federal territory, or on murder charges from the military. By the '60s, however, West, Morris and the Anglins could look around the dining hall and see that nearly twenty-five percent of the cons were African-American. And increasingly they were emerging from the big eastern cities on heroin charges.

"There were a lot of dangerous blacks there," Battles said.

After the 1954 Supreme Court ruling in *Brown vs. The Topeka Board of Education*, Alcatraz officers had tried integrating the cell blocks, but both blacks and whites balked and administrators backed off, the blacks remaining on Broadway. Interracial incidents—more common years after Alcatraz closed—were infrequent and reflected the racial separation. The 1960 Clymore–Gilliam incident, in fact, was one of the few interracial stabbings on Alcatraz.

Partly because of a higher percentage of Negro prisoners, the BOP was beginning to hire more black officers. In 1961–62, Battles worked with at least three other African-Americans on Alcatraz.

West, Morris and the brothers had plenty to worry about. Not only because of the Gilliam stabbing, but other reasons as well.

A highly vocal, aggressive, bitter social protest known as the Black Muslim movement was just then in its infancy, and several newer Alcatraz cons were members. The movement leaned on religious precepts and was based on defiance of whites. Black Muslims demanded respect while espousing overt racism, something that whites had practiced for decades but now found threatening. Lincoln Molless, AZ 1567, a Muslim who arrived on Alcatraz on a forty-year narcotics conviction, demanded that spring to be sent to segregation because a few of his Muslim brothers were confined there. The Muslims caused a slow down at several meals. They communed on the yard. It was a beginning, and they were viewed with fear.

No one knew, least of all West, Morris and the brothers, how deeply the new racism would manifest into their territory. The four debated how to handle them. Morris, gulping the last of his coffee, quickly said, *Bumpy Johnson worked with me in the brush shop. He might be able to influence 'em.*

Everyone knew "Bumpy." He was the last of the big-time gangsters from Harlem but he was top drawer. Fifty years old, smooth and savvy, Johnson, AZ 1117, was serving his second stint on Alcatraz. Most everyone liked his deep, resonating laugh, his unhurried style and natural confidence. Even guards liked him. Notes in his file called him "dignified," "energetic," "intelligent," and "cooperative."

"Guys that had the big money," Battles said, "were the nicest to deal with."

Carnes, who played chess with Bumpy, looked up to him and maybe felt protected by their friendship. "Popularity is power in prison," he once said. "People didn't touch you if you had friends."

Johnson got his name because he knew the bumps in life, spending more than twenty-five years in New York state prisons like Sing-Sing, Attica and Rikers Island, and federal joints like Atlanta and Alcatraz. Known as the "Al Capone of Harlem," like the Chicago mobster, Johnson had a supportive family, a large circle of dangerous friends and strong political ties. He ran Harlem's prostitutes and its drug trade. His gang was the enforcers. Yet,

Bumpy Johnson, on Alcatraz twice.

Bumpy was no thug; he was genuinely sophisticated. And once romantically involved with a white woman named Helen Lawrenson, a legendary raconteur, author, and an editor at *Vanity Fair* magazine when it was the epitome of style and glamour. Their liaison was a 1930s and '40s example of "radical chic," the mix of hot Harlem jazz, smartly dressed gangsters and white society women.

"Everyone feared him," she wrote in an *Esquire* profile after he had died, "some hated him." She quoted a prosecuting attorney who called him, "one of the most vicious criminals in Harlem."

"I never found him anything but kind, considerate, polite and protective," she wrote, "and like many tough men, vulnerably sentimental . . ." She called him immaculately dressed but not flashy, a terrible dancer, and a proud, elegant, powerful black man—something of an anachronism in the pre-civil rights days.

One night she was dining with him minutes before he was to meet a rival on a street corner for a prearranged gun duel. Bumpy was eating with gusto. Lawrenson found it hard to believe he was so calm. "I'm hungry," he explained. Someone signaled and he was out the door, while Lawrenson sat, poised, frightened. She heard gunshots. A few excruciating minutes later, he appeared, sat down and ordered up a banana split.

"What happened?" she asked.

"Nothin'," he said. "We both missed."

On Alcatraz, Bumpy was housed in B-111, on the Broadway flats near the dining room and far from the four men. Everyone could see he had power. But could he keep the younger guys in line? And did he have any say over the Muslims?

West rubbed his lower lip, looking from man to man.

There's just a little problem, Morris said.

West glared at him.

Bumpy's in seg. Contraband.

West looked away, then looked back, his eyes narrowing.

Breakfast was done.

2

OUTSIDE THE CELL house, in the warden's office, the December custodial staff meeting was underway. Warden Blackwell, Associate Warden Dollison, Captain Bradley, all the lieutenants, the heads of industries, culinary, mechanical and medical services, as well as the staff training officer were present. A correctional officer took notes. Everyone had a chance to talk. They discussed security, special inmates, custodial changes, or revisions in procedures. Lieutenant Ordway, a cantankerous, cigar-smoking New Englander who was the longest employee on Alcatraz, requested that something be done to clean up the west gun gallery. Painting the ceiling had resulted in considerable dust and paint chips setting on the gallery and Ordway thought it prudent to clean it up. He also reported that there were numerous leaking faucets in the kitchen, as well as a lot of lint from the dryers lying around the industries floor. Ordway was a stickler for cleanliness.

The monthly reports also detailed the number of officers on duty. In December, although Alcatraz was authorized to employ ninety-eight officers, it had ninety-one.

3

THE MONTH ROLLED on. West had obtained a six-inch tapered piece of metal. He rolled one end with white hospital tape, shaping it so that he could hold it like a gun. Now gouging out holes was a lot easier.

But it was becoming a bigger challenge to hide the lines of drilled and plugged up holes, and the chance of discovery was mounting. He began casually leaning his guitar case in front of his vent. Photos show that John hung a long raincoat from a ledge above his sink. He stuffed extra towels around the drain pipe below the sink, and hung a string across the back of his cell to hang more towels. Morris no longer slid his accordion case under his bed as had been required. Now it lived in front of his air vent.

Each night, two men resumed digging while their two partners watched with their mirrors and the band played on.

They'd been at it for six weeks, and the drilling was beginning to seem tedious. Not only that, but West felt the blacks had by now all caught on. He felt they were watching him in the dining room and on the yard. They'd hush up whenever he came near, or talk in a language that even he couldn't understand.

One night after the supper count, when the day watch officers were departing the cell house, West heard the main gate open and close as each man left, but he was distracted, getting his tools out of his mattress. Suddenly, a shadow passed over his cell. "It startled the hell out of me," he told Carnes later. West looked up and saw an officer cruising by, looking back at him. "He looked right at the stuff I had in front of me."

West scrambled to conceal the tools. The officer passed, oblivious. West was stunned. Then, suddenly, he realized he had probably been in a shadow and the guard hadn't seen his tools. Just as he relaxed, one of the tools fell off his bunk and bounced on the floor with a loud *ping* and a metal roll.

The officer stopped.

West froze.

In prison, metal on concrete is instantly recognizable. It can only mean contraband—a shank, a bar spreader, a file, a drill.

"I almost shit!" he said. His throat muscles clenched around his windpipe.

The guard, who was just passed West's cell, did not move. He seemed suspended in time, as if making a decision. Then, he took a step. And another. And incredibly, he moved on. He did not turn around.

West blinked back his panic. His heart racing, he hid his tools and tried to calm his nerves. "All this goddamned work—worrying, sweating, scheming," he growled to Carnes, "and I get busted on a fluke shit thing like this." West told Morris they'd have to suspend digging for awhile; he felt the officer would return and shake his cell down. Morris may have found West's stupidity just a little irritable; *he* wouldn't have been that careless. They hid their tools in a towel, passed them down the line to another con, and they waited for the shakedown they felt sure would arrive.

CHRISTMAS, IN 1961, falling on a Monday, was not quite the happy holiday West had predicted. No one was out of his cell like he had said.

He had finished the top row of holes and was now working down. But digging little holes was beginning to lose its allure. West was anxious to move forward, get the supplies. Stealing.

"Blackie" Audett, serving in the officer's dining room in December 1961.

That's what juiced him now. But so far he had nowhere to hide the stuff. And other things were commanding more of his attention. They still hadn't taken care of the blacks.

But that too was about to change.

The day after Christmas, Bumpy Johnson walked out of segregation and into the main line. He was greeted heartily by his friends and sat down for his first meal in the dining room. West was soon to discover that Johnson would not return to his job in industries. Instead, he was placed in cell house maintenance. West couldn't believe his good luck. As soon as it was prudent, he set about to ingratiate himself to the smooth big man. Bumpy remained in maintenance until May 1962.

Most assuredly, West, Morris and the Anglins could never be sure if he, or anyone, could keep the blacks from squealing. Bumpy was a leader and many blacks looked up to him. But whether a fifty-year-old black man had any sway over the angry, young Muslims is unknown.

Each night as they dug more holes, was one more night they were being watched. Sometimes, they waved. Just the thought of it made West's jaw clench. The only thing that West could dare count on, was that everyone—black, white, Hispanic, Native American—all of them were united in their hatred of the Rock.

Not much to go on. Because the risky part was that more and more prisoners were being told about the escape attempt in an ironic effort to keep everyone quiet.

4

HAPPY NEW YEAR, suckers, they told each other.

Just another heavy meal, just another bitter cold day in the yard. Except for guys in seg, of course, some of whom may not have cared it was New Year's day, one of whom discovered *after* the holidays that his father died Christmas Eve, but his mother delayed telling him so it wouldn't ruin his holidays.

Ruined them anyway. In retrospect.

"Cell house in unusually good condition for New Year's day," the lieutenant wrote in the watch log. There had only been "a few small fires" that night, with "no damage and very little debris." Steak dinner was served that day; the lieutenant called it excellent. "Table knives used and all accounted for," he wrote.

For West, January wasn't so bad. So what if it was so cold and wet that fog just drizzled into rain, then pelted the concrete in sheets, making the sky as gray and ominous as the bay. He'd had no disciplinary reports since leaving D block in May 1961, and the lieutenants were impressed. Just listen to what they wrote about him: West "performs his tasks in an exemplary manner, is dependable, cooperative and requires a minimum of supervision;" he's "pleasant to talk to and responds in suggestions," and "gets along well with officers and inmates." The cell house officer called him an "excellent worker around the cell house," a man who "prefers to work alone." West had even donated blood.

Most of the time it wasn't even an act. West rushed through everyday, laughing almost. Everywhere he went—up on the scaffolding, into the A block supply area, into the dining room, in his cell—everywhere presented opportunities that would aid in this escape. Three times a day in the dining room he could plan and conspire with his buddies. The men he saw at work on a daily basis—Carnes, Kent, Boggs, Clarence Anglin, Glenn May, Bumpy Johnson—all had potential for ideas and transport.

Each day officers could hear the squeak of the wheels as he pushed the three-story scaffolding into place. He was jovial, bantering with them as he climbed to the platform with his paint can and brushes.

But the scaffolding worried some. Captain Bradley ordered the lieutenant to tell the OIC to get the ceiling painting completed, so the scaffolding could be removed. West and the others were told they had to step it up. *No problem,* West cheerfully told the officer. But inside he was seething. Now he'd have to come up with a new plan.

Overall, West appeared to be a changed man. Even going into his cell at night, laying around until the music hour. Tedious as the digging was, he knew it was part of a much bigger adventure. After drilling holes to the right for about fifteen inches, then heading south for ten, West was now doubling back and lining up little holes under the vent. The feeling was just like the first time he'd broken into somebody's house, his whole body tingling with the thrill of entering and the fear of discovery. It was almost like a sexual experience, the atmosphere charged, every hair on his arms alert, making him almost weak with anticipation. The problem was, after each subsequent crime, West could never get back to that first intoxicating feeling of being alive. Until now.

Morris felt it too. But he knew discovery was always hiding in wait.

By now, the conspirators had devised better methods to signal each other if officers approached. West and Morris were using electrical wire strung between their cells. Clarence had a long piece of twine which he passed out of his cell bar each night to John's adjoining cell, where it was hooked to John's cot. One would wiggle it and the other would catch on. It was perfect. During the day, these items were concealed.

On Thursday, January 11, the day watch lieutenant reported in the watch log that Officer Herman had found two tines from a table fork in the inmate kitchen toilet. "Unable to find fork," he reported. Officers wheeled over the portable metal detector on the noon mainline "without results." They figured someone might have honed a shank to knife a con.

ON FRIDAY, JANUARY 19, Morris was given five days' furlough for "maintaining a clear institutional record." His furlough card showed that he was on vacation from work and could go to the yard almost any time. He was also given a Prince Edwards cigar. His report complimented him for being "quiet . . . orderly . . . friendly . . . with a good attitude. He seems to stay out of the picture."

He burst out of the cell house on Saturday, a cold, gusty, wet afternoon—not the kind of weather Morris liked at all.

In fact, that night the seas were so high and choppy that the boat repeatedly slammed into the pilings, damaging one of them. Then something incredible happened; that morning snow began falling. On Sunday, January 21, the first real snowstorm in thirty years blanketed the entire Bay Area with as much as an inch and a half. On the yard that day, hardened cons were like little boys, gathering up snow, hurling snowballs through the air. It never got above thirty-seven degrees on Sunday, and that night the lieutenant reported that the cell house temperature was fifty-four degrees. He called the powerhouse operator to divert more steam to the cell house. The boat was still banging against the piers so much that at 4:30 A.M., he called the pilot and asked him to take it out on the bay to keep it from destroying the island's slip. By 7:00 A.M., the cell house temperature was still fifty-four.

The snow quickly melted by Monday, and, by Thursday, the temperature had returned to normal. Novelty over.

Morris spent his week taking extra yard time, noodling on his accordion and reading in his cell. There would be no working on the escape attempt during the day. But he thought about it constantly.

He had studied the wooden boxes that left industries every week for transport off the island. They were stacked with clothing for the military and gloves for the Atomic Energy Commission, and bound with strap banding about eleven-sixteenth-inch wide. He wanted some of that. He could hide a strip of it in the bottom of his shoe and drag his feet through the metal detector. But if he got caught, he'd go to seg, and he doubted if West or the Anglins would wait for him.

Maybe the dockworkers, who loaded the boxes onto barges,

Several groups of prisoners went to the dock regularly,
among them the garbage collecters.

could cut off a length of banding and sneak it into the clothing
room when they delivered stuff there. John could insert it in fresh
clothes, and on bath day Morris would have it.

The dockworkers also delivered stuff to the kitchen. Maybe
West or May in their rounds could move it to him.

Morris had already brought stuff through the metal detector.
But the easy stuff.

He smirked. The metal detectors were old and notoriously inaccurate. Called by cons the "snitch box," they were tuned by con-
trols on an oscilloscope that determined how much metal could
pass without triggering the alarm. But Morris knew that sometimes rookie officers tuned them poorly. And brass, copper or
aluminum were not detectable. Neither was wood. Morris had
walked through with several skinny metal screws about two-and-a
quarter-inches long, some washers and nuts—all brass. He had
also sneaked a small block of wood with a brass screw in it. Not
once had the metal detector snitched him out.

He shuddered. He picked up a pack of Wings, lit a cigarette
and tossed the pack back on the metal fold-out table. All the planning, all the supplies that they needed other cons to bring up—it
was enough to drive him nuts.

5

THAT MONTH, FAR away in another world altogether, Associate Warden Dollison was approaching U.S. Attorney General Robert F. Kennedy in a dinner receiving line. Dollison was in Washington, D.C. for a BOP conference. As he was introduced, Kennedy gripped his hand and, in a quick aside, said, "You're going to lose your happy home." Dollison felt a pang of regret. He knew exactly what the attorney general meant.

The next month, on Alcatraz, the *Foghorn* contained a brief announcement that caught everyone's attention. A sometimes gossipy, sometimes prosaic monthly newsletter, it served the hundred and fifty staff members and their families, half of whom lived on the island. It detailed transfers, civil service news, the island's women's club news, its potluck dinners, teen parties and frequent visitors.

On page four was a note that the new maximum-security prison in Marion, Illinois, then under construction, was ahead of schedule and would be ready for occupation in March 1963.

Marion was rumored to be replacing Alcatraz as the new super max pen.

Few of the staff, or their wives, wanted to leave San Francisco to go to scrubby, drab prison towns in southern Illinois and elsewhere. And, in the winter and spring of '62, that began to seem probable.

That spring, Dollison told employees that nothing definite had been decided and that Alcatraz could go on for years. It was obvious that nothing could be gained from admitting to employees that Alcatraz would close. But few were convinced, and some began job shopping.

Perhaps it would begin to seem fortunate that cons like West, Morris and the others were on their best behavior, because staff morale was worsening.

Nonetheless, at the January 24 custodial meeting Warden Blackwell told the lieutenants to keep the officers alert. He urged a continuous effort in the shakedown procedures. "Although we have tool proof bars," he told them, "that's no reason for complacency. Bar spreaders found in the past would no doubt snap this type of bar with little difficulty."

The lieutenants felt the pressure. They were short six officers that month, and it was always the day watch that was compromised.

6

IN EARLY FEBRUARY, J-Dub showed two metal files to a con named Hank Gates. Gates (not his real name), who had arrived in August on a twenty-year kidnapping and auto theft charges, was said by Tom Kent to be "an asshole friend of John Anglin's." John told Gates he gotten the file off a con who worked in industries. Named the guy, even.

Although they focused their fears on the black prisoners behind their cells, West, Morris and the Anglins were their own worst enemies. West had obviously invited numerous guys in. According to Juelich, Morris had also extended invitations. ("That set well with everyone," he said, "because they knew he meant it.")

"Word went out that the guys were going," said a former con named Frank Hatfield, AZ 1296, "but you'd have to go over to B block."

Now, apparently the Anglins were bragging about it.

Gates lived on B block third tier, just above them. J-Dub was so excited about what they were doing that Gates didn't even have to prod him. He told Gates exactly how they were digging, with what tools, and how they planned to get out. He bragged that Morris "was a good helicopter pilot," that they planned to steal a 'copter, fly to the desert and hide out for four or five months. Gates was impressed. John may have even mentioned how big they planned to build the raft—six by fourteen feet—big enough for five or six guys. Told him they were going to San Francisco, that he'd timed the island boat and figured that was the shortest distance.

The next time Gates was racked into his third tier cell he looked for the vent. He spotted it. That night Gates told the guy next to him, Philip Stones, a bank robber sentenced to twenty-six years and one day, who'd been on Alcatraz for an escape attempt since June 1956.

Stones (not his real name) had been described by a former warden as "one of the most desperate men on Alcatraz." In 1959, while attending a trial out of state, Stones had swallowed a pouch containing five metal pieces of contraband, some as long as two inches. While trying to dislodge it, he had snuffed it up his nose. Doctors had to remove it from his nasal passages. On Alcatraz, Stones had worked as a plumber's helper in the pipe chase. He may have realized how easy Anglin's idea might actually be.

On Tuesday, February 6, Lieutenant Fred Mahan wrote in the watch log that an officer had reported a kitchen ladle missing. The following Sunday and Monday, two more ladles were reported missing. Gates and Stones were in business. They started digging little holes around their vents—moving from top left to right— exactly like West had described he was doing.

"That's what you had to worry about," Kent said, "a bunch of tough guys who wanted in."

"They figured all they had to do was make a hole in the back of their cells and be ready," Carnes later said. *"Without asking permission,* they just started making a hole."

Prisoners operated on a strict social hierarchy. If you didn't cell or work near a high-ranking con, you didn't move on him— you had to be vouched for by one of his friends. Asking questions about somebody's business was not advised. Quizzing about an escape attempt, or joining up uninvited could be, as Carnes called it, "a killing thing." Gates and Stones had told at least one other man. It wouldn't be long before West got wind of it.

7

ALTHOUGH BLACKWELL URGED everyone at the February cus-todial meeting to keep the staff alert, he made a startling pro-posal, which underscored his concerns.

Dollison, Captain Bradley, who chaired the meeting, all six lieutenants—Ordway, Severson, Mahan, Miller, Weir and a new man, B.F. Delmore, who had just arrived—as well as other depart-ment heads, were present. Officer Dick Waszak took notes. After the old business was dispensed with, Warden Blackwell made an announcement that surprised everyone but Bradley.

Blackwell wanted to shut down the road tower at night.

Some of these supervisors looked up sharply. I can see Ordway's eyes narrowing into a critical focus. Lieutenant Mahan, a well-organized, efficient supervisor, may have been stunned. My father, a circumspect man, probably blinked back his alarm; this was the first he had heard of it. Bradley was probably not surprised, because as captain of the guards, he would need to have been consulted on the elimination of any security positions under his command. In fact, it's likely he had worked with Blackwell on this proposal.

The road tower was one of only two towers that operated twenty-four hours a day. Located opposite of the dock tower, along the south side of the prison building, it had a sweeping view from the west-end industries area, across the prison yard, the prison, the west road and east into the resident's compound. Blackwell was proposing to permanently shut down half the island's perimeter security from 4:45 P.M. until 8:00 A.M. every night.

"They couldn't operate the institution without the dock and road towers!" Bergen said later, "Those two were vital."

Blackwell figured he could save three staff positions, and he wanted to replace them with another boat operator to expand the daily boat schedule and another administrative secretary for the front office. He felt he could also justify it to the BOP by assigning an officer full-time as cell inspector. He asked for comments from those present.

Judging from the shocked tones of officers interviewed later, some of these men must have been astounded. But it was also telling that their concerns were quickly justified.

According to the captain's monthly report later sent to Washington, about the only objection raised was that boats could land undetected on the south side of the island at night. But that was quickly shot down when someone pointed out that boats could land anyway, on the west or east edge of the island. It had never been a problem. Nor would anyone outside the institution know that the tower would be shut down at night.

Someone else immediately saw the advantage of expanding the boat schedule. The limited number of trips to San Francisco had always been inconvenient both for the staff—who had to keep the cell house on a fast pace—and for residents, so that everyone could get on and off the island on time.

Blackwell pointed out that cons were safely tucked into their cells at night. They'd have to cut through cell bars, then get through the window bars to escape. Given that, he said, manning the road tower at night was a poor use of staff time.

Bradley agreed. They had figured that by shifting another stationary lookout position to that of a patrol, especially between 6:00 and 8:00 A.M. and again from 5:00 to 6:45 P.M., that the vulnerable period, when kitchen inmates were out of their cells, would be covered. My father remained silent. Although he later told me he thought it was a bad idea, he was under the impression that the suggestion had come from Washington, and didn't dissent. He would soon regret his restraint. A few minutes later, when it was his turn to speak, he stated that the pounding of the bars was a project he wished would get immediate attention. (By dragging a mallet or a night stick across bars, officers could detect different sounds and quickly determine if a bar had been sawed.) And Lieutenant Delmore, the new man who was assigned as the day-watch lieutenant, responded that this would soon be started.

Bradley wrote to Washington that "everyone seemed to be in agreement that this would be a definite improvement in our program, without loss of security."

Blackwell wrote in his proposal that the associate warden, the captain and all the lieutenants "agree that these two posts can be

The road tower had a sweeping view of the south side of the island including the industries area, top photo, the prison and its yard, left, as well as the east end near the family quarters.

safely eliminated, provided additional coverage is available inside the institution for bar and cell inspections." He stressed that inmates inside the cell house would have to get through "two sets of bars—their cell and the outside window—to effect their escape."

It seems inconceivable now, but it's obvious from their statements that they were focused on the bars. Although they knew the bars were not as tool-proof as had been believed in the past, they were lulled into thinking that the walls were secure. At least the exterior walls were solid. But no one considered that the inside walls were vulnerable. They didn't realize that the concrete, in many respects, was just like quicksand.

8

NEITHER DID WEST, Morris and the Anglins know how lucky they really were. In fact, from their perspective, the obstacles were beginning to mount.

They had each dug scores of holes. And as long as they only had tiny camouflaged holes hidden behind towels or guitar cases, no one would notice. But sooner or later, they would have to break out bigger chunks of concrete, the grill would have to be removed and a fake wall section would need to be built. This would take weeks, during which each man would be extremely vulnerable to cell inspections. Discovery of even one exposed wall would mean that the entire institution would be searched.

They talked guardedly about the best method of doing this at meals during the day, warning each other, Morris and West urging the anxious Anglins to move slowly.

It was just too exciting. One night in February, while Clarence held a tiny mirror out of his cell as a lookout, John took out a three-ring binder and ripped it in half. He drew a four-by-eight inch rectangle on it, then cut it out with his razor blade. He knelt down and slid the piece of cardboard into the recessed vent. It fit.

Next, he drew a diamond-shaped, cross-hatch pattern on the rectangle and began cutting pieces out of it. The razor blade was sharp, but small and awkward. He needed to make four cuts for each side of each diamond. More than seventy diamonds meant almost three hundred cuts through canvas-backed cardboard.

Within minutes scratches and razor skids tore at his fingers. It took several nights of hard work to finish the pattern. Then he painted it green—the cell color. When completed, it was neat and precise. He hid it in the recess just in front of the real vent, then hung towels and his raincoat in front of it.

Next, John persuaded one of his artist friends to give up his little wooden box used for paints and brushes. All the artists had one. Leon Thompson, AZ 1465, figured his was about eight by ten inches and about five inches deep. John tore off the lid and the bottom, and cut down the two long sides to about nine inches. Once he glued on a new side, he then attached it to his newly cut fake vent.

He shaved the edges down until it fit neatly into the recess of his wall. Then he draped his towels over the sink pipes, completely covering the fake vent, and drifted off to sleep.

"Rained all night," a lieutenant had written in the watch log on February 13, "Routine quiet watch."

ON ALTERNATE NIGHTS, Clarence was doing the same thing, using one of John's twelve-by-sixteen-inch canvas art boards and a small "George Washington" brand pipe tobacco box. After several evenings of cutting and fitting his fake vent and box, he laid it into the recess of his grill.

John was becoming more reluctant to leave his cell each day for work. He was edgy and insecure about being found out. On Thursday, February 22, he went into the sick call line complaining of dizzy spells. He wanted to lay in. Four days later, he complained of vague discomfort in his upper gastrointestinal area. He remained in his cell that day. May, Carnes, even West could swing by, pop something in. But laying in also meant that officers would probably pick someone else's cell to search.

That night, a black con on the third tier was trying to honk out "Kansas City Here I Come" on his saxophone. Someone else was playing a rather morose version of "Moon River." No one ever thinks that hardoned cons liked the same sappy tunes as did the public, or that murderers sometimes did their time knitting or crocheting, even on Alcatraz. Other guys with guitars were trying to strum out Johnny Cash tunes, like "Folsom Prison Blues," anything

The fake front with its cell wall, top photo, with the back, made from tobacco boxes, which fit snugly inside the vent openings .

to drown out the pouring rain that was hitting the cell house roof. And John was breaking off little pieces of metal in the vent grill.

The metal was thick and brittle and tore at his fingers. Soon, with the jangle of songs bouncing around the cell house, John was banging on the metal with his shoe. It took several nights to clean it all out. When he finished, he stood up, walked to his cell front and looked back. He grinned. The new fake grill and its little box fit perfectly into the vent opening.

Over the next few nights, he began to chip out concrete between the holes. But only to three inches deep. They had talked about this: officers frequently checked the utility corridor. For now, J-Dub only broke out the concrete on the cell side, deep enough to fit a fake wall. The remaining one to two inches on the pipe chase side would remain intact.

He broke the concrete by inserting several spoon handles into several holes at once and slamming down on them with a shoe. As noisy as this could be, the screeching sounds of "Over the Rainbow," "Ring of Fire," *that friggin'* "Mary Had a Little Lamb" and now—horridly—"Tonight" from *West Side Story* all jangled into one lousy, caterwauling mess.

By then, Clarence and Morris were also beginning to construct their own grills. West told Carnes, "Just a matter of days and we'll be into the utility corridor."

Within a week, John had chipped out enough concrete to fit in his new L-shaped wall section. It was made of canvas art board and was now attached to the new box vent. The whole thing slid perfectly into place and John molded it to the wall with soap and paint. He had even tapped tiny finishing nails into the back of the box to act like hooks, so that when he exited his cell, he could pull back the vent wall section using the hooks. Who said the Anglins were dummies?

But if everyone thought drilling a hundred little holes and chipping out a few of inches of concrete was hard work, each man soon discovered that that was the easy part.

John soon saw that there was an iron frame imbedded around the vent. *Shit,* he said leaning back on his haunches. *We're gonna need saw blades.*

9

ON TUESDAY, MARCH 13, Blackwell sent the road tower shut-down proposal to Washington.

That same day, Glenn May was awarded two hundred days "good time" off his sentence for his work as an electrician.

May had written out a request to the warden that month, ask-ing about a mural project he wanted to paint. He must have thought that the climate had changed on Alcatraz so much that he might actually be allowed to paint a mural. "See Mr. Dollison," Warden Blackwell wrote on his request slip, "I am not the art ex-pert."

On Wednesday in the watch log, there was some confusion about two missing ladles, which were later found, then another missing ladle, which eventually was found in a garbage can.

That day, Morris ordered a *Spanish Made Simple* instructional book and a Berlitz Spanish book. It was generally known among cons that Morris was planning to go back to New Orleans or Mexico.

A week later, Morris was also given an award of one hundred and fifty days restored good time as an "incentive for continued clear institutional record."

Four days after that, John reported to the sick line, complain-ing about pain in his right shoulder which he said he'd been suf-fering for the past four to six weeks. He laid in.

10

WEST'S EXCITEMENT DIMMED. The digging was harder than he thought, taking longer, and he was getting bored. Cutting little diamond shapes in cardboard was also drudge work. He itched for something new.

That's about when the March issues of *Popular Science* and *Popular Mechanics* made their rounds on Alcatraz. Each maga-zine first went to the man who subscribed, then to other cons on the route list. Both magazines had articles with photographs on the top new designs in life vests. The officer assigned to censor magazines obviously didn't notice the articles, and soon the magazines were pitched onto West's bed.

West flipped through the pages. *Popular Science* talked about the 6,000 water deaths every year—many of which were not actual drownings, but panicked, thrashing victims of shock or heart failure. The article featured photos of several styles of life jackets—casual sailing jackets with air bladders inside which could be inflated with special pull-out tubes, and "Mae West" style life vests, named after the sassy, prodigiously endowed, comic actress, with yokes that wrapped around the neck to hold the head afloat.

West seized on the idea. He liked the "Mae West" design. It was simple to make. Even the *Popular Mechanics* article recommended the yoke vest as the best type for holding a man upright and keeping an unconscious man afloat face out of the water.

He was charged. He talked it up to Morris through the bars. He kicked it up at chow the next day, and again at lunch. He figured they could get even more raincoats and make the life vests out of that.

The Anglins may not have been as excited. *We been chippin' four months,* Clarence complained, *and we're not even into the chase yet. Now you want to pile more work on us?* J-Dub agreed, it'd take too much time.

It's back-up, West argued, *in case the raft fails. That water's cold. We could die tryin'.*

Morris agreed.

The brothers were derisive. *Hell, we been swimmin' in Lake Michigan,* one of them said, *Besides, we won't BE in the water.*

Clarence eyed Morris and West. *Ain't you in "the boat" yet?*

It's tempting to think of the brothers getting up and noisily returning their trays, cocky and grousing along the way. West was a stir hustler, they decided, thinkin' up more stuff for them to do—*shit, he was stallin'.* It would take too much time. *It'd already been too much time.* The Anglins had grown up near rivers and bays, *Hell—alligators, coral snakes, water moccasins.* They weren't afraid of cold water and fake tales of man-hungry sharks circling the island. They knew they could swim the San Francisco Bay. Moreover, despite years of confinement, both men still felt close to their families. John, especially, had lived longer outside of prison. He had bought cars, he had a common-law wife waiting for him—with kids even. Prison was just not where he saw himself. West's plan would only slow them down.

West and Morris may have lagged behind them, threatened and sullen, West dropping his tray noisily on the dishroom pass through. There may have been a deep philosophical split between the two sides. West and Morris were longer-term prisoners, both far more institutionalized. Not only was swimming not their usual summer activity, but they had no families waiting for them—no lives outside of prison. For them life outside was much less predictable. They were more comfortable and better fed inside, than out.

For them, it was the escape plan itself that juiced them the most. After all, "freedom and liberty," Kent once said, "are only secondary to the primary purpose—perfecting the escape." It was just more fun trying to escape, than being out on the lam.

If there was a fight over whether to make life vests or not, it didn't last long. West had made up his mind and they would do what he said.

One can imagine West on the yard, consulting with a few guys, tossing a tiny pebble back and forth in his hands, watching the guards on the yard wall. One man in particular, a lanky con with narrow, lop-sided face and hair that stuck up like he'd slept badly, may have provided the best idea. The tall guy slinked back to his cell, ducking under the doorway. He'd have to spend hours working out the idea on paper, crumbling up and tossing each bad design into the toilet to be flushed out to the San Francisco Bay. It would need to be a simple idea.

Ultimately, it would be ingenious.

Eventually he got back to West and told him to grab some common supplies: raincoats, of course, some lengths of half-inch wide canvas straps, binder clips, several Windex bottle "dipsticks," and some good waterproof glue. *That's important,* he told West, *get some good glue from industries, glue that'll hold in water.*

It would take nearly a month to design, obtain supplies and set up the sequence.

IN THE MEANTIME, obtaining saw blades was crucial. Morris got some of that strap steel banding from the industries boxes.

When they finally came up, he spent several nights etching teeth on one side and turning them into six or seven handmade saws.

West went to his old buddy, Carnes, who had said he knew where some blades were hidden.

Carnes had been in segregation for six years after the '46 escape attempt. He was in cell 25, he told me years later. "One day an [inmate] orderly came through." The man told Carnes that some hack saw blades were hidden in his cell. And Carnes says, "Yeah, where?" The orderly told Carnes about a tiny, rectangular hole in the steel door jam where the barred door closes. When Carnes looked at it later, it almost looked like a latch had once been there; now it was just an empty hole. The orderly told him that a con who had celled there years before had hooked some saw blades to a paper clip and lowered them down inside. But before he could retrieve them he had been moved to another cell. "Don't you think it might be rusted by now?" Carnes asked him. *No*, the con said, *he put grease on it and painted it. All you gotta do is drop a string down there and pull it up.*

In segregation, guys didn't have too much to do except think up schemes.

Days later, as planned, the orderly interrupted the guard just as Carnes was entering his cell but before the door closed behind him. Carnes lowered a string down the hole and quickly brought up the saw blades.

He eventually smuggled them to Larry Trumblay. Trump and Teddy Green worked out an escape plan in 1957. They collected bar spreaders, wrenches and other tools which Trump hid in the base of his toilet and camouflaged with soap. Officers uncovered the tools, but the saw blades were not among them. Carnes said they were still in circulation. He went back to Trump.

"And they finally wound up in West's hands," Carnes said proudly. "They were a little worn—been using them for one thing or another through the years—but they found their use."

Kent derided the story, "Carnes was bragging," he said, "They were useless."

But Carnes never bristled easily. The point, he would have retorted, was that saw blades were already inside and readily available.

And it was true. J-Dub obtained four saw blades, swiped from the kitchen bread-slicing machine. He hid them in his cell. Every other night, he was sawing those cross bars around the vent. Each night he'd slide them into their hiding places. After he was finished with them, he pasted them to his cell wall with soap, then painted over them. They wouldn't be discovered until Lieutenant Weir inspected the cell in August, and scraped them off the wall with a fifty-cent piece. But by then the escapees were long gone.

11

SOMETIME THAT MONTH, West put in an appearance before the classification committee. Sitting at one end of a highly polished, rectangular table, he faced a large, usually stern, group: the warden, associate and captain, the day watch lieutenant, the superintendent of industries, the medical technical assistant and, in those years, a religious leader and an educational instructor. On a typical day the committee reviewed twelve prisoners, a tiring, sometimes contentious task for them. Some cons got nervous; they'd become defiant, belligerent, sullen, sarcastic, obsequious or grandiose. Carnes said his hands would begin to sweat hours before he was called out. "I refused to go once," he said, "because I looked at the list of inmates and I knew by the time I got there, they'd be angry."

There would be a list of bank robbers with assaults and parole violations, and comments like "no food handling" stamped on their files; drunken losers who'd kidnapped seventy year olds; an old, tough back-room abortionist who'd bombed an airplane in which forty-one people had disappeared; cop killers, rapists; rickity-tickity mobsters, like Frankie Carbo, with bizarre medical complaints; cons with pages and pages of slicing and dicing. For prison administrators, it could be demoralizing.

West had always been uncooperative and cynical. Today he was "friendly, almost cheerful." He had made a stunning turnaround in his work and behavior record.

"The lieutenant in charge of quarters reports that subject has done an outstanding job as a painter in the cell house," his file later stated. Only in retrospect would the next comment be revealing: "He works seven days a week, including all weekends."

The classification committee members were impressed with West's turnaround. They couldn't know that each night he was breaking off pieces of his grill, digging deeper through his cell wall, stealing and hiding supplies and planning how to get his squadron up to the roof.

Nor did they know how much they were actually aiding him.

The committee awarded West fifty days good time off his sentence. He slinked out of the meeting, his tongue wetting his lips.

AT THE MARCH custodial meeting the day watch lieutenant was happy to report that the painting project was nearly completed. Fifty percent of the cells were painted, and the ceiling was done. But he was wrong. West had not yet finished the ceiling. A big portion over B block still needed painting, but he hadn't told the officer that. He simply said he no longer needed the scaffolding, and the officer just assumed the ceiling was done.

CLARENCE AND JOHN were also on their best behavior. The marked insolence that characterized most of Clarence's attitude toward authority had been toned down to "associates mostly with the 'hoodlum' element but has not caused any trouble. . . . If he has any trouble it may be with his brother." Clarence liked his job. "Doing a fair barbering job but appears conscientious," his record reported in 1962. At his classification committee hearing in March 1962, Clarence was commended on his good adjustment and encouraged to continue. He "seemed disinclined to prolong his appearance before the committee." He had had no visits since arrival. He had no funds in his personal bank account.

By now, Clarence had textured his fake wall section with soap chips, which when painted with the green paint that West had provided, looked remarkably similar to the real wall. Smelled like soap too, even decades later.

John was described as being "not much of a mixer, appears to prefer his brother's company." In the yard, he lifted weights. It was also noted that "he seldom does anything to draw attention to himself." The classification committee also found him "not overly eager to discuss his case." He had had no visitors. He had never had more than $25 in his personal account and in the spring of '62, he had $7.27.

By then, John had cut through some of the iron frame using his files and saw blades. With his vent gone, he was now reaching through the hole to gain better leverage to break off bigger pieces concrete. He was also constructing a fake back wall. He would soon be entirely through the wall.

12

ALL WAS NOT perfect, however. One night as he poked his arm out of his cell vent, J-Dub saw a black con in cell B-145, across the pipe chase, move into view. He clutched. Several days later, watching the mess hall line, he told the others, *That's him, the gimp.*

Nathaniel Harris, AZ 1509, ten years, narcotics, a new "fish," was a short guy with a droopy right eye and a badly damaged right leg from an automobile accident. He was forty-one years old, described as an aggressive, "die-hard racial agitator," by a Leavenworth warden because of his open relationship with a white con, which provoked violent resentment from both races there.

A friggin' wolf, John had spit out in his poor-boy drawl. Harris probably gave John the willies, watching out his vent with his one good eye. There was no way that Harris would not eventually have seen John crawl out of his vent.

WEST WAS NO longer worried about the blacks, however. He was beginning to hear from his friends something far more pernicious. Others were digging out too. It came to him in only bits and pieces—first as a rumor, then more details—until finally he got their names. Gates and Stones were digging around their vents. Then West was told that it was the Anglins who'd brought them in.

He slammed his fist on the table at breakfast one Saturday. Later, gripping his cell bars, he furiously whispered to Morris. Knowing well that it was more dangerous to go after Gates and Stones, he focused his wrath on the Anglins, talking them up as *slathering red-neck idiots.*

"He wanted to kill them both," Kent said.

By the time the B block flats were levered open for lunch, West was in a towering rage. The brothers avoided him, knowing that an explosion was imminent. That afternoon, West stormed out onto the yard. He took off after John, poking him in the chest, salting his tirade with profanities and slurs, accusing him of wrecking *his* deal, exposing *his* plot. West, who was five and a half feet tall, looked all the world like a ticked off terrier, leaping with every bark, while J-Dub, who had a good five inches on him, stood his ground like tough mongrel.

You got no beef with me, J-Dub came back.

If you don't shut your mouth, West said, *you'll get a knife in your back.* West may have counted on John becoming intimidated. He knew that sneering accusations and maniacal outbursts flustered and humiliated people. But when Clarence sided up, the brothers stood like a brick wall.

Go climb up your thumb, Clarence spat out, red-faced and livid. They were sick of his bullying and bitching. *You're not running this dump!*

Guys sitting on the steps could see the whole yard and figure out what was going on, Carnes had said.

But West was not about to cave in. *You keep this inside,* he snarled, *Or I'll slice your friggin' neck.*

Cons saw without looking. Guards scanning from the yard wall spotted the clash and locked on. No one knew how far it'd go.

"They almost came to knives out on the yard," said Carnes.

But West was signifying, Alcatraz lingo for posturing—what later cons would call "selling Wolf tickets," probably to Gates and Stones.

Another con sauntered by, *Cool a few,* he said under his breath, *The heats on the gun,* indicating the yard wall guards. West stopped cold. It ended as quickly as it began, the three men separating to different sides of the yard.

To the fifty or sixty guys on the yard, Carnes said, it was proof that something big was going down. "It's a small community," he said. "Nothing could go on that you couldn't figure out. . . . You can tell by the expression in their faces, you start piecing things together, you know where they cell. . . Practically everybody standing around knew what was going on."

Friends of Gates and Stones urged them to back off—everyone knew what West was capable of.

But West cooled down quickly. Soon he was acting as if noth-

ing had happened. His intentions had been signaled. His little tirade put Gates and Stones on notice and was a warning to the Anglins as well. He continued firing .22 caliber eyes at them, calculated to make them shut up. He told Morris through the bars that they would probably cut him and Morris out, if they could; they were unpredictable. He said that he wanted only one Anglin working up top. Morris would have to go *every* night. He could *not* have them up there alone together.

West was so confident that he later bragged to Carnes that he didn't care if *whole joint* came out behind him, so long as he made it. But it was just a show. In the weeks since January, things had gotten messy. He wanted this to work—more than anything in his whole life. Now, especially, because so many cons knew of the plot, were supplying tools, saw the digging, or had even joined up. The pressure was mounting. It was *his* rep at stake.

Gates may have gotten scared. He stopped digging after only eight holes. He "jiggered" for Stones, but then backed out of that. Stones persuaded a man called "Big," who lived on the other side, to watch for guards. And he continued digging.

~~~

Part 4
April Fools

APRIL 1962 WAS a cool month, especially if you lived on Alcatraz Island.

About half the staff, or sixty-five families and a few bachelors, lived on the island, mostly because they wanted to.

We lived in buildings that surrounded an old U.S. Army parade ground down the hill from the prison—Sixty-four building, which straddled the dock and the parade ground, four cottages reserved for lieutenants or higher administrators, a duplex with our family and the captain's family, apartment buildings A, B, and C, and three structures up top reserved for the medical, the coast guard and the warden's families.

About seventy-five kids lived there, most of us crossing on a boat every day to schools in San Francisco. It had been a cold, gusty winter. I remember stomping through puddles on the parade ground as the wind nearly knocked me off my feet, seagulls squawking and flailing in every direction. The snow fall that January was delightful. By April, the days were brisk but sunny, and you could smell summer coming.

I felt little concern about my safety. A small number of prisoners worked with officers on the dock or near our homes, but they were locked down by 4:30 P.M. We never questioned our fathers' control of our neighborhood, nor did out mothers burden us with their fears. Men had died during escape attempts, but those had occurred so long ago that it never seemed to touch our lives. There existed an almost absolute belief that no harm could come to us other than that which might mushroom during the Cold War. It was Russia we worried about—not prisoners up the hill. We lived in a low-crime neighborhood.

We stayed out as late as we could, playing pickup softball or basketball games on the parade ground, sitting on lover's bench

The annual watermelon feed on the dock for the island families.

overlooking San Francisco, or running down to the Officer's Club to go bowling or for dinners and parties. We strolled back to our apartments late at night, shouting, flirting, giggling. It never occurred to us that frantic, dangerous cons like West, Morris and the Anglins could be planning to break out of the building.

April was exciting if you were a San Francisco Giants' baseball fan. They were at their peak that year. The incomparable Willie Mays, Willie McCovey, Orlando Cepeda, the Alou brothers, a new Puerto Rican kid just up from the minors, named Juan Marichal, who had a beautiful high, left kick. Marichal would pitch the season opener that month with ten strike-outs, the Giants trotting off the field with a 6-0 win against the Milwaukee Braves. And the Giants would go on to win the pennant from their rivals, the Los Angeles Dodgers, to compete in the World Series with the New York Yankees.

There would be other, more momentous events in 1962: the U.S. would establish a military presence in Vietnam, a country almost no one had ever heard of, Marilyn Monroe would die of an apparent drug overdose that summer, and the Cuban Missile Crisis would bring us to the brink of war in October.

But in the spring of '62, even Alcatraz seemed at the center of the news. The movie, *Birdman of Alcatraz,* was released in April, starring Burt Lancaster as Robert Stroud. Stroud, of course, was actually the Birdman of Leavenworth, and at that time was residing in Springfield, Missouri. Only Hollywood—and the rest of the nation—thought of him as the Birdman of Alcatraz. Mickey Cohen returned to the island days later, having lost an appeal on his fifteen-year income tax evasion sentence. We grabbed popcicles down at the grocery store in Sixty-four building and gossiped about his girlfriend, stripper Candy Barr, whom we all hoped would pay us a visit. *Days of Wine and Roses,* starring Jack Lemmon and Lee Remick, was filmed near our dock in San Francisco, and one day on the boat, I leaned over the railing and waved to two actors in a small rowboat who were their doubles—an almost exciting moment.

Up top, far more momentous things were happening, and April would prove to be, as T.S. Eliot once wrote, the cruelist month.

ON SUNDAY, APRIL 1, Morris ordered a concertina for twenty-eight dollars. He had been playing on the standard-sized, prison-loaned accordion. Now he wanted one of his own. The warden's secretary, Walter J. Bertrand, a dapper, handsome man who lived in San Francisco and frequently obtained guitar strings, clarinet reeds and sheet music for inmates, charged Morris' account and gave it to the cell house officer to deliver. Morris was polite as usual when the officer handed it to him. A small accordion-like instrument, it was a beautiful, little seven-by-seven-inch, polished mahogany box with genuine steel reeds.

It's not clear if he had already conceived of the idea. In fact, Kent said the idea had come from Glenn May. FBI agents and Alcatraz investigators thought it came from a May 21, 1962, *Sports Illustrated* magazine article on inflatable toys and equipment—an issue that wouldn't come to Alcatraz for another six weeks. But soon, either Morris or Glenn May would dismantle the keys and adapt the musical instrument as a bellows which Morris would used to inflate the raft.

That Sunday was also the quarterly officer rotation. Officers usually remained on a shift for three months—the day watch hospital shift, say—then were rotated to another position on another watch. West may have initially been unaware of who worked where, something that was occupying his thoughts of late. But by the middle of that week he knew.

A husky, left-handed, former pro-baseball pitcher named John "Jerry" Herring was the day-watch cell house OIC. From West's perspective that was good: Herring had already served in that position over the winter, when West had blazed his trail to the top of the block.

Alert, stocky, and as solid as the Grand Coulee Dam, Herring had written "Springfield or Leavenworth" on his 1956 civil service application. They sent the twenty-two year old to Alcatraz. But he liked it there; within three years he converted to career. A man's man, who talked sports at work but was pensive at home, Herring lived with his wife, Ruthann, and two children on the third floor of C building with a commanding view of San Francisco from his living room window.

By 1962, Herring had already distinguished himself as a junior officer by calmly escorting two-time attempted-murderer Roland Simcox, AZ 1131, to seg, after he fatally stabbed Edward Gauvin, AZ 1134, in 1957, and by alerting police that car thieves were working the city-side Alcatraz dock.

New, young or uncertain officers were usually tried out on the periphery—towers or the gun gallery—where they were no harm to themselves or to others. Herring worked inside, in TU, the barbershop, the hospital, the yard and the main gate. He'd spent six months in the culinary department, supervising thirty cons, all of whom had ready access to an alarming array of professional carving, filleting or butcher knives. You needed to be on your toes. Described by some as capable, steady, and by Warden Blackwell as having "some potential as a lieutenant," Herring would go on to a distinguished career. After promotion to senior officer at Alcatraz, he would transfer to the Federal Medical Prison at Springfield, Missouri, where he would become a correctional counselor, a sought-after position, which went to well-liked and intelligent officers. In 1975, he would be given an Outstanding Performance Evaluation. At Milan, Michigan he would become a unit manager and a staff trainer, eventually retiring at La Tuna, Texas in 1984 as captain.

As the cell house OIC, Herring was in the position held for many years by Lieutenant Mitchell. He supervised movements in and out of cells, the dining room and the yard, directed officers in cell searches, pat downs, bar ticking, and supervised the inmate orderlies. Despite his obvious acumen, Herring quickly came to officers' minds when they spoke of less experienced men pushed by Blackwell's management style into key positions to gain experience. One officer joked that on Alcatraz Herring "didn't know the difference between a convict and a seagull." Although he was a good officer, at age twenty-eight, Herring barely had six years' prison experience.

West, at age thirty-three, had eighteen.

The shift changed at 4:00 P.M., but West could have cared less about who worked the evening or morning watches. It was Jerry Herring he was after.

West was also concerned about the day watch lieutenant.

He had hoped Severson would be the day watch supervisor. A big man, a perennially cocked eyebrow and a pompous attitude, Severson was sometimes referred to as "Utah," or, behind his back, "the warden" because he had once been warden at a Utah state penitentiary. He was well educated but irritatingly pedantic. "Severson tried to act like the boss," said Juelich, "but he didn't get the respect." It was said that Severson gave West his cell house maintenance job, and thought he had influence over West.

"West was Severson's boy," said Lew Meushaw, who observed the lieutenant numerous times standing at West's cell talking to him.

West figured Severson was the industries lieutenant that quarter because he only came into the house in the morning and at lunch. But that would soon change.

West noticed that that Lloyd Miller was the day watch lieutenant and it disappointed him. Miller was all-business, smart and not easily intimidated. He was outside of West's circle of manipulation.

Miller's relief, however, was Maurice Ordway. He worked the day watch on Fridays, Saturdays and Sundays, then worked the evening watch on Mondays and Tuesdays. Known as "Double-

Tough" or "Hardway," Ordway was nervous, passionate and peculiar. He had a slam-the-door mentality. Cons thought he waddled like a duck and sometimes when he angled into the house you could hear a chorus of "Quack-quack, quack-quack."

Ask an evening or a morning watch tower officer what his most important job was and he'd say: watching for the lieutenant, *"especially* if it was Ordway," said Bill Rogers. At night, the lieutenant patrolled the island and signaled the tower officers with his flash light to keep them awake. Ordway would sneak around, try to flash his light at odd times, from high up on the balcony of Sixty-four building, or down low along the road, or behind the tower along the shore. If you were a new officer still on probation, you could be fired on the spot if you didn't flash back.

"He always [tried] to give the impression to both cons and officers that he was the tough, unyielding boss of the cell house," said former officer Larry Quilligan, "but I don't think he was fooling anyone other than himself."

Ordway lacked other characteristics for promotion. He relied on baiting officers into compliance and barking out orders. He apparently was not a well organized supervisor; he would never

The dock tower, on the opposite side of the road tower, operated
twenty-four hours a day.

wear the gold shield of the captain's rank. But he was a good officer and even cons could see that.

"Ordway was strictly rules," said Carnes." 'Don't do this!' 'Don't do that!' 'What are you doing up on that gallery?' 'How come this man ain't locked in his cell?' 'One movement at a time around the institution!' 'How come the mess hall door's open—and you opened up the door of the isolation unit?' "

But West had a talent for sizing people up. Ordway was a stickler for cleanliness and from West's point of view, not the sharpest blade in the grass.

2

BY NOW WEST was becoming a fanatic about the plan, thinking about it constantly. Sometime he would stop what he was doing and just stare. They needed supplies but had no hiding places. They needed to move forward but were stalled out on digging little holes. They needed to get up to the ceiling, but he hadn't set up that part yet. Then he would kick himself: this was the fun part.

They were entering a new and more dangerous phase, and everything needed to go perfectly—one step at a time, in sequence—and he had to plan it all out. He still worried about cell searches. He fretted over bringing in the Anglins. At mealtimes, he was sharp, at times sulky, teetering between desperation and distraction.

Baby 'gator, the brothers snickered behind his back.

He kept his eyes on Herring, gauging how the officer conducted himself. Herring was young and cocksure. West would have liked that; it would have been a challenge. But he had other things on his mind too.

Sometime in April, maybe at lunch one day over vegetable beef soup, omelets, fried potatoes and coleslaw, West announced that he wasn't going to break through his entire wall.

That got their attention.

We don't all need to go up, he explained. *Morris'll work on the ceiling vent. One of ya'll 'll go with him,* he indicated to the Anglins. J-Dub and Clarence exchanged looks.

I kin work on the vent, Clarence protested.

No, West would say curtly. *Morris. He's the smallest. Besides, two of us need to stay behind and make stuff in our cells. Then the night we go—ever'thing's ready—me and one of you can pop out the back of my wall.*

Well, I'll be going up, Clarence said a tad defensively.

Fine, but if we're all up, nobody's downside to watch. I'll be up there everyday. I can tote stuff up.

When'zat gonna happen? J-Dub asked.

West cocked his head in Herring's direction. *I got a plan,* he said.

BUT THE PLAN was cut short on Wednesday, April 11.

While West and an officer were getting supplies out of A block in order for him to paint another cell, he noticed several officers hovering around the west-end desk talking to the Herring and the lieutenant. More officers than usual. He nonchalantly asked his escort what was up.

Shakin' down the whole place, the officer replied, *top to bottom.*

West acted casual. From the corner of his eye he saw the officers break up and some begin to climb the C block tiers. Others left the cell house.

When West was locked inside a third tier B block Broadway cell and went to the bars, he had a commanding view of C block. He put down his paint can and brushes, and slowly covered the bed with a small tarp. He watched as an officer began walking down Broadway dragging a mallet across the bars along the flats. He smirked. "Bar-tickin'" everyone called it. The officer tracked down Broadway and out of West's view.

Another officer walked up to the second tier, and another to the third. As West watched from the corner of his eye, he could see they were tapping every bar.

"Very monotonous," Officer Rogers said. "Some of the bars were quite high and you had to get an extension ladder and crawl up there to pound them." He was referring to the bars above the third tiers.

"How in the world they thought anyone could climb up there and saw them is beyond me. But you have to pound them anyway. You pounded cell bars too. . . . Any time [they] had extra men,

that's what they did—pound bars," Rogers said. "We hated it, the inmates hated it, the lieutenants *loved* it."

"Two or three guards, all day long, with rubber mallets," said Juelich.

But this wasn't "extra men," this was an institution-wide surprise shakedown, West could see that. Within minutes the OIC racked open a set of cells and West saw other men disappear inside them to shake them down. It looked to West like they were actually going to shake down every cell in the house. He suddenly felt sick to his stomach. *Had they been ratted out?*

He tried to remember how many things he had in his cell—spoon handles, saw blades that John had given him, a little bottle of cell paint, extra bars of soap. Then he tried to visualize the holes in his back wall. *Would they notice the uneven concrete?* His heart pounded. Paint dribbled down his arm, tickling him, and he absent mindedly wiped it off.

A good shakedown, George Gregory indicated, started at the top. Then he would leaf through books, personal papers, fold back photographs, flip through paintings, open paint boxes, and examine the hinges. He picked up everything—packs of tobacco, tooth powder, shaving brushes and mugs, shoes, slippers. They'd even look at your letters. Some officers were so good, you'd never know they had been in your cell.

Next, they removed everything from the shelf, pulled it down and examined the edges.

"They'd just scrape a groove in the shelf," said Rogers, "push in a sharpened table knife, and cover the groove with putty or soap." Carnes said he once found a piece of steel inside the hole where the bolt attached to the shelf.

They'd find "bushels of knives," Gregory once said.

"Guards were almost insane about security," Carnes noted, "It was almost like a religion." And he knew. Officer George DeVincenzi was waiting for the main line to be racked out for work once when a paper airplane floated down from the third range and landed at his feet. Spellbound, he picked it up. Inside was a note saying that Carnes had a shank and had threatened to kill someone. They tossed Carne's cell, real good, and found it. He cursed all the way to segregation.

Anything—extra razor blades, saw blades, drills, nuts, bolts, hollowed out tubing to make a bar spreader, powder to blow things up—could be discovered. Shakedowns had even uncovered fake guns at times—made out of soap, or wood and a short metal pipe. Other things were considered contraband. Leon Thompson made a sewing needle out of a paper clip. He stripped individual threads from towels to sew buttons on his pants. With enough patience, however, a paper clip could be turned into a key. Even slit someone's carotid artery. So that would be confiscated.

"We had so many places to hide things you'd never believe it," said Juelich. "The toilet bowl. Or you might hollow out a piece of your chair leg, or the bed leg. Mop ringer handles was another good place."

After an officer finished a cell, he went into another and began all over. West lit a cigarette. He tossed the match in the toilet and peered out of the bars.

A good cell searcher ran his fingers along the tops of the barred door. Then he checked the bottom bar; sometimes someone would glue or tape a knife under there. He checked the toilet for broken, soaped-up seams. He checked the vent to see if things were tied behind there. He checked the *vent.*

West blew smoke out of his nose like a dual-exhaust '56 Chevy. His heart was racing. John already had his fake grill up. West had never seen it, and he didn't know how neat John was. But Clarence was a slob, he knew that. *Christ!* he thought, as he sucked on his cigarette, *Friggin' boat's probably sunk now!*

The game for cons was to hide things in unique ways—a drill hidden in some cleanser, a razor blade sewn into the hem of a blanket, a nail tied to a string and hung down the sink drain.

For guards, the game was finding stuff—period.

If officers suspected a con was packing steel, they threw everything out of the cell, piece by piece. It would really mess a con up; some stuff he'd never see again. The mattress would be examined for tears, or a new sewing job. Sometimes a guard would even take it out and run it through a metal detector.

Christ! They all had stuff in their cells! Morris' file was hidden near his toilet. He had a piece of metal under his mattress. West had an eight-inch piece of scrap metal under his bed and an ice pick buried. Clarence had a blade attached to his writing stand and John had multiple tools.

West watched officers as they marched down the C block rows. Each time they found something, he got more nervous. At lunch, everyone was racked back to his cell and West whispered to Morris as they stood for the noon count, *We're screwed! They're checking the whole house.* Morris passed it to the con next to him, who passed it down the line to the Anglins.

"C! Inside!" an officer yelled and the C block flats were racked opened. "C! Second tier!" West and Morris could hear the cell doors crack open.

Morris told West to calm down. *Nothin's gonna happen.*

"B Flats!" Their doors slid open.

At lunch West was visibly shaken. *Those vents better be tight.*

They look, they see, J-Dub said, biting his thumb nail, *Big deal, we go to D, we come back, we start over.*

Fuck that, Morris said, *you'll never go back to the same house.*

They'll scrape down every inch, West added. *And then the snitches'll come outta the woodwork.*

Morris looked steadily at the Anglins. *Can you carry your tools this afternoon?*

Yeah, Clarence said, *but I'll be clinking like an old truck.*

Well, get 'em out of your cell, Morris ordered.

I can take yours, West said to Morris, *How many you got?*

Couple of spoons, some blades, Morris replied.

I got my own stuff, West snapped.

I got the snitch box, Morris shot back.

Clarence poked at his food. *Who the hell did this?* he wanted to know. *Fuckin' ruined everything.*

Get rid of the tools, Morris replied. *Leave some stuff out, like the canvas boards, make it obvious, so they don't look harder. Then don't worry about it. There's too many houses to search.*

Back in their cells, John checked the wall where his blades were pasted. He passed other tools through the bars to Clarence, who took them into the barbershop that afternoon. Morris passed his tools to West who slid them in his socks, up his sleeves, and down his pants. *I feel like the fuckin' tin man,* he joked, as they were racked out. *The Wizard of Oz*—everyone seen it in the joint a number of times.

That afternoon, while everyone was at work, the remaining cells were shaken down. Then the auditorium, the clothing rooms, TU, the shops, the roof, the entire institution—interior and exterior—was given a thorough shakedown.

Everyone was quiet at supper. No one had heard anything.

That night, none of four worked on their walls. And the caterwauling music roared on.

3

DAYS PASSED. GUARDEDLY, the four men began to work on their escape again.

When West got all the stuff for the life jackets, he got back to the lanky guy with the funny hair. They met on the yard one Saturday and the guy described how he could do it in three steps.

The next night, West pulled his own raincoat off the peg and spread it on his bed.

The navy surplus raincoats were generously cut and had plenty of material at the back. Slipping a razor blade lengthwise down the back, he stripped out an eighteen-by-fifty-eight-inch piece of material, and threw the rest aside.

He folded the bottom about two-thirds of the way to the top. Inside the bottom fold, he slipped a long strap of canvas all the way through, extending it out each side, then glued it into the fold. Next, he glued the two panels together at the sides and the top to form a large air bladder. This would lie on a man's chest with the straps tied around his back.

At the top of this bladder, he cut a twenty-inch hole, big enough for a man's head to slip through. The hole was not a complete circle, however. At its lowest point, about where a man's clavicle would be, was a two-inch high protrusion, into which West would insert the Windex bottle "dipstick" for inflation. He would use a binder clip—a large, black clip used to fasten a sheath of paper together—as a stopper. The vest was designed so that the user could lower his head and grip the dipstick with his mouth, especially if, while floating, the vest would begin to lose air.

The remaining top third he folded backwards, then folded it again under itself, like a finished collar, or a flap on a soft leather brief case. This part would be free of the front panel and, when inflated, would form a sort of pillow for a man's head.

When completed, the life jacket was eighteen by thirty inches in the "Mae West" design.

The adhesive West obtained was later identified by the FBI as a "rubber adhesive." It was amber in color, rather than opaque or white, meaning that it consisted of about twelve percent rubber to about eighty-eight percent solvent and would not dissolve in water. No doubt West had asked around for the best possible glue. It was a flammable contact cement, much like model airplane glue or superglue today. It could have been found in a furniture refinishing, tire repair or shoe repair area, and was readily available on Alcatraz. Later, investigators would find a small plastic bottle of a "Rem-Weld" brand book repair glue that the men had left behind. That was a white, opaque glue which would dissolve in water. When it was discovered, officers and cons began to believe that West and the others had used a water-soluble glue, and some would deride them for their stupidity. But, in fact, West had thought carefully about this.

He pressed the seams tight until they bonded, and then he laid the jacket flat under his mattress while he slept that night. The next day, he gave it to Morris to carry down to the shops.

For years it was rumored among staff and prisoners that the life jackets were sewn in industries. And, when viewing them, it was easy to see that someone had used a sewing machine. The stitching was not original to the raincoat's design, and was, in fact, contoured to the life jacket's modification.

There were only two places on the island where the life jackets could be machine stitched—the clothing or the glove factories. Both shops were the two largest on Alcatraz, each utilizing about thirty-five to forty men—several of whom could be persuaded to help out.

Getting it into a shop would be a simple task of wrapping it under your shirt and walking it down. Upon arrival, however, the task would become trickier. The vests needed to be stitched down both sides and over the straps, then sewn around the neckline and up both sides of the protrusion—without anyone seeing.

If it were done in the clothing shop—where it would be easier to hide while sewing—you need look no further than Larry Trumblay or Teddy Green who celled near Tom Kent and were said by Kent to have been marginally involved, or West's friend, hipster Billy Boggs, who would be found to be "deeply involved in the escape attempt"—all of whom worked in the clothing factory for many years.

A former prisoner, who wished to remain anonymous, and who

was on Alcatraz from 1953 until 1959 and did much of the pur-
chasing and payroll in industries, said that the glove shop would
have been the more likely area, however. Those machines were
larger, using large needles to sew thicker thread for the leather
gloves that were sometimes ordered. And the thread on the life
jacket was larger than normal.

If the glove shop were the likely destination, you might theo-
rize that Homer Clinton, played a part in the caper. Also known
as the "Green Lizard" because he had once swallowed whole a
live lizard, Clinton was easily led, emotionally immature, childish
and extremely disruptive. You might remember that he had used
a spoon handle in 1958 to cut his Achilles tendons. While in segregation from December 27, 1959—after he tried to topple the
dining room Christmas tree—until April 1962, he had more than
twenty disciplinary reports. He sliced his heel skin again with West,
Clymore, Boggs and the others. When he finally got out of segregation on April 4, 1962, he was assigned—you guessed it—to cell
house maintenance with West. On May 10, he was reassigned—
you're right again—to the glove shop where he remained until

The life jackets were machine-stitched in the clothing or the glove shops.

September. Clinton was easily manipulated; West was the supreme manipulator.

Just the fact that industries was involved answers other important questions as well. Over the years outsiders have often speculated that officers must have been involved in this escape attempt. After all, how could West and the others hide the vests in their cells without being discovered? The answer is simple: the vests were never hidden in their cells. To do so would be folly. Instead, the raw material was smuggled into the industries building, sewn at opportune times, then hidden until they were needed. A different shop was shaken down by an officer every night, but if a life vest were found, it would not implicate anyone in particular. Cons would act shocked, disavowing any knowledge.

It is likely in fact that very few items constructed and used in this escape attempt remained in West's, Morris' or the Anglins' cells. Everything was probably hidden either in the A block supply area or in industries until the moment when one of the four men got to the top of the block. Once that would happen, West would call for the items one by one, and they would be taken up top that night to be hidden even more deeply. Prison officers did not need to be used in this caper. *The cons could do it themselves.*

But with industries involved, this escape attempt took on wider dimensions. Not only were more cons used in smuggling and sewing and retrieving life vests, but now, more officers, more lieutenants and more industries employees were failing to notice what was going on. Especially since the institution-wide shakedown on April 11 had uncovered nothing but "nuisance items."

It was a masterful scheme—and a stunning indictment.

4

AT WORK, WEST took his cues from Officer Herring, mostly talking up pro-ball with the ex-pitcher. He no doubt teased Herring for scuttling his minor league baseball status for a job as a prison guard hanging out with cons like him. Herring was part Native American, stoic and not easily flattered, but he was amused.

West was the eager show-off, bursting with ideas. Leaning on his push broom one day, he casually told Herring that he needed to paint the ceiling above B block. Herring might have even been surprised. He thought the ceiling was done. *Oh no*, West said, *still got a little section over B block.*

Within minutes, Herring and West were up on the third tier, noisily setting up a step ladder so Herring could climb above the third tier and unlock the bar door onto the top of the block. Herring climbed back down, told West to watch himself, and returned to the floor. West made sure to make lots of noise, sometimes even yelling down to Herring at his desk at the west end. That morning, he had his paint can and brush, his turpentine and rags all staged up there with him. He also brought up the floor sweep.

"Herring locked West inside the utility corridor by himself," Dollison wrote in a later memo, "and permitted West to work at the top of the block without supervision."

Officer Irving Levinson was stunned. He told told Herring, "I wouldn't trust West as far as I could throw a piano."

"I felt genuine admiration for the little son-of-a-bitch!" Carnes later exclaimed about West's chutzpah.

Officer Ron Battles opened the third floor utility corridor one day while West was up there, painting. He was shocked to see West working alone. "I backed out of there!" Battles said. He went down to the floor and said, " 'Herring! You got an inmate on top of the block!' "

" 'That's been approved,' " Herring shot back.

IT WAS THE first blunder leading to the success of this breakout. Only two cons on Alcatraz worked without supervision: the gardener, who remained visible to the road tower officer, and a prisoner who worked inside the warden's house. No one was allowed in a utility corridor or on top of the block without an officer escort. Some thought the reason was to limit homosexual activity. But the real reason was far more vital to security.

When Alcatraz was transferred from the U.S. Army to the BOP, new tool-proof bars were installed on B and C block cells and new fences and towers were erected. But not enough money existed to secure everything. And among the items that had never been properly secured were the ceiling vents. They were fixed with two square bars—the old bars—which could be easily spread. As West knew by now, all but one or two had been dismantled and their vent openings cemented over.

"The weakness in the vents was known by everybody!" Phil Bergen exclaimed years later. Bergen had been shown the vents in his first few days in 1939 and given a lecture about their vulnerability. "The only way to insure that that area was never compromised was to have a rule that no inmate *ever* be up there without on officer."

That rule was observed as long as he was captain. But Bergen transferred in 1955, and his replacement, Captain Emil Rychner, had in turn been replaced by Captain Bradley. And the message apparently had not been passed on. Lieutenant Lloyd Miller said years later that he "never dreamed of a weakness in the ceiling." He had worked there for five years and obviously had not been told. Herring didn't know, or it's probable he wouldn't have allowed West up there alone.

It's possible by 1962 in fact, that only a few men actually knew the real reason. Among those would have been lieutenants Ordway, Severson and Mahan, all long term officers. But they might not have been aware that West was up there alone. West was supervised by the OIC—not the lieutenant. And West might have refrained from going up there when Ordway was day-watch relief lieutenant. And certainly the dock, industries, evening and morning watch lieutenants would not initially know. It's possible, in fact, that few officers knew West was up there alone. Even years later, some were unaware of how much West was responsible for the success of this attempt. But Severson knew. This was a *maintenance* escape and Severson had given West his maintenance job. "West was a sneaky, very agile fellow," Severson said when I called him years before I had been told about his own involvement, "If it wasn't for West, they'd have never gotten out."

Then, sadly, when Herring said that "it had been approved," junior and senior officers backed off, assuming that Captain Bradley or the warden or the associate warden had approved it. They didn't question it. Prisons operated on a military model, with junior officers just like army privates. They never volunteered, nor complained, and they kept their mouths shut. No one dared go above his immediate superior to suggest that something was wrong.

"They'd label you," said Ed Deatherage, who was a junior officer there from 1959 until April 1962. "When you tried to go to the administration, they'd label you as a do-gooder—'Don't worry about that, kid.' "

"Everybody was pretty closedmouthed over there," said Officer Herman. "You didn't squeal on your fellow officers."

"They made it difficult for younger officers to talk to superiors," said long-term Alcatraz officer Don Martin.

"If a concerned 'old timer' mentioned any dereliction to a lieutenant and suggested a remedy," said long term officer Karlton Moore, "(I tried it once or twice) he was promptly told 'Suppose you let *me* run the cell house and *you* run your job.' . . . They will absolutely accept *no* suggestions from anyone lower in rank than the captain."

"Several of us made comments about why [West] was up there unsupervised and the story was he was locked in up there—there was nothing he could do," said Officer Fred Freeman.

"When Mr. Herring was questioned about this," Associate Warden Dollison wrote in a memo, "he stated that West was painting and was always under either visual or audio supervision. I asked Mr. Herring where he was standing in relationship to West when he could hear but not see him. Mr. Herring replied that West was on top of the cell block and that he, Herring, was standing on the flats and could hear the slap of the paint brush."

Conceptually, West's working on top of the block unattended, to Herring, seemed no different from his working alone up on the scaffolding. It was just an incremental change. But that tiny step from the scaffolding to the top of the block had what mathematicians call "exponential amplification."

"West was supposed to be painting," said Officer Freeman, "and all the time he was working on the roof."

It was a monumental blunder, which would pale, however, in comparison to West's next new thing.

5

ON SUNDAY, APRIL 15, evening-watch Lieutenant Ordway had

written "Routine," in the watch log notes. On Tuesday, he also wrote, "Quiet, routine—no incidents." On April 18 and 19, Lieutenant Delmore had written, "Very quiet shift," and "Quieter shift." The next night he wrote, "Routine."

On Saturday April 21, Blackwell and Bradley went fishing together with their wives at Lake Berryessa, and it was a "quiet watch" that evening.

"Two hundred and eight knives issued for the noon meal—all returned," Lieutenant Ordway wrote on Easter Sunday, April 22. "Quiet day—no incidents."

"Foggy night—routine otherwise," Acting Lieutenant Dick Barnett wrote on April 23.

By Wednesday, April 25, John had completed his ten-by-fifteen-inch hole and had broken through his wall. That night he crawled through for the first time.

The corridor was dark, narrow and salty with a urine smell. The black con, with the one good eye, watched from his vent as John duckwalked over to Clarence's cell and quietly rapped on his vent. When Clarence's face appeared at the opening, J-Dub's lips parted in a tight con grin.

While Clarence covered for him, John began working on a little box and a wall piece that would fit on the utility corridor side. He was in and out of his cell several times, fitting it and slapping concrete around the back fake wall, so it could slip out easily, yet still seem natural.

No one on the evening watch heard anything. "Routine night," Delmore wrote in the watch log.

BUT WITH JOHN out, West became even more frantic. He urged Morris to hurry—get out, get on top—warning Morris that the Anglins could *not* be up there alone.

The pressure was building in other ways as well. Now that John was out of his cell, he would need a decoy.

Clarence had pocketed locks of hair from the barbershop floor, which at night he tied into little pony tails. They had obtained a length of green 12-gauge ground wire, which Glenn May had suggested as a foundation. West had retrieved some cement powder and a sealant known as cement paint. Anyone could have provided oil paints.

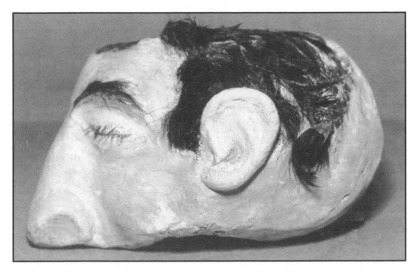

The first mask was small enough to hide behind the vent.

That night, after lights out, John balled up the wire into a circular shape and packed it with a slurry of cement he made in his sink. He hid it in his cell to dry overnight and then hid it behind his cell vent. This first mask was designed to be small enough to easily hide. About nine inches wide and as little as five and a half inches in height, it was not a complete head, but a half-head in profile. Cut off just above the eyebrow and just below the nose, it had no mouth or chin. It was a face with only an ear, a closed eyelid, an eyebrow and a large nose.

Next, John took a piece of red wire—a small gauge perhaps from an electrical tester—and molded it into an oval shape. Using cement or soap, he formed a rudimentary ear, then attached it to the head. Once the profile dried, he overlaid its surface with a layer of cement paint—a substance composed of finely ground cement and paint powder used to seal and brighten concrete building surfaces.

Then it was painted a washed-out pink color. The flat scull cap was dabbed with black paint or an ink stain. When finished, John slid it through the bars to Clarence, who then patched human hair on top. He laid out several wafts of hair on the eyebrow line and put wisps of hair where a closed eye would be. It was sloppy and rough. The hair was clumped in patches. John giggled as soon as he saw the finished head. With its prominent ear and nose, it looked like a pig. The brothers began calling it "Oink." John hid it behind his fake grill.

CLARENCE WAS STILL completing his hole. Now, however, he worked with renewed vigor. And he wanted to get up top. On the way back from supper one night in late April, he poked J-Dub into switching cells. John reluctantly agreed. When Officer Herman cocked open the B block flats, Clarence entered John's cell.

Once the musicians cranked up, he set up Oink on the pillow and crawled out the back, replacing the fake wall. He waited for his eyes to adjust, the salty effluvia nearly bowling him over. He felt fairly certain he could sneak up quickly before any guard would notice. Besides, guys often slept in at odd hours.

Although it was dark, he could see the lighted ceiling above, and each cell had a tiny vent which emitted a weak shaft of light. Within a minute he could make out the maze of old pipes. He followed them up, deciding that they could support his six foot, one-hundred-and-sixty-pound frame without rattling against the wall. He grabbed a little cold water pipe and hitched himself up onto a big cast-iron waste pipe.

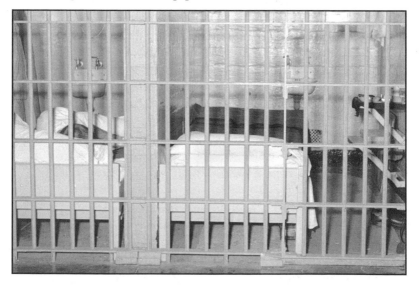

It wasn't unusual for cons to sleep at any time during the day.

Each handhold led to another step. On the second and third tiers he had to avoid the two-by-twelve-inch planks running down the middle of the corridor, which guards used to check behind the cells. Clarence had never been a careful man. Impetuous, with schemes that rarely panned out, he usually left telltale signs of his criminal trespass. It took an exhausting amount of time and concentrated effort to climb to the second and third tiers.

By now men along B block knew of the breakout. There were six men digging out of their cells, others next to them, or behind them, who could hear or see what they were doing. Soon, cons would start hearing strange, small sounds from behind their cells.

A con in cell B-352 heard a slight noise coming from his vent. Alert, he sat up. It sounded strangely like an echo through a pipe.

Heh! he may have hoarsely whispered to Martin McNicholas in B-350, *You hear something?* McNicholas, AZ 1442, a bank robber on a twenty-year sentence who arrived on Alcatraz on the same train as did Kent and Morris, hadn't heard a thing, but he knew something was going on along the B block flats. He'd been waiting for it.

When Clarence got to the top of the cell block, he didn't look down. One misstep—one tiny slip—and he could fall three stories. He secured his footing, leaned across to the top of the block with one hand, then the other. When he was secure, he pushed off with his legs, hoisting himself onto the top of the block.

A thick layer of dust billowed up into his face. Clapping his hand over his face, he stifled a sneeze. He could feel his heart pounding in his chest. Somewhere just below him that same con was squeezing out that same song, "Moon River," which by now everyone was ready to kill over. Despite all the other angonizing tunes, he could clearly hear that one.

Crouching low, he scanned the top of the cell house, starring first down at the west gun gallery. He had been told the guard always remained on the lower level to cover the floor guards, and seldom climbed the ladder to the second level. Clarence knew the east gun gallery wasn't manned but he shot a look anyway.

He was beginning to get hot, perspiration clinging to his denim shirt, heat radiating up to his neck. He stood gradually to a half crouch and took a few guarded steps, glad that he had thought of changing into his tennis shoes.

Just in front of him was the big air exhaust blower and ductwork that extended to the ceiling vent. He could see that the duct could be easily disassembled. A motor sat beside the blower on a metal box, unused and disconnected.

He wiped his palms on his pants.

He had brought along a handmade screwdriver. But he quickly realized that the screws connecting the ductwork were not regular slotted screws, but hexheaded sheet metal screws. His screwdriver was useless. Besides it would take two men—one to hold the duct while the other loosened the screws. He stood examining the ductwork a long time, trying to memorize everything. He didn't want to go back down. That familiar feeling of breaking and entering had stoked his senses. But the honking and screeching in the cell house was pounding in his brain.

The con in B-352 knelt by his vent and squinted. It was too dark, he couldn't see a thing. But suddenly, as Clarence began his descent, he could hear it. *Christ!* he exclaimed to McNicholas a minute later, *what's goin' on?* McNicholas probably snorted like he didn't know; he had told no one, but he had been compiling a list of mileages from Alcatraz to ten different landings around the bay. First on his list was "Alcatraz to Angel Island," which he correctly noted as about a mile and three quarters away. It was the opposite direction from San Francisco, which was only a mile and a quarter away. Anyone going toward Angel Island was crossing a bigger expanse of the bay with swifter currents. But it was U.S. Army property and mostly empty. Few people. No cops. From there, you could practically jump across to Marin County and the freeways that would lead north or south into the country. That was exactly where West, Morris and the Anglins were planning to go. It wasn't known if McNicholas had compiled this list for himself, or for someone else.

Clarence descended the pipes to the floor, then pushed in John's fake wall section and crawled back into the cell.

That night in hushed tones, he told J-Dub everything he had seen. They talked long into the night, drifting into derogatory comments about West and Morris. They may have planned then to ditch them once they hit land, just like West and Morris had decided to do to them.

I got West back, John whispered.

Clarence, excited, sniffed, *Whadjado?*

Fixed his back wall, J-Dub answered. West had cracked it and had asked him to stuff a line of cement in there, so the guards wouldn't notice. *Fixed it real good,* J-Dub said, chortling.

The officer strolled by for the evening count and they dummied up. He never noticed that they had switched cells.

The next morning, they switched back. That night, Clarence was heated up; now he wanted to get his own wall open. For the next couple of nights, John crawled out to help him break off bigger chunks. When Clarence's wall was completely opened, they began working on the fake back grill.

Officers checked the utility corridor periodically, using flashlights to illuminate the walls. On the second and third tiers, they would bounce along the planks, holding onto pipes for safety, seeing painted cell numbers, even old U.S. Army graffiti. But West, Morris and the Anglins celled along the flats. There was no reason why the fresh cement, which looked like a glob of slurry the color of gun metal and which contained no aggregate, could not be distinguished from the old 1912 concrete.

NOW THAT A second man was about to get out of his cell, another mask was needed.

West didn't share the Anglins' amusement over the tiny pig face, and he may have groused about it to Glenn May. Over the years several men have theorized that someone other than the Anglins worked on at least two of the masks. Billy Boggs is a possibility. He took an art class that year (something else that was new on Alcatraz). In his file was a note from his teacher for his "rapid progress in painting." And there were others who have been mentioned from time to time. But Tom Kent flatly stated that Glenn May contributed more to the dummy masks than anyone realized. And that's a good theory for several reasons.

May, the polite, lanky, ghostlike figure who floated around the cell house repairing electrical equipment, was, according to Juelich and others, one of the best artists in the cell house. "Devotes all his spare time to painting," his file stated, "and is regarded as one of the better inmate artists." His portraits, probably copied from pictures in magazines or personal photographs, were typical of the highly stylized, often idealized prison artwork. When he transferred from one prison to another his personal property listed numerous colored pencils and brushes, seventy-eight tubes of oil paint, cans of gesso and glue, bottles of varnish, sponges, rulers, drawing boards, books on watercolors, landscapes, trees and figures. He frequently sent paintings to his family.

Whether the electrician, counterfeiter, expert lock picker and artist was a co-conspirator in this escape attempt, or even a willing participant, is debated.

"May wasn't brave," said Officer Meushaw, "He was easy to scare." Meushaw had heard that May was forced into an escape attempt at Leavenworth that got him transferred to Alcatraz. And there was some truth to it. The Leavenworth warden wrote that May had been forced to join because of his lock-picking ability. Meushaw thought May might have been threatened by West, or sucked into the plan little by little until he was in too deep to get out. But like many cons, May presented a different picture to different people; in his file it was written that he "fears no inmate."

May no doubt obtained the electrical wire used in the first three masks, and certainly in the second mask, which contained a strand of wire with a thick cording on it, like the kind seen on table lamps or vacuum cleaners from the 1930s.

And the second mask differed strikingly from Oink.

Its foundation was made of wire and concrete, like Oink's, but on top of that may have been a layer of plaster—an easier medium to mold. This head faced east—opposite of Oink—which faced west. It was also a full face, and modeled in the round, like an actual head would be. It was unusually large, with a long ski-slope nose and a fully developed, authentic looking ear, appearing as if the artist worked after lights out, feeling his own face to gauge size and relationships. It was painted in tones of orange rather than pink. Its eyebrows and eyelashes were cropped and neat, unlike Oink's, which were sloppy and glued in clumps.

There were some oddities: the eyelashes, meant to resemble a sleeping man, were curved upside down. And the top of the head down to the neckline had been painted with a strange lime green color, over which the hair was placed.

But the hair, rather than being splotchy as was Oink's, ap-

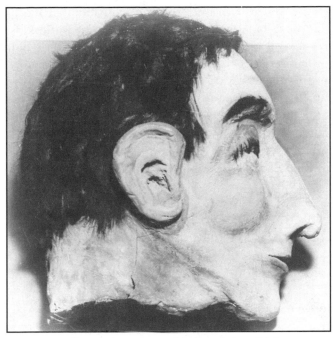

Oscar was more sophisticated than Oink.

peared combed, neat and straight. This mask actually had a hairstyle. In fact, it was a remarkable "face," almost lovingly constructed. Vibrant, colorful, its artistry and heft were impressive. When John and Clarence saw it, they thought it resembled an uncle and began calling it "Oscar."

Although it was said later that the brothers made this mask, that satement may have been made to guard the true identity of its artist. Men like May left a trail of documents in their files—extensive lists of supplies, requests and comments by officers on their interest. There were no such documents in either Anglin file (other than one document requesting canvas boards used as the fake walls). When the brothers transferred from Atlanta, to Lewisburg and Leavenworth, then to Alcatraz, none of their property cards listed any art supplies transferring with them. There were two portraits of their girlfriends found in their cells on Alcatraz and later sent by authorities to the Anglin family. But the portraits are not signed and look suspiciously sophisticated, like those from someone with more advanced art experience. In

the last few years, at least one Anglin family member has begun
saying that both boys were amateur artists even while kids. But
those claims seem specious, designed to revise the long-held impression that the Anglins were clumsy and doltish. Far more telling is the absence of any document in their files showing them as
having any interest in painting or sculpture.

And the difference between Oink and Oscar is obvious even
to the amateur eye: someone with talent made the second mask.

Oscar was given to Morris. When the time came, it would be
hidden on top of the block. For the time being, John used Oink.

6

WEST CONTINUED WORKING on top of B block, painting the
ceiling and hatching his plan. Today, it can be seen where the
"slap of his paint brush" stopped midway across the ceiling over
B block. The other half remains unpainted.

Clarence had told him that the sheet metal ductwork was held
together with hexheaded screws, so West obtained a clamp which
someone had made from parts of a bed. While painting one day,
he was able to loosen the screws. But he left them in place.

Now West began to set his grand plan in motion. One morning while up there, he grabbed a push broom, and began sweeping dust and dirt into a large mound. He pushed the mound of
dirt over to the edge of the block. Then with a quick thrust, he
flung it off the edge. Dirt cleared the third tier overhang and
floated down to Broadway like a sack full of hundred-dollar bills
streaming from an airplane.

He pushed more dirt over to the outside B block and flung it
over that side. With each stroke, more dirt cascaded down, landing on the tiers, billowing onto cell blankets, falling to the floor.
When Lieutenant Ordway walked into the cell house, he could
hear it crunching under his feet. He jerked his head back, looking up angrily for the source. The lieutenant ordered OIC Herring to have that stopped immediately and get it cleaned up.

At lunch, Herring told West he'd have to stop sweeping.

Hell, it's dirty up there, Mr. Herring, West was said to have ut-
tered. Then, appearing to muddle over the problem, he suggested

that maybe he could just hang some old blankets up there, keep the dust from falling. *That way I could clean it up and it wouldn't bother nobody. And I could finish painting the ceiling.*

Herring stood for a minute, saying nothing.

You should see it, Mr. Herring. I cain't paint with all that shit. I'm gonna have t'clean. I could hang a coupla blankets, sweep up, paint, 'n' take 'em down in no time.

West was proposing to hang blankets in front of bars. When Herring appeared to have stalled out on that idea, West may have invoked Captain Bradley's wish to have the job finished, upping the pressure. After all, the ambitious young officer wouldn't want to stand in the way of the captain's wishes.

What happened next will never be precisely known. Stories from officers and prisoners have varied, and it's difficult to determine who heard what, and who was relying on third-hand stories.

Lieutenant Lloyd Miller said that Herring had sought Ordway's permission for West to hang them, but "Double-Tough" snorted and said no—*No way.*

According to Carnes, Officer Herring doubled back to West saying that Ordway wouldn't approve it. West argued, saying that Ordway was *not* in charge of the cell house, *he was just the relief lieutenant.* He probably got a little hot and reminded Herring, that *he* was officer-in-charge, *not* Ordway. Then like a good little manipulator, West backed off.

Carnes claimed that Severson somehow got involved, and others have backed that up. But documents don't put Severson in the cell house at that point. In fact, he's nearly absent from cell house records for much of this quarter, and it appeared as if he was working in industries. But perhaps West caught up with him at lunch that day, and complained how he couldn't get his work done. Severson might have told West he'd see what he could do.

Although not all of Carnes' stories could be said to be true, he had one thing going for him: he worked in the cell house everyday. He could have easily overheard the conversations.

Lieutenant Miller, however, said that Herring went directly to Captain Bradley and asked for his approval to hang the blankets.

Nodoby knows who approved it. But it was approved.

Herring got on the phone that afternoon and told clothing

room officer to send up a few blankets the next day. J-Dub worked in the clothing room. When West saw him at supper, he told John to hold off a couple of days—*make up excuses, whatever.* He wanted Herring to be on his days off. *Then,* West said, *send plenty of 'em.*

WHEN SEVERAL BALES of blankets arrived in the cell house on Herring's day off, West quickly took them up to the top of the block and strung them up.

B block, like C, was split in two by an aisle known as the "cut off." The east half of the block, where the target vent was located, contained fourteen cells on the outside and thirteen on the Broadway side—that entire block being approximately seventy-five feet by twenty feet wide. West hung about two hundred feet of blankets around the entire section—completely encircling the target ceiling vent. When Officer Herring returned to work a day later, he was said to be stunned.

West acted puzzled at the officer's reaction. " 'That's what they sent up,' " Carnes said West told the officer. " 'I thought you ordered that many up. So I put 'em up.' "

"Then Ordway comes through," said Carnes, "looks up, says, 'Who put those blankets up there?! Take those blankets down immediately!' "

West was ready for that, Carnes said. It was his genius to turn any crisis into an advantage. He ran to Herring and said, " 'I heard what that stupid ass said.' He started screaming: 'Who in the hell runs this place anyway? I did a lot of work putting this thing up there! And *I* did this! And *I* did that!' "

Carnes called it one of West's little maniac bags. "He was good at that kind of thing."

In other versions, West bellowed to Herring that Lieutenant Ordway was *not* in charge of the cell house. *He comes in here and tells you how to run the cell house!*

According to Carnes and other officers, Severson then got involved, getting into a fight with Ordway over it, each man trying to outdo the other, to prove that he was the boss of the cell house. It was a magnificent manipulation and West had read both men like a book: they were the two biggest egos in the building.

The blankets remained. And it became the second catastrophic blunder in this escape attempt—crucial to the scheme. Prison bars exist solely to keep a man inside while you watch what he's doing. Not only could two men work on top of the block each night while hidden from view, but the top of the block was the *only* place big enough to build a raft.

"It was against everything we were taught!" said Deatherage.

"I'd say there were maybe thirty or forty blankets around there," said Officer Virgil Cullen.

"Ordway didn't want 'em up there," said another officer, "but he couldn't get them down."

"There was plenty of 'em hung up there," said Rogers.

"That's where the officers were not doing their job!" Warden Blackwell stated. "They would have had those blankets removed. The cell house officer and the lieutenant that's working around there, if they saw those blankets up there, they would have 'em took down right away. And found out what's going on up there."

What's more surprising than knowing that several officers were duped into allowing the blankets to be hung, is that in the coming weeks, all six lieutenants were in and out of the cell house and would have had the authority to question the judgment of allowing them to be hung. But they, in turn, may have been as reluctant to question the captain's authority as any officer. And there's another possibility. There had been so many policy changes, such strong intimations that the island would close and a prevalent feeling that those in charge were rank amateurs that perhaps the morale had sunk so low that men no longer really cared. Because as Carnes later said, "If there was any lax in security, it was those blankets."

Officer Deatherage had worked on Alcatraz since 1959. He liked San Francisco. That spring, the officers were talking about the "new Alcatraz" that was being built in Marion, Illinois and Deatherage began to worry. "They were talking about sending me to Marion," he said. "I didn't want to go." So he quit that spring. According to the *Foghorn*, his last day was April 28, 1962. The blankets were up by then, he said.

"West was the head man on that deal," Lieutenant Mahan later said.

"And everyday," Carnes said, "West thought of some new reason to go up there and work."

~~~

Part 5
Under Cover

THE BLANKETS WERE hung four stories atop Broadway, just above the third tier overhang, recessed about two feet. Unless someone pointed them out, you could walk into the cell house and never see them.

"They weren't noticeable," officer Don Martin said. "They *were* visible but they weren't noticeable."

News traveled fast, however. Officers groused about it to each other and a torrent of accusations came pouring out later. It was "approved," or officers' comments were "ignored," or nobody did anything about it. But, after the blankets were hung, denial set in. After all, security on Alcatraz seemed invincible. Even Jeulich thought "nobody was looking for anybody to cut out of their cells."

And, as often happens when something inexplicable occurs and people can't fit it into their world view, the blankets slid into the scenery. Everyone forgot about them. Above the eye, recessed, "approved," they became easy to *not* see. They were, in fact, hiding in plain view. West only needed to convince a few day-watch officers that they were necessary to his cell house improvement project. Days passed, and they were still up.

Speculation would later focus on Captain Bradley. He'd been given high marks at other institutions, yet Pat Mahoney described him as "totally out of his league on Alcatraz." He was described by several men, both cons and officers, as having an ability to become friendly then cold, and certainly his actions during the subsequent investigation proved that to be the case as he sought to target some for blame and to shield others. He showed his inexperience, or favoritism, by placing men like Herring, with less than five or six years' service, in key assignments to give them

Preceding page: Warden Blackwell and Captain Bradley.

experience. It's not known whether he sought approval from Dollison or Blackwell, or alone gave the nod to Herring when the blankets went up. It's not known if he took sides in a fight between two lieutenants—Ordway and Severson—because he liked one better than the other, or whether he assumed Herring would have an officer up there with West, but forgot to mention it.

And ultimately, it's impossible to tell who actually approved the blankets to be hung because of one striking ommision in both the FBI and the BOP written reports: the blankets were never revealed. They were covered up.

And Bradley was dead by the time they were publicly revealed.

IT WASN'T AS if Blackwell and the captain weren't focused on security; they appeared to be. Witness the April custodial staff meeting, held on May 2, when Blackwell talked about the "ever existing dangerous atmosphere in which we work." He named several prisoners and recited their criminal pasts. You can bet West, Morris and the Anglins were not among those named. He again urged his staff to "not fall into an air of complacency," stating, "We cannot relax for a moment." It's easy to see why he would drive home this point, because he then announced that Washington had approved his plan to shut down the road tower.

And Bradley said that it would become effective immediately.

At roll call that night officers were given a brief summary of the meeting and "warned about being too complacent." *Warned* because they were losing a nighttime security position, and they needed to be even more alert.

On Sunday, May 6, a Bureau official visited Alcatraz to assess the dining room modernization. He was driven around the steep island in Blackwell's new golf cart, he visited the cell blocks, the industries and the mechanical service. He was shown the new four-man dining tables, the new plastic dish ware, and he even sat for a meal. "The inmates appeared to be under excellent control," he wrote in his five-page memo, and the personnel were proceeding in "a dignified, business-like manner." He made no comment about the blankets—which he probably never saw. But he did comment that the staff repeatedly expressed their "apprehension" about the "their future and the future of Alcatraz" given rumors that the prison would soon close.

By then, Morris had removed the keys from his concertina, turning his sweet, shiny mahogany instrument into a bellows to inflate the raft.

And by that Sunday, the road tower had shut down. Officers on the evening-watch and May 6 morning-watch noted it in the watch log.

"Dismaning tower two was an extremely stupid thing to do," said Rogers. "The inmates weren't supposed to know about it, but of course they did."

It's likely that few officers who lived on Alcatraz even told their wives about it, not wanting to worry them. But many of them may have slept less soundly.

It was risky behavior that Blackwell would later vehemently deny had happened. "We needed all the security we could get," he cajoled. "Logic would tell you we would not shut down a tower." A few minutes later, he said, "If I ordered the shutdown I must have been terribly off center." But it had been his proposal.

And because of the tower shutdown, other changes occurred. Another post, colloquially known as the "kitchen cage," located outside the prison on the northwest edge near the basement windows, was manned when kitchen workers were out of their cells and up and down the basement to send supplies up the dumbwaiter. The kitchen cage was manned to make sure no one escaped from the basement windows.

But because road tower was closed at 4:45 each evening until 8:00 each morning, the kitchen cage was altered in the evening hours and the early morning hours from a stationary post to that of patrol.

Thus, Alcatraz was set up for its second escape attempt that year, an attempt which would occur at precisely the time when both posts were unmanned.

One week after the tower shutdown, the boat schedule was expanded to include a 2:00 A.M. run.

"They shut down tower two to hire another boat operator!" exclaimed Mahoney, who added that by then the old boats were running almost twenty-four hours a day, and now included trips at 5:15 A.M. as well as an optional 2:00 A.M. trip.

Jim Hudson in the kitchen cage in earlier years.

"They robbed the custodial," said Lloyd Miller under his breath.

"We done things over the years that we thought were improvements in the prison and it really wasn't," Blackwell said, telling me a bigger truth than he thought I would come to understand. "It was an improvement in *our* working conditions. Making *our* lives a little more bearable."

On May 11, Morris was the third man out of his cell.

"Routine night," the lieutenant wrote in his watch log.

THAT MAY, BRADLEY'S dream came true. It was announced that he was getting a promotion with a pay raise and returning to

Leavenworth as captain. He must have puffed up like a peacock, feeling as if he were returning to Leavenworth as the big shot. But West, Morris and the Anglins would soon cut him down. Only weeks later Bradley would write a brooding, self-defeating comment in a memo, that it was "most discouraging to note that these inmates were able to work over a long period of time without any of our personnel discovering it."

Without acknowledging his role, yet admitting too much, he stated, "It is obvious now, but it appears that somebody should have accidentally stumbled over it."

An amazing deception given that the blankets were there for everyone to see.

"It certainly looks like loose security on Alcatraz," an FBI agent later wrote.

"He took the blame," Kent said, "because he involved himself in the blankets."

But as Lieutenant Miller mused, "I doubt that Captain Bradley would have made such a decision without the warden's okay."

2

WITH THE COVER up, the pace of stealing and climbing pipes accelerated.

West began sneaking up more supplies during the day: painting tarps, gloves, a long pole, several types of glue, wooden planks and a long white cord.

Morris and Clarence coordinated their moves at supper. They had agreed to move everything up top—the life jackets, the raft pieces, the concertina and the paddles—where everything would be hidden inside the blower. The masks would also be hidden up there too, which meant that one of them would have to climb up top, open the blower, retrieve them and send them down every night. The men were prepared to climb in and out of their cells and up and down the pipes several times each night—all while cons on all three tiers could hear or possibly see them.

Remember, the main gate screw is right below you, West warned. *Anytime the lieutenant comes in or out, you better be on your toes.*

John squinted, *It'll be a friggin' miracle if we pull it off.*

We din' come this far to get caught, Morris said. Without missing a beat, he looked at Clarence and said that they probably wouldn't get much done this first night. Ultimately, he would be unprepared for how little they would get done.

Supper ended. Cons walked back to their cells and stood by. "B! Outside!" an officer shouted and their cell fronts were ratcheted open and shut behind them.

Within minutes the officer began passing out the mail and the medicines. Morris put on his tennis shoes, tying and snapping up his shoelaces. Clarence was uncovering the handmade wrench, which he slid into his pocket.

When the music finally cranked up, Morris retrieved Oscar and Clarence pulled out Oink. They placed the masks on their pillows, stuffed their beds with rolled blankets, opened up their fake walls and climbed into the utility corridor. It was Morris' first time up. He climbed slowly, deliberately, never looking down. They had about an hour before the music stopped—not nearly enough time.

Morris had brought up a real wrench stolen from maintenance and a glob of grease wrapped in paper that he probably swiped from an industries machine. Once up there, Morris allowed himself a brief moment of smug pleasure. He could barely make out someone squeezing out the notes to "Over the Rainbow."

He climbed over the electric fan sitting next to the blower and stepped to the east end of the block. He gently fingered the blanket, looking down on the floor. What he saw startled him; West was right, the main gate was right beneath him.

He turned back to the blower and saw the section of the duct that he could remove. He began turning the sheet metal screws, guardedly at first, as if he were working on a time bomb.

Clarence worked on their delivery system. The pipe chase was so dark it was impossible to see down to the floor. And they needed to know exactly where the bottom was so that when the masks were lowered they wouldn't bang noisily or become damaged. Remember—they were on top of the block with cells on either side and below them. Up there, the pipe chase, running along the middle, was little more than a three-foot wide, three-story crevice filled with pipes. They had to step onto a narrow concrete but-

The air blower at the top of the block, with the blankets
behind it spattered with paint, and the ceiling vent
after the duct work had been removed.

tress to get from one side of the block to the other. One little
misstep and you could fall three stories like a rag doll, banging
into pipes and wooden planks to certain death below.

Clarence knelt down at the edge and tied one end of the white
cord to a water pipe that ran along the edge of the block. He
began lowering the other end of the cord slowly down the pipe
chase, searching for light from a cell vent which would tell him
when the third tier floor was located. When he found it, he marked
it by tying a knot in the cord. He let out more cord, until he came
to the second tier, tied another knot, then finally found the first
floor, tying a third knot.

After Morris loosened all the screws, he motioned to Clarence
to hold the duct while he removed each one. Together they eased

off the duct and silently laid it on the floor. Both stared at the ceiling hole for a minute. Two guys on the three range were calling out chess moves—*Bishop two to white nine,* one of them shouted, barely audible above the musical cacophony.

Morris climbed atop the blower. Clarence handed him two planks of wood which Morris placed on the blower's rim to sit on. Tilting his head as far as it would go, he looked into the black hole above him.

THREE STORIES BELOW, John checked his cell front. Satisfied that he was in the clear, he took down a raincoat from the peg. He had managed to wear several raincoats from the clothing room without officers realizing it. He had also slipped a couple more to friends who then passed them back to him. Clarence had arranged to casually put one on in the yard, placed by another guy who wore it out of the cell house. Cons frequently wore their raincoats on the yard, even in the spring and summer. That's when the gulls nested on Alcatraz and raised their young. It was a lot nicer to be strafed in a raincoat than a woolen pea coat. John now had six raincoats in his cell and he had to get rid of them tonight.

He cut them into pieces and rolled them up. Then he opened his cell vent, located the cord and began jerking on it, trying to get their attention up top.

MORRIS WAS STILL squinting into the hole. The back of his neck ached from the extension and he idly rubbed it. He couldn't see much.

Clarence was squirming around, first on one foot, then the other. Morris shot him a quizzical look.

I gotta pee, he mouthed, and when Morris smirked, he shrugged.

Morris went back to looking into the hole. It was about eighteen inches in diameter, big enough for all of them to get through. Two half-inch reinforcing rods crossed the opening. That was simple, he thought, after studying them. They were old, square rods. He could probably spread them.

But there was another set of bars above the rods, a heavy iron grate. In fact, it looked like someone had taken an old bar front and cut a round section out of the middle where the cross bar was located. Then soldered that inside a circular bracket. The whole unit—the bars inside the bracket—had been squeezed inside a sixteenth-inch metal sheeting which encircled the hole. But it was so dark, Morris couldn't see how the unit was attached nor where to begin to cut it out.

In time he would discover that the bracket was attached by rivets—what West later described as "tapins," which may have been iron workers' slang West knew from his work in the Savannah, Georgia shipyards. Rivets are short, thick bolts used to fasten two metal plates together. They are fired to a white heat, and when tapped into a hole they spread at the other end to form a tight seal. Hence the expression "tap-ins." Had Morris known this, he might have become discouraged. But he couldn't see this at first. Instead, he focused on the bolts that attached the metal sheeting to the sides of the opening. They were probably prison bolts, he surmised, designed to break off when tampered with.

Somewhere beyond that was the roof vent. It was too dark to see, but Morris could feel a breeze on his face. He languished in it for a minute, rubbing the back of his neck. He was hot and the cool air felt good on his forehead.

Whaddaya see? Clarence whispered. He'd already gone over to the cut-off side and quietly urinated into some rags.

Morris gave him a questioning look. *Couple bars I can spread,* he murmured. *A whole 'nuther set I don't know about.* He looked up at the vent again, then at Clarence. *They're attached to this— metal housing. Maybe I can just drill the whole thing out, I dunno.* He started to climb down.

Whadaya doin'? Clarence asked.

Time's up, Morris said, easing off the blower. *We gotta get out of here.*

The music was blaring in the background, a jangle of squeaks, honks and discordant long tones that was giving him a headache. *We need a bar spreader,* he whispered. *Can't do nothin' 'til we get that.* Suddenly they heard a sound that was closer—a "whither-whither" sound—and they both turned towards the pipe chase.

The cord was jumping against the pipe. Clarence knelt down it and jerked it a couple of times. J-Dub, responded with a pull. The signal. John tied the cord around the rolled up raincoat pieces, jerked it twice, and Clarence began hauling it up. But the pipe chase was an obstacle course with large waste pipes, narrow water pipes, electrical conduit and those long planks suspended down the middle of two and three range. The big roll snagged on everything. Clarence would twirl it, moving it a few inches at a time.

Suddenly the bell rang out, loud enough to cut through the music. Clarence shot Morris an anxious look. The bleats and honks ground down to a few guitar strums ending on a D minor. Slowly, they began hearing instrument cases being snapped open. Clarence's pulse beat faster. Now any noise might be detectable by the main gate hack. And soon the cell house officer would start his 8:00 P.M. count. He jerked the roll up, untied it, and they placed it inside the blower.

Clarence climbed back down the pipes, retrieved his mask, then crawled into Morris' cell and got his. He placed both of them in a little bag made of raincoat fabric, tied it to the cord and jerked on it. Morris hauled it up and placed the bag carefully inside the blower. In the meantime he had applied grease to each sheet metal screw. Now he gingerly replaced the duct and turned the screws. But he didn't turn them all the way—just enough so that everything looked intact.

Quickly giving the place the once over, he slipped back down the pipes. He looked through his fake vent to check his cell front, gently pulled the vent opened and flew through the hole like a rabbit.

Whadja get done? West asked at his cell front after Morris had replaced his fake wall.

Nothin'. We didn't get nothin' done.

3

THE NEXT DAY Morris got someone to put together a battery-operated light. A small, thin plastic box was found—perhaps one used to hold drill bits. The con poked a hole in its edge big enough to squeeze a tiny light bulb. Inside, he placed a Ray-O-Vac pen-light battery which he held in place with paper and a wad of plaster made up in his sink. Next, he took a common office product—a file binder clip which Kent may have provided—and placed it between the bulb and the battery. It was a little shaky, but it lit up. And soon it was in Morris' hands.

Morris also worked on devising a bar spreader, a tool known to every con in every joint. The best one's are made of short hollow tubes which are threaded inside both ends. Then you find a couple of bolts, and nuts, and screw them deep inside the tube. Turn the nuts, and the bolts extend, pushing everything out of the way.

West began calling in his favors.

He wanted the first life jacket to come up from industries.

He needed some scrap wood from the furniture refinishing shop. He needed brass screws, nuts and washers. Someone in industries found a piece of partially-stained plywood and cut it into an eight-by-twelve-inch rectangle. A two-foot length of board that fit comfortably in a man's shirt was also found. Both pieces were drilled precisely so they could be attached. They came up from industries separately—the rectangle stuffed under someone's shirt, the long stick in someone's pants leg, or along the side of his waist. Soon West would have both in his cell.

Within a couple of days he had the first life jacket in his cell. That night after supper, he glued strips of raincoat material down the side seams to seal the machine stitching, and another strip around the neck line. He checked his cell front. He reached up and twisted his light bulb until it flickered off. He still had plenty of light to see. He poked the Windex bottle dipstick into the protrusion. The binder clip, which would be used as a air plug was near by. He checked his cell front again. *One thing about cons,* he thought to himself, *we got great side vision.* Sitting on his bed where he could see out, he put the life vest over his head and tied it at the back. He then lowered his chin, took the dipstick into his mouth and began inflating it.

SOMEONE ELSE BEGAN making the third mask.

May had obtained black electrical wire as its base. Portland cement, and possibly plaster, were also used. This mask faced west, but like Oscar, it was painted in orange tones rather than pink, its eyelashes were cropped and thick, and its "skin" was smooth. Its

The finished handmade life vest

lips appeared painted with a faint lime green color. Underneath the hair line lurked a convincing, but strange, purple color. It was heavy and nearly one-and-a-half times the size of a normal male human head. And like Oscar, but unlike Oink, this mask had a hairstyle—a dark, soft, curly, almost jaunty hairstyle. Its hair and the smooth luster of its surface were delicate, and almost lovingly done. But there was something else, something far more striking: this face actually had bone structure; its facial contours were extremely lifelike. This mask, in fact, was the crowning achievement of all four.

When finished, it was placed in a bag and hauled up top where it was hidden inside the blower with the others.

THAT NIGHT, MORRIS made his second ascent, taking the bar spreader and the penlight with him. He opened the blower, retrieved the bag of masks, and lowered them down the chase. Clarence caught them and set them up in their cells. He crawled

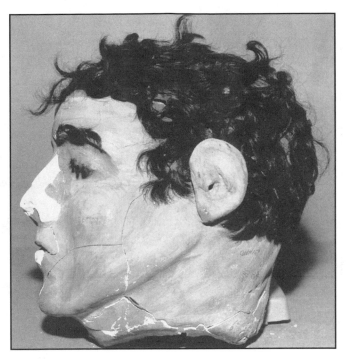

The third mask was the crowning artistic achievement.

over to West's cell, ignoring the dust, the intense urine smell and the occasional curious con peeking out his vent. West handed out the first life jacket. Clarence tied that to the cord and jerked on it. Morris began pulling it up. Then Clarence climbed up. Although they had coordinated their moves, it still took nearly half their allotted time to set everything up.

Once Clarence was up top, he dropped the cord to John, who began tying more cut-up raincoat pieces to be hauled up.

While this was happening, West uncovered his long stick and the rectangular piece of plywood. He inserted two, two-and-a-quarter-inch brass screws, nuts and washers into the holes and screwed the two pieces of wood together. It was a perfect paddle. The long, skinny screws protruded about an inch and a half, but West didn't notice, or else, he didn't care.

He pulled out his fake vent and placed the paddle into the chase for J-Dub to send up.

The old square bars inside the vent were the first to be spread.

WHILE CLARENCE WAS pulling supplies up, Morris began working on spreading the reinforcing rods. Working with his arms over his head, he jammed the spreader between the metal sheeting and one of the rods. The bar spreader was too long, but that was okay. With the music as cover, he could make noise. He took his shirt off, wrapped the sleeve around the spreader and began pounding it with his wrench to wedge it into place.

Once he had it place, he used the wrench to turn the nuts. Morris had done this many times in his twenty years behind bars. It was tough at first, but then the metal would fatigue. Very quickly the back of his neck began to ache again and his arms burned. He stopped frequently, rested, and began again.

It would take three nights for him to turn the nuts and widen the rod enough for them to eventually squeeze through.

When Morris finally got his shaky little penlight to work, he lifted it through the rods and peered up through the hole. He examined the iron grate to see if the bars passed through the

The iron bracket was riveted inside the ceiling vent opening.

bracket and into the sheeting in the wall. Didn't look like it. The bars were cut so they fit neatly into the circular bracket and it was the bracket that was attached to the sheeting.

But then his heart sank. The brackets were riveted.

And as he studied the bracket he began to see that each leg had two rivets. Six legs. *Twelve* rivets. Later, Morris and West talked about the tapins. They must have decided he could drill through them because worked stopped while a drill was found. By this time West was nearly out of control. The OIC was quizzing him about getting those blankets down, he heatedly told Morris. Morris just looked at him, and smiled, *not my problem.*

AT LUNCH THEY discussed possible drill ideas and someone hit upon a barber clipper. *Maybe that could work.*

Clarence found an old electric barber clipper in the barbershop, slipped it to West who kicked it to Glenn May. It was an old-style, black, professional unit with an on-and-off toggle switch at one end and screws attaching to the blade head at the other end. May unscrewed the head and replaced the blades with a drill bit. This took ingenuity and time. The blades were oscillating; a drill needed to turn. Then, because the motor would make noise, a thick, wide strip of gray felt cloth was wrapped around it and attached with black electrical tape.

IN THE MEANTIME, cons all over the house were participating in little ways. Over in B-208, near the barbershop, Billy Boggs was compiling names and addresses of some of his friends and relatives in California. He would write them down on slips of paper and give them to West.

Someone else ripped up his raincoat and made two little bags. One bag, when glued, was about six by eight inches and would fit inside another bigger bag. Two bags would insure that their eventual contents would remain dry. The ensemble was passed to West, who would place Bogg's contact names and addresses inside. West would then pass it to John and Clarence who would add their possessions.

McNicholas, up in B-350, was also making a small bag out of raincoat material. It's unclear why he might need what he hoped would be a waterproof bag, unless he intended to go out behind them. It would be found in his cell after the escape, along with the list of mileages to ten points around the bay.

4

WITHIN A FEW DAYS, Morris and Clarence were ready to make their next ascent, taking the barber clipper with them. West had received the second vest from industries and was ready to hand it out the vent. He had called for more wood and was putting together another paddle.

After setting everything up and getting up top, Clarence had spliced the clipper to some electrical wires from a nearby junction box and strung it over to Morris. Morris detached the duct, set up the planks and climbed up the blower. He turned on the penlight and marked where the rivets were located.

He needed to work quickly. They were already a half hour into the music. Some *sick fuck* was trying to play "Moon River," and sounding more like whiny cow. *God, I hate that song,* he thought as he switched the clipper on and off quickly, testing the noise level. Clarence stood by the blanket peering down to see if the main gate officer reacted. He didn't; Clarence gave Morris the thumbs up. Morris turned the drill on again, touched the rivet, then snapped it off. A chill ran up his spine; it felt loud to him. *It's okay,* Clarence signaled impatiently. Morris turned it back on and began trying to drill out the bolt.

After several minutes of pressure, the drill bit suddenly broke off the barber clipper. He stopped to fix it.

Morris turned the clipper on again. The old familiar neck ache returned, and with it, his irritation. He tried to push the drill bit behind the bolt but there was little wiggle room. He turned it on. Within seconds, the drill broke off again. He caught it just before it dropped to the floor. *Friggin' motor's too weak.*

He waved anxiously to get Clarence's attention, pointing to the wrench. Clarence stopped and exchanged the barber clipper for the wrench.

Morris tried to squeeze the wrench between the metal sheeting and the sides of the bracket, hoping to bend it a little. But the *damned* wrench was too thick. After a few tries, he gave up and put it down.

Annoyed, he waved at Clarence again, pointing to a screwdriver.

Lifting the screwdriver above his head, Morris immediately felt a stab of pain in his neck. He jammed the screwdriver behind the bracket leg, angling it back and forth, pushing deeper, trying to pry it away from the metal sheeting. But the rivets were tight. The thing was tougher than he thought! Perspiration beaded up on his forehead. He was tense. The quarter-inch iron was rigid. Neither would give an inch.

He stopped. He *hated* this! *It was tougher than digging through a friggin' wall.* Frustrated, a deep feeling of resentment welled up in his chest. It was just like people *all of his life* who wouldn't let him to do *anything. Go anywhere!* That old feeling of wanting to run away. That's how he dealt with everything. *Get the HELL outta here!* He rubbed the back of his neck, and pushed the screwdriver between the metal, twisting and angling it. *Stupid, friggin' idea.*

But soon his frustration was overcome by a new feeling—a ferocious determination. He rocked the screwdriver back and forth,
willing it to separate the leg away from the sheeting. Suddenly it
bent. Just a little, but it moved!

Dirt and pieces of rusted flakes of metal tumbled down and
mixed with his perspiration, dripping from his brow into his eyes.
He wiped his face with his sleeve. He raised his arm again, slipping the screwdriver behind another leg of the bracket. He was
hot now, and furious. He could actually feel the veins thicken in
his neck. He rocked the screwdriver back and forth, pushing
harder. *Forcing it* to bend. *Willing it.* Within minutes his shirt was
drenched in sweat. But the iron began to give and suddenly, it
inched slightly, freeing up a tiny space behind the rivet.

But just as suddenly, the cell house bell rang out and the music ground to a screeching halt. Silence engulfed the house. Morris stopped, relieved, busted, pissed. Triumphant. He wet his lips,
then wiped them with the back of his sleeve, turning his hand in
an unconscious moment of exhaustion and then letting it fall to
his side.

SMACK! came the sound so fast he didn't know what he'd done.
It crashed into the blower, banging the edge of the block, twirl-
ing and plunging down the pipe chase, sideswiping one pipe then
another, clattering, rattling, echoing, falling headlong down three
stories, crashing onto the floor like a thunderclap.

Dead silence hit the cell house. West and John heard it. Tom
Kent, way over in C-236, heard it. If Kent heard it, Teddy Green,
three cells down from Kent, heard it. And Boggs, up at the front
near the dining room heard it. Carnes and Juelich and the blacks
along Broadway all heard it. Probably everyone in the house heard
it. The wrench!

West started rummaging around in his cell, someone else
snapped the clasp on his guitar case, others banged down cups,
someone yelled out, *Heh, quit throwing things up there!* Someone
else called back, *Ah, shut up,* and several cons laughed.

Morris exhaled in short bursts. The sound echoed in his mind
over and over.

What the hell was that? West demanded in a hoarse whisper a
half hour later, when Morris climbed back into his cell. Morris

evaded the answer. *Friggin' motor's a bust,* he spit out. He yanked his blanket aside and rolled into bed.

Christ! West said through clenched teeth. *Everybody in the joint heard that!*

We'll be thinking of some other idea, was all he would say.

Shit! West whispered madly. *We're screwed.*

5

WEST LAIN AWAKE much of the night. They still had two life jackets that needed to come up from industries. Another paddle. He had to keep Glenn May from panicking. *They're going find out!* May had exclaimed. West told him to *SHUT UP.* He had his own problems.

Broadway cons in B-137, 139, 141, 143, 145, 147, 149, 151 and 153 knew exactly what Morris and Clarence were doing every night. Cons between West and John—in cells 142, 144, 146 and 148—as well as others located on the second and third tiers knew what was going on. Eyes were acknowledging eyes. Some may have spoken guardedly about it once the subject was broached. Others may have even been too afraid to say anything. And although some cons would *never* know about it until days before the actual escape, others beyond the B block cutoff, and even over in C were very aware. And any one of them could go to the authorities. West tossed and turned all night.

He didn't know the half of it. Snitches were everywhere. And there were hints all over the institution.

Way back in February or March, George Gregory was escorting cons when he began to sense a feeling of urgency from one of them, a man who had confided in him before. Gregory was a smart officer; he did nothing—it would arouse suspicion and put the man's life in jeopardy. He waited. But every time an opportunity arose for the con to say something, it was quickly dashed by another con's approach. At the end of day, Gregory strolled down to the boat. He couldn't shake the feeling that someone wanted to tell him something. But Gregory was injured in an accident on the dock on April 2. He never returned to the island and retired.

Sherman Calloway, AZ 1219, over in C-131, had heard the tool as it crashed down the pipe chase. An obsequious, hyperactive, fussy homosexual, he was described by Carnes as "one sick individual," and by a chaplain as "one of the most disturbed men on Alcatraz." He was in prison for kidnapping a seventy-year-old man while in a drunken stupor. Calloway was a somewhat clueless, tragicomic figure; on a personality test once when asked to fill in the sentence, "If I am left behind . . ." Calloway had written "I will be there later." He was ostracized on Alcatraz, not because he was flamboyant, which was unique in prison in those days, but because he was a known informant. Calloway never went to the yard for fear of being killed. Consequently his face was ice-white. Some suspected his hair was stained black with ink. Cons would risk getting disciplinary shots rather than sit with him in the dining room.

Calloway was an equal opportunity "stoolie"—he ratted out cons *and* guards. But you could never tell with him. Some stories were true; others weren't. My father thought that cons sometimes planted lies with him so he could run the false information to officers.

Calloway approached an officer. This man didn't have a sterling reputation either. A "busybody," but one of the better shakedown men, he was rumored to be supplying Bumpy Johnson with cigars. After Alcatraz closed, he was transferred to another institution and relieved of duty for handing a contraband letter from a con to someone on the outside. Calloway told him that "something was going on over on B." The officer said he'd "look into it."

Or, at least, that's what Calloway said later.

West decided it was time to work other angles. He casually approached Stones on the yard one day. Stones, still digging, now had thirty-six holes around his vent. In oily, all-is-forgiven tones, West told Stones he should stop digging for a couple of days. Plumbers were working in the pipe chase near his cell.

Stones was unmoved. But West was persuasive. They might see your drilling, West said, his eyebrows raising in a moment of assurance. *I'll let you know when it's safe to start up again.*

Stones reluctantly agreed to stop digging. West never got back to him to tell him it was okay to start up again. At least, that's what Stones told authorities later.

In another B block cell, a con sat staring at his wall, deciding whether or not to write a letter to the warden. It was gnawing at him. He had his reasons and he knew details. He also knew his life would be in danger if other cons found out. Reaching a decision, he took out a Big Chief tablet and began writing down everything he knew about the escape attempt. When he finished the page, he folded it three times, addressed it to the warden, then laid it across the bars for the guard to pick up. He lit a cigarette, blowing out the smoke in a moment of fear mixed with resolve. He waited, hoping the hack would soon pick it up. At lights out, he drifted off to sleep, sure that the guard would stroll by and get it. The next morning, the letter was still there, mocking his resolve. He snatched it off the bars, ripped it up and flushed it down the toilet. Or so he later told authorities.

Shakedowns were now mentioned more often in the watch log, as if men were heeding Blackwell's warnings. On May 7, Lieutenant Ordway wrote that the utility officer shook down the kitchen and the clothing room. The next evening, Officer Battles again shook down the kitchen, then went down to industries to check the clothing shop. The hospital was thoroughly checked on May 13; and on May 16 and 17 the library was completely shaken down by three officers. Yet, night after night, lieutenants heard nothing, often writing "routine watch," or "quiet shift" in the watch log.

All was not quiet, however. Officers Herman who now worked the evening watch, began to feel that something was not quite right. It wasn't anything he could put his finger on. But when he thought back on it later, he remembered that he became aware that prisoners were playing their musical instruments a little too loudly.

Warnings, missed opportunities, noises, empty shakedowns, loud music, quiet shifts, blankets softly swaying along the top of the block; why hadn't anyone compared notes?

6

IN THE MIDDLE of May, a block orderly casually told a cell

house officer that the vacuum cleaner was broken. The officer told Glenn May about it and May set about to repair it.

Opening the motor cover, the electrician saw two motors inside—one to power the suction and the other to drive the brush dowels. He studied the alignment for a moment. He figured he could remove a motor and rig it so it would work again. Although the officer checked him periodically, May was able to plunder the motor and jury-rig the vacuum cleaner. Outwardly cooperative, inside May was a bundle of nerves. He was in deep.

Days later, at around 8:40 A.M. on Tuesday, May 22, in fact, West was painting in the kitchen while May was in there examining a broken appliance. Two cons attacked AZ 1444, Daniel Contreras, in the dish room, beating him over the head with a brass pipe. He was pummeled into unconsciousness. Several other cons jumped in and officers immediately flew into the fray to separate them.

In the melee, West smuggled out the motor.

THE NEXT NIGHT, after setting up his bed, Morris hauled the motor up to the ceiling. This time it was John who climbed up with him.

While Morris set up the vacuum cleaner motor, John began working on a pontoon for the raft. An ambitious project, the raft was conceived as a six-by-fourteen-foot platform with fifteen-inch pontoons on each side. John and West had cut up so many pieces for the life jackets and the raft that the FBI later estimated they had used material from fifty-five raincoats. John had originally wanted to reinforce the floor with material from the canvas laundry bags. But that idea had been sacked.

The first air baffle, measuring twenty-one inches by six feet and two inches, was hand sewed and glued at the edges. He set it aside. Then he began working on an air valve which would be used to inflate the pontoon. He inserted a short piece of stolen pipe in the middle of a round piece of plywood and attach it to the pontoon with eight stolen nuts and bolts.

When rolled and sealed, this pontoon would form the short end of the raft. But it would not be fifteen inches in diameter as planned. A twenty-one-inch rolled piece of raincoat would only

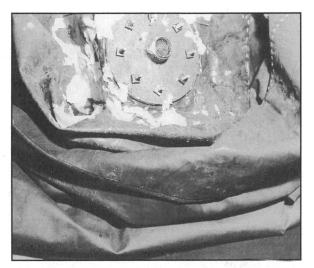

The first air baffle had a wooden valve and was left
behind. Note the hand stitching above right.

yield a-six-and-two-thirds-inch diameter air baffle. After working
on it for several nights, J-Dub became unhappy with it. It may
have been the wooden valve he didn't like. He threw the section into the blower, where it would remain until found by
officers later.

He started again, making another pontoon with a rubber valve.
It's unknown how big this one was, but it's likely that it was a similar size; the longer a seam on an air baffle, the more potential for
leaks. J-Dub would also make other modifications before the raft
was completed.

WHILE HE WAS laying out the raft pieces, Morris had finished
hooking up the vacuum cleaner motor. Everyone thought it was a
great idea. The motor had a large threaded, turning bolt that
could be used as a drill. It rotated at a high speed and they must
have thought he could drill out the rivets with pressure and friction. While the music was echoing around the cell house, Morris
got up on the blower. He flipped on the switch. The motor whirled
on—screaming out. John's head snapped back. Morris, shocked,
hit the switch. He jerked the wire out of the wall.

Infuriated, he returned to staring at the black hole again.

7

BY THE END of May, they were all becoming frustrated with
the lack of progress. Preparation took so much time that they
barely had time to work. They had hidden so many articles in the
blower—the raft pieces, the vests, the concertina, the paddles,
the bag of masks—that digging some of it out without harming
other items was difficult. J-Dub had hammered a nail in one end
of a pole that West had brought up and used it to hook the raft
pieces from deep inside. That helped. But Morris still hadn't jim-
mied the ceiling vent. The raft still wasn't completed. Everyone
was getting anxious. West was almost hysterical. *I can't keep the
blankets up there forever!* he had threatened them, *Sooner or later,
they're gonna get suspicious!* That made everyone even more frantic. They began discussing remaining up top longer. J-Dub and
Clarence were all for it; Morris didn't like it. He wasn't sure the
masks could make it through a count. But everyone knew they'd
have to go soon, or something would go horribly wrong.

THE NEXT NIGHT, Morris and J-Dub carefully laid out their
masks, propped up their blankets and clawed their way up top.
This time they were going to work longer, actually leaving the
masks in place during several counts. *We'll see who the dummies
really are,* West had said sarcastically.

Morris knew that drilling out or around the rivets had been
a bust. ("You couldn't pull that thing out with a tractor," West
would tell Carnes later.) He now knew he was going to have to
saw each rivet.

They loosened the duct, hauled out the raft pieces and J-Dub
started working on that. Within minutes, he had laid out the raft
pieces into a discernable pattern.

Morris climbed up on top of the blower and settled in. Reaching through the reinforcing rods with one arm, he slipped a screwdriver behind a bracket leg. It was incredibly awkward working
above his head between two reinforcing rods, trying to force a
tool between a rivet and a piece of iron, twisting it so that the leg
would bend a little—enough to get a saw blade in there. But the
more he studied the bracket the more he noticed that some riv-

ets were not seated properly. He smirked. *The guy that put 'em in had as many problems as I'm havin' gettin' 'em out.* Every fiber in his body was directed towards this little opening. He squeezed the screwdriver between the tiny space and began rocking it back and forth.

Two hours must have elapsed. Both men were still working when the music hour drew to a close. J-Dub had looked up anxiously at Morris, who ignored the now-silent cell house. John took his cue and continued working on the raft, but now his ears were tuned to every sound. Morris now had both hands around the screwdriver, pushing it, twisting it, angling it to move the bracket just a bit. Every once in a while he stopped, rested his arms, then started up again. He was making slow, steady progress.

A minute later, the click of the main gate alerted them both, as the officer opened it and the lieutenant stepped in. Morris stopped. He could hear the sound of his own breath; he could feel his body tense. The officers talked quietly. John silently stepped over to the Broadway side, parted the blankets and looked down. He saw the top of his hat as the lieutenant meandered down Broadway. When he could no longer see the lieutenant, he silently crept back to his raft. They resumed working. Minutes later the lieutenant walked back down Broadway. West, Morris and the Anglins all lived in constant fear now. Every time the lieutenant walked by their fears pounded to the surface. They knew any con could get a trip out of Alcatraz by snitching them out. And although it could happen at any time, it was the lieutenant's stroll that brought the fear forward.

About forty-five minutes later, around 8:00 P.M., John stood up and gestured to Morris, tapping his index finger on his left wrist; it was time for the count. They were so attuned to the officers' patterns that they knew within the next few minutes, he would walk the tiers, counting heads. They both stopped, Morris glad for a rest.

Most officers started their rounds at the west end, counting the flats first, then doubling back to the stairway, climbing up to the second tier, then the third tier. When finished, they walked back down to the floor and started counting on the east end of the block. After that, they crossed Broadway and did the same thing on C block.

John crept to the edge over the outside of B. Just as he parted the blankets, he saw the officer slide by underneath him on the third tier. A jolt of electricity shot through his body. He wasn't expecting the officer to start at the top. J-Dub puffed out his cheeks and cast a sideways glance at Morris. The officer moved past, down three range. Soon, John could no longer see him, and he knew the hack was turning toward the Broadway side, counting the black cells. Within seconds he could hear the plop-plop of the metal stairs, as the guard stepped down to two range. *Jeesh! What a boring job,* John thought. *Sucker's gotta count all day and all night.*

John fingered the blanket silently. He couldn't follow the guard anymore; the third tier overhang prevented that. And he could barely hear his footsteps on the metal walkway. Still, he waited. It would be the first time the dummy heads had been counted.

Down below, in B-140, West sat at his metal desk, pretending to read. He was also deeply listening to the guard's footsteps. His life vest was flattened out under his mattress, the paddle also hidden. He shot a look under his sink. Everything in his cell look normal. But this was the test. Would the guard think John and Morris were asleep? West thought he heard the screw step down from two range to the flats, but he wasn't sure. He was scared, the book in his hand was shaking. He was ready. If the guy stopped at J-Dub's cell, curiously lifting the blanket, or spoke to the dummy, Clarence would have to handle that. But if he stopped at Morris' cell, West would have to divert his attention. Say something. *Heh!* he'd admonish, *he's not feeling good. Leave 'im alone.*

It seemed to West like a lot of time had passed. Every hair on this body stood on end. His heart was pounding in his throat. *God! What's takin' so long?* West began to wonder if he should stand up, hold onto the bars, glare at the guard as he passed by, dare him to stop and notice the dummy mask. *Shit!* He wished he could see.

Up top, J-Dub was becoming alarmed. He could see nothing, hear nothing. He nervously shot Morris a look. But Morris was silently sawing on a rivet, moving his arm up and down, seemingly oblivious.

John's eyes widened. He looked away.

West held his book. But his mind was racing. Should he go to his bars? Had Morris even fixed his bed properly? West felt like every pore in his body was listening. He felt like screaming. It was just like hiding in the forest with men and dogs all around you, the dogs howling as they pulled at their leashes, nearing your scent. Every color—even in this drab gray and green place—was shockingly bright.

Suddenly the guard appeared at West's cell—West felt a jolt—and he passed by, oblivious.

West waited a second to peer out his bars with his mirror. He could see the guard stroll down the flats. He hadn't noticed.

J-Dub heard the *whither* sound and looked over to the pipe chase. The rope was jumping. His cheeks widened into a lopsided grin. The dummies had worked!

The two men had just a few minutes before lights out. Then things would get even more hairy.

ON TUESDAY, MAY 22, Lieutenant Ordway reported in the watch log that prisoners Contreras was still in a coma after his beating and was given a breathing tube. On Wednesday, it was reported that he was "holding his own." But on Thursday, he "appeared to take a turn for the worse." That day Lieutenant Miller reported on the day watch that a shakedown crew in the library had uncovered two books with cut out pages containing a brass knife, sandpaper, wire and two steel, toilet flush rods. Otherwise, it was a routine shift. That Thursday evening, Lieutenant Delmore reported it as "quiet." On Friday, May 25, Delmore reported that the telephone system was failing, and Mr. Langley was called in to service it. Dick Barnett called the morning watch "quiet—no incidents." On Saturday, Ordway reported another library shakedown, and that night it was "quiet."

"Very nice ham dinner," Lieutenant Miller reported on Sunday, May 27. "Giant size portions—quiet day—movie in P.M."

Lieutenant Delmore reported a "routine evening" on the Sunday evening watch.

On Monday, May 28, 1962, Lieutenant Severson, now working inside the cell house, called the evening watch a "quiet shift."

That watch log entry—May 28, 1962—was the last entry at the

bottom of the page. After that, there are no more entries until Thursday, June 21.

THE MAY STAFF meeting was held on Tuesday, May 29. Ordway was now on annual leave and would be gone for nearly a month. With Acting Lieutenant Gregory gone, that meant that Alcatraz was down two lieutenants. In fact, not including annual leaves, Alcatraz was below its authorization by five officers.

Bradley reported that shutting down the road tower "has not hampered the routine nor has it jeopardized our security." But he emphasized that "as inmates realize that those positions have been vacated, certain desperate ones may try us." He urged extreme caution at all times.

When it came time for Associate Warden Dollison to speak, he announced: "This may or may not be significant." Mr. Bennett, the plumber, had reported that his inmate assistants had been acting strangely lately, especially in their conversations. He noticed they were discussing something in small groups and then would break up whenever he approached. Dollison also stated that Bennett had heard the date, "June 4" mentioned.

June 4 was exactly one week before the breakout.

Warden Blackwell, on May 29, 1962, with a board showing that
although Alcatraz was authorized for ninety-nine officers,
it had ninety-four.

ON FRIDAY, JUNE 1, Warden Blackwell wrapped up his last day before his two-week fishing vacation at Lake Berryessa. It was his first real vacation in a year and a half and it had been approved by Washington. Dollison became the acting warden; Bradley, acting associate; Lieutenant Fred Mahan, acting captain.

My father said later that he felt unsettled, but he couldn't put his finger on it. He had driven my mother, Evelyn, to the airport at the end of May, where she would fly to Washington, D.C., to visit my older sister. He didn't mention it then, but in later telephone calls, he did. So concerned by his comments, my mother would cut short her vacation and return home early.

Others noticed that Alcatraz had settled into an eerie quiet, as if everyone were waiting for something to happen. It was almost *too* quiet.

Earlier, Dollison had asked Bradley, who was anxious to depart the Rock and settle in at Leavenworth, if he would stay until Blackwell returned from his vacation.

Bradley hesitated. He badly wanted to return to his old stomping ground now as captain. He couldn't wait to assume authority over an inmate population of 2,000 and a correctional staff of hundreds. He wanted to leave behind the gray, pea soup summer fog, and return to warm summers and fall colors.

But, of course, staying two more weeks was the right thing to do.

Had he left, his promotion would have been assured. He would have skirted criticism and maybe, even, responsibility.

Staying would change all that.

‍‌‍‌

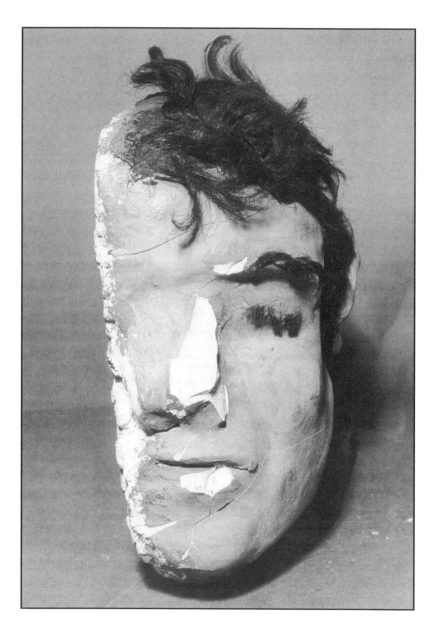

Part 6
Countdown

IT WAS FRIDAY, June 8, and it had come to this: Blackwell had been gone for almost a week. The blankets had been hung "for at least a month or more," Officer Herman had said. Everyday West had to stall cell house officers who wanted to know when he would be finished up there. Every supper, he was agitated, jamming food in his mouth, pointing with his fork. *I can't keep them up much longer!*

Keep cool, Morris told him.

By now Morris had inserted thin, handmade saw blades between the rivets and the brackets to sheer them off. *We're making progress,* he told West. *You concentrate on getting' the last life vest up. And we need something to hide stuff in.*

There's a five-gallon can of cement paint up there, West said, *use that.* Then to anyone, he said, *We still don't have the last mask!*

That's taken care of, Clarence said.

The raft . . . ?

. . . Is fine, said J-Dub.

Then all we're waitin' on . . .

. . . Is the hole in the roof, Morris finished.

West sat back, exhaling. *I just don't want anything to go wrong,* he said, his eyes shifting around the dining room. A con at the next table idly looked over. Officers casually strolled among the tables.

Only man's gonna get us noticed, Clarence warned, *is you.*

SOMETIME JUST BEFORE the escape a fourth dummy mask was made. For reasons that are unknown, portland cement, plaster, even the electrical wire that Glenn May had provided, were not used in this mask. Maybe that weekend they couldn't put their hands on the supplies. Maybe there were no more supplies to get.

Instead, Clarence ripped a bed sheet into strips, and that night, wrapped it over and over until it formed a flat, headlike shape. He moistened a bar of soap in his sink and squeezed off a slice. He then pressed it onto the cloth. The soap was slippery and moldable. But he had to work fast because the soap quickly dried and lost its adherence. He attached a slice, then another, blending them together and molding them into a face.

He made an ear and a nose out of soap. Just when the face was nearly finished, the top of the ear cracked off, and had to be moistened and reattached. He hoped it would remain intact long enough to fool the guards. Later the nose would again fall off and have to be reattached.

The color of this mask, the sloppy, haphazard appearance of the eyebrows and eyelashes, as well as the way the hair was attached in globs rather than neatly styled, was similar to Oink. Given that it was made out of cotton sheeting and soap, however, this face was remarkable. It remained in Clarence's cell. Soap chips and tiny ponytails of hair were also later found around his toilet.

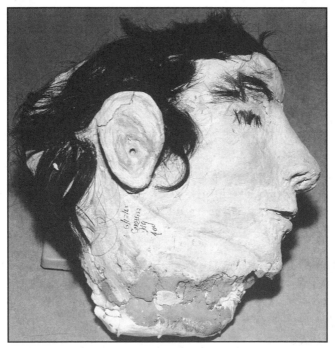

The fourth mask, made of soap chips over cotton sheets.

CLARENCE WAS NOTICEABLE in other ways as well. The next day, Sunday, June 10, cons drifted into the yard for dominoes, horseshoes and softball. It was a warm, sunny fifty-five to sixty degrees. Juelich was sitting in the sun along the stairs when something caught his eye. He swiveled in its direction. Clarence was meandering from one friend to another, "shakin' everybody's hand," Juelich said, incredulous, "saying good-bye."

2

THAT EVENING, MORRIS silently ascended to the top of the block just as the music cranked up. He got the masks, lowered them, and he and John prepared their beds. Clarence prepared his bed using his new mask and went up too. For the first time, both the Anglins were up there with Morris, which made West irritable and nervous. Obliviously to his moods, they dropped the cord down the pipe chase near his cell, so he could signal them when to haul up the last of the stuff.

Morris climbed atop the blower. Immediately, his arms and neck muscles began to ache, in a way that now felt oddly comfortable.

John was hand sewing and gluing the final pieces of the raft

Their workshop on top of the block.

together. He hoped to test it by inflating it with the concertina.

Earlier Clarence had cut up four strips from a canvas art board, which were approximately two by twelve inches in length. Now he glued three strips together, lengthwise, using "Rem-Weld" brand book repair glue, which he'd probably obtained from Carnes or Kent. He slid two small, broken pieces of mirror on each end, with crumpled up book binding tape behind them, then glued them into place. When they dried, he glued the fourth strip into place and set it aside to dry. It was a periscope to peer out onto the roof.

He then began helping John.

Working together, the brothers became more animated, murmuring, whispering, jostling each other. At one point Morris had to tell them to *quiet down*. They jabbered and sometimes argued over the raft. Later, Clarence silently stepped over to Morris. *We're 'bout done,* he whispered excitedly. Morris, distracted as he was cutting another rivet, looked down and said nothing. Clarence turned back to the raft, helping John examine the seams.

You couldn't blame them. Pulling off the biggest escape in history. That Sunday might have been the best part—the excitement, the anticipation, the final feverish touches. Although they may not have realized it, they were now doing the one great thing for which they would always be remembered. John was no longer the unemployable, third-grader who never finished anything. Clarence was no longer the tough-guy wannabe. No matter how far they got in the next few days, they had now gone farther than any other con in Alcatraz history. They would enter the history books, not as anonymous nobodies, but within the spotlight along with men like "Ol' Creepy" Karpis, "Doc" Barker, "Machine Gun" Kelly, Mickey Cohen, Frankie Carbo, *hell,* they would have said, *even Al Capone.*

John motioned to Clarence to help him flip the raft so they could check the back side. *Bustin' from the tightest joint in America,* he snickered to Clarence, *gonna be so cool,* he snapped his fingers noiselessly and cocked a wide grin. He couldn't wait to grab his girlfriend, squeeze her real tight. They were dreamers, the Anglins.

They flipped the raft back on the right side. Later reports hinted that they may have vulcanized the raft seams—using wooden planks to press them against a copper hot water pipe. While FBI agents assumed they did, their labs never tested the discarded pontoon to see if heat had actually been applied.

IT WAS NOW near midnight. Somewhere just south of the island, a ship silently plowed through the bay. A steady stream of car lights across the Golden Gate Bridge made the span look like a string of pearls. On the cell house roof, seagulls launched themselves off the edge, their cries quickly fading as they flew towards the bay. Overhead, the lighthouse beam circled, flashing the roof every five seconds.

Inside the cell house, the lights had been turned down for almost two hours, and it was now mostly quiet. The dummy masks had made it through several prison counts, the guard never noticing that both Anglins and Morris had been asleep since 8:00 P.M. West had silently sent up the third life jacket. And he was now working on the last jacket. It was so quiet, even the Anglins had settled into hand gestures. Morris, his neck aching, his arms exhausted, took a break from his tedious job. He was now fashioning a fake rivet out of soap for camouflage. He had made seven of them but he had almost that many to go.

Gazing idly down at the brothers, he suddenly focused on what they were doing, Something wasn't right. Morris silently slid off the blower and closely examined the shape of the bundle of raincoats. They had left off once side. And the whole thing was smaller. What he saw now was small, triangular-shaped raft. *What the hell is this?* he demanded in a whisper.

The Anglins looked up, startled.

He hunched down, gestured towards the raft, *It's s'posed to be a rectangle. Four* sides!

Don' need a fourth side, Clarence assured him.

Whaddaya talkin' about? Morris replied, leaning closer to Clarence's face, *You can't put four men in a triangular raft!*

The brothers didn't know what to say. It was true, they had decided upon a six-by-fourteen-foot, rectangular raft. But they'd had grown up along rivers and lakes; rafts weren't square. They weren't rectangular. They were like boats—pointed at the bow and wide at the stern—triangular. But, of course, the Anglins hadn't told anybody they were changing the design. *Four men'll do fine in this raft,* Clarence said. He hated being challenged.

It's not what we decided, Morris said.

What the hell does that matter? J-Dub asked.

There's four of us, Morris said slowly, like he was talking to a child. Morris had had no experience with water sports. When they talked about a six-by-fourteen foot raft he had figured each man would sit in a corner, balancing it out. That made sense to him. Now they'd gone and changed it. *Where's the fourth guy gonna sit?*

Clarence was almost dumbstruck. The Anglins knew everyone would sit in the middle, cushioned by the surrounding baffles of air.

We don' need four corners, was all he could muster.

Hell, we don't! Morris shot back. *It won't be stable.*

Suddenly, a click echoed throughout the house. They froze. The main gate cracked open three stories below them. Someone stepped into the cell house, exchanged words with the officer, then strolled down Broadway. The three men remained as if in a trance.

When the footsteps faded, Morris hissed, *What the hell else you been skimping on?*

Fuck you! Clarence shot back. *It'll take too much fuckin' time to make 'nuther one.*

J-Dub piped up, *We know what we're doin', you sonofabitch!*

Cons on B third tier were awakened by the furious on-rush of angered whispering. Even third tier C block cons across the aisle could have heard them. All the way down the flats, West heard them. "I thought they'd get busted—all the noise they were making," he said later.

Anybody can see it's not stable, Morris said, his lips barely moving. He picked up one end of the deflated bundle of glued raincoats. In an exaggerated whisper, as icily as he could, *This is my life you're screwin' with,* he said.

Rafts ain't square, Clarence snarled.

There's four of us, Morris repeated.

Clarence stood up. Everything in his movements said he had had it. *We done ninety percent of the work here,* he said, *and I'm sick of you and I'm sick of West!*

You ain't done nothin' if that thing don't work, Morris said, standing, meeting his gaze.

You little cocksucker, Clarence snarled, moving closer, *I'll be so glad to get away from—*

Suddenly, his shoe knocked a tool along the floor.

West heard that. Alarmed, he jumped off his bed and quickly flushed his toilet. Morris and the Anglins heard the toilet gurgle, then hawk throughout the house. They stared at one another, glowering.

Okay, J-Dub said, raising his hands in an pleading gesture, his eyebrows lifting, *okay.*

Neither man wanted to back down. West was right, Morris thought to himself, the Anglins were morons. Pointing at the crumpled olive green material he said, *That won't last two minutes.*

You don't know what your talkin' about, Clarence said.

Morris was still seething as he slowly mounted the blower and resumed working.

He was fed up. Suddenly he regretted ever getting involved in this scheme. None of them knew how much trouble all this had been. Sawing rivets with a homemade blade, wedging his arms between bars, working for hours with his arms above his head. Never knowing if they could even *get* out.

He let the cool night air beam down on his face. None of this meant anything if that raft didn't hold. *You stupid sonofabitch,* he remembered one of his friends saying to him. *You trust them? I was with them in Leavenworth.*

Busting through the roof vent was the toughest part. It required more than strength. West was too impatient, Morris knew that. The Anglins would have given up, or worse, made too much noise.

Morris was always a misunderstood character. Carnes later referred to him as "just a guy digging a hole." My father thought his superior intelligence, his stoicism and willpower, made him the only man who could keep the Anglins quiet. In the movie, *Escape from Alcatraz,* Morris was portrayed by Clint Eastwood as a man who was motivated to escape because of the warden's threats. Everyone knew the Anglins were too simple to have pulled off such a complex scheme. Few were aware of what West had done. But no one had ever really understood what "Ace" had accomplished. Aside from his bitter sulking, Morris was probably more Eastwood-like now than at any other time—self-righteous and brutally determined. It's true that West had moved mountains to get them up there. But Morris had done what none of the others could. With his sheer will, he had ripped a hole into the sky.

BY ABOUT 2:30 A.M. he had removed most of the rivets. He told John to get him some rope. He tied a knot around the grate, then flipped the other end of the rope over a strut that was part of the vent hood. He didn't want the grate to fall back and clatter onto the rods, so he used the rope as a pulley. Then he began working on the last rivets.

After about an hour the iron bracket was free. He carefully pulled the rope, lifting it up, then gently lowered it on the two reinforcing rods. Since he couldn't remove the rods, and since the roof vent was still intact above them, the grate would have to remain in place for now.

Gimme the light and the periscope, Morris whispered to Clarence.

He still had attitude.

Clarence handed it up without looking at him.

DOWN IN HIS cell, West was finishing up the last jacket. An eerie calm had settled over him. Up top, they'd finally stopped quarreling. Everything was nearly finished. He'd done what he'd set out to do. He got up and washed his hands in his sink. After six combined years on the Rock, he had orchestrated one of the greatest escape attempts in history. As he wiped his hands on a towel, a sly grin crossed his lips, a calculated, all-knowing, self-satisfied smirk. He'd done it, he congratulated himself. He'd orchestrated it. And, like the conductor before the crowd, he would take the last bow.

MORRIS HAD NEVER understood how the roof vent was designed, but now, as he fumbled with the light and maneuvered it through two sets of bars, it was suddenly revealed to him as if he'd always known.

The vent was constructed out of sheet metal and designed simply so that neither rain nor birds could slip through easily. He could see that it was made in three parts. The top part was a foot-wide band about forty-eight inches in diameter. This was attached by six struts to an inverted cone in the middle, which insured that raindrops were directed onto the roof. The third part, a band of about twenty-five inches in diameter, fit into a frame on the roof and was attached by six little sheet metal screws.

Six tiny screws. That was *all* that remained between him and freedom. The half-inch screws didn't even have nuts on them. He could twist them out using two fingers.

He laid down the penlight and pushed up the periscope. It took several agonizing minutes to coax it through the rods, the bars and the struts. It was pitch black. He couldn't see a thing at first. But as he jiggled the periscope, the lighthouse beam circled around and for a second the roof was bathed in a soft, wispy light.

He saw two big, black tanks directly in front of him—*water tanks?* Directly behind them was the lighthouse, looking like a black obelisk with a softly illuminated window on top. He watched the beam circle around, bathe the roof in light, then circle past.

The cell house roof as it might have appeared to Morris.

Five seconds later the light came around again. But the tanks obscured everything except the lighthouse. *Wait a second.* The beam circled again. He could just barely see a parapet along the east rim of the building. That was good; maybe it went around the whole building. *There. Yes!* He saw something else; something that looked like a tower. After studying it, however, he realized it was an entance from the cell house to the roof, encased in glass.

He angled the periscope to the right, but the awkward position made it impossible to see. He lowered it, rested his arms a minute, then awkwardly jostled himself into the opposite direction. Lifting the periscope into place, he gazed across the west side of the roof.

He saw the cell house skylights to his immediate right, faintly illuminated from inside, and farther to his left, more skylights. The lighthouse beam circled, painting the roof in a soft haze. He saw the 250,000-gallon water tower dead ahead of him. He'd never seen it look so small. Usually he viewed it from down on the yard where it loomed above him. Now he was looking directly at it. The light circled again, a soft, pale beam sweeping across the roof. He saw wooden catwalks which the guards walked on. The beam crossed over again. There was a parapet all right, around the entire rim of the building. He waited until the light swung around to take in the whole roof.

Whadduya see? Clarence said, a little too sharply.

There's no guard tower, he whispered back.

No tower? J-Dub asked.

I don' think so. He was too tired and irritated to elaborate.

By 3:30 A.M., Morris had the fake rivets in place with the rope holding the bracket. John was wrapping up the last of the raft.

Clarence stepped over to a five-gallon can of cement paint and began gently prying it open. Stuff needed to be hidden—the spoon handles, the vacuum cleaner motor, the barber clipper, unused electrical cord, nuts, bolts, files and the pen light. The plan was to protect Glenn May, Kent had said, because if the electrical stuff were uncovered, it would point right to him. One by one he dropped everything into the paint. He left the lid off, so the paint would harden, covering the tools inside. The can sat resolutely, over by the blower. Morris and the Anglins thought no one would think to crack it open.

By 4:00 A.M., they had returned everything back inside the blower. They turned the sheet metal screws in the ductwork and climbed back down to their cells. Exhausted, ragged, they crawled into bed.

3

THE WAKE-UP BELL shook the cell house like an earthquake, ripping Morris out of a deep sleep. It was 7:00 A.M., Monday, June 11. Morris stood for the count, whispering to West that the grate was out of the way.

"B! Outside!" the lieutenant barked. Along the flats, the cell bars cracked open and rolled across the metal with a deep roar. Morris and West stepped out.

They left off a pontoon, Morris said as they strolled down to the dining room.

So?

They—changed—the—design—of—the—raft.

Turning a corner, passing a guard, West remained silent. *Big deal,* he thought, *what's upsetting him?* The first pontoon hadn't worked, that's all he knew. Then West was supposed to make another pontoon, but he just hadn't gotten around to it. He assumed the Anglins had made the last one. As he and Morris moved into the dining room and up to the steam table, West could see from the corner of his eye that Morris' jaw was clenching. Both got their trays and utensils and Morris picked up a box of dry cereal and a carton of milk. A kitchen worker slid two fried eggs onto a dish, Morris nodded, and the guy scooped up some hashed brown potatoes. He grabbed some toast, a slab of butter and some catsup. West got his food. Both picked a table, sat their trays down and strolled over to the coffee urn, real casual-like.

Why'd they do that? West asked, scanning the dining room.

They wanna go tonight, Morris said without moving his lips.

Are we ready?

The raft's not finished, Morris said, leveling his gaze at West.

When they were all seated, *Whatsup with the raft?* West asked. *You left off a pontoon?*

Yeah, but it's stable, Clarence replied defensively.

Have you tested it? West asked.

There's no problem, Clarence said, evading the question.

John liberally salted his eggs and grits. *We got the boat!* he said. *Morris got the bars out. Now all we do is get the roof vent off and that's a snap.*

Morris' eyes narrowed. He poured milk into his cereal, stirred it, and scooped a spoonful into his mouth. *Nothing was a snap,* he thought, *and it wasn't gonna be.* He saw himself emerging onto the roof, running across it, shimmying down a pipe three stories. A shudder went up his spine. Maybe tie a rope around himself just in case. He saw himself down at the bottom of the building, climbing fences, getting the stuff over the barbed wire. He'd never been on the northwest side of the island, but he'd asked around. Once they got to the shore, they would inflate the raft, get in and float off. He pondered for a moment. *We might have to push the thing out into the bay.* He had heard the shoreline was full of boulders. He thought of wading out to his waist, trying to get in without swamping it, getting seated, all while the waves grabbing and shoving. It'd be easy for the first three guys to get in. But the last

guy would have to hold onto the raft and climb in all while the
currents were pulling it further out to sea. He was *not* going to be
the last guy in. Suddenly he was pulled back to the present. The
others were looking at him.

You ready? Clarence was demanding.

Hell, yes, he said, crunching a mouthful of cereal.

WHEN MORRIS RETURNED to his cell, he was surprised to find
a copy of the May 21, 1962 *Sports Illustrated* magazine on his bed
with a page folded back. Someone had obviously pitched it in
when he passed by before breakfast. That would be the Anglins.
Opening it to the page, his eyes immediately moved to a picture
of a triangular shaped raft. It looked pretty good. He stared at it
for a moment then tossed it aside. It would have ticked him off.
He wouldn't have liked being one-upped by the Anglins.

The lieutenant's whistle screamed out. Officers cocked back
the levers and the cells rolled open. As Morris walked out, he felt
like he had drank too much coffee. But outwardly he was calm.
Clarence, grinning and as cocky as a rooster, practically pranced
into the barbershop. West sailed around all day, eyeing Carnes,
Kent, May, Bumpy, Boggs, all his friends and conspirators. John
was hyped up, eagerly chinning himself from the pipes, giggling,
broadly hinting to his coworkers that tonight's the night. He
knocked off work early, remaining in his cell that afternoon.

One can imagine J-Dub preparing for his departure, moving
things around his narrow cell, deciding what to take, what to leave
behind. At one point, he slipped an envelope of photographs off
his shelf. He may have laid each photo out on his bed. Shots of
his mom, his brothers and sisters, photos of his girlfriend—
seventy-eight pictures altogether—many of them identified on
the back. He lovingly examined them. He missed his family. Maybe
he even reflected on his life a little, realizing that he had never
made anyone very happy. But that was about to change. *They'll be
thrilled! Escaping from Alcatraz! Fuckin' free men again!* He gathered up the pictures, a letter, and put them in the homemade
double-wrapped bag. West had already put nine slips of paper in
with all the names and addresses of people to contact.

John stopped for a moment, looking at an Alcatraz receipt

Clarence had included. True to character, Clarence had wanted to prove to *anyone* that they had escaped from Alcatraz—in case no one believed them. He'd show them the receipt. *See? Now gimme your fuckin' car keys!* John stuffed that back inside the smaller bag and closed both bags tightly.

Five thousand miles away in Ruskin, Florida, on June 11, the very day the Anglins would slip away from Alcatraz, their mother, Rachel Anglin, was finishing a letter to Clarence. It appears that she dictated it, perhaps to one of her daughters, because she had broken her arm.

The letter was newsy with details about one of his sisters' wedding, which was to be held at the house in five days, and doubts about whether anyone was going up north to do some cherry picking, and talk of going to see Alfred, who was still in Atlanta penitentiary, and about family members who were going to work at the summer camp snack stand, and that the fish—brim, trout and shellcrackers—were really biting at the pits, and that was about all Dad could do even though he wasn't working now, and notes about an insurance form she'd sent to John, but not him, because she already had good insurance on him, and that since she expected to hear from John soon, she'd close for now.

Within a couple of days she would realize that he never got the letter, that he had departed the same day it had been written. And she would cry. She was just like many mothers of Alcatraz inmates; she stayed in touch and forgave and forgave.

4

PROMPTLY AT 4:00 P.M., Charles Herman checked in as the cell house evening-watch officer. He made a count, checked it against the day-watch officer's, then called it into the control center. They racked the population out for supper.

The day-watch OIC left the cell house and walked down the hill to his apartment on the island. He took off his coat, loosened his tie, sat down and opened a can of beer, staring blankly at the San Francisco skyline. His kids crowded around him.

Up top, Herman took over. It would be nearly his last day with the federal prison service.

West, Morris and the Anglins sat together for their last meal on the Rock. Although cons sitting near them may have been aware that their time was close, they could gather no clues from the four men. Supper ended and everyone returned to his cell. All four men exchanged their oxfords for tennis shoes, each snapping his shoelaces tightly.

At 5:30 P.M., Herman made another count, rounding the tiers and filling out the count slip. He passed out medicines, then the mail. "It was mentioned at that time," he later wrote in a memo, "about a light being left on in A block across from the Anglin brothers' cells and I said I'd see what I could do."

"At that time [Herman] is certain the Anglin brothers were in their cells," Captain Bradley wrote in a memo, "as they complained about the light in A block being too bright and they were unable to sleep."

ABOUT THAT TIME, around 6:00 or 6:30 P.M., when the bay was a deep blue but the sky was still almost white, a group of us older kids met outside on the old army parade ground and teamed up for a game of softball. It never got above sixty degrees that day, typical June weather in San Francisco, and it was a cool, clear night with little wind and no fog. Most of us were in Tee shirts and light sweaters. Our parents could see us from their apart-

ments surrounding the concrete. I only had one or two days of school left, so I could afford to goof off a little. Years before, a maintenance crew had painted a baseball diamond on the concrete with two large, yellow boxes for home plate and lines to all the bases. They painted it at an angle so fly balls were not aimed at apartment windows. We divided up into two teams and the pitcher began warming up.

UNKNOWN TO US, Herman was having some difficulty in the cell house. "There was excessive playing of instruments," he later wrote in his incident report. Two black prisoners, on the Broadway inside cells, "were warned to play more quiet[ly] or their instruments would be taken away." Herman was relieved an hour or so later when the noise stopped.

By 7:30 P.M., he had frisked the kitchen workers and racked them back into their cells. He passed out the packaged cigarettes to B and C block inmates and exchanged razor blades—picking up the old blade on the bars in exchange for a new one. Although in the past, prisoners had locked razors, now the locked razors were used only in segregation. It was pretty simple; you had to leave a blade in exchange, or you went to seg.

He made another count and filled out the count slip. "Called in my 8:00 P.M. count to the control center," he wrote.

With Warden Blackwell and Lieutenant Ordway both on vacation, several positions needed to be reassigned. Although documents from the end of May until about July are incomplete, missing or tampered with, it appears as if Severson took over the day watch and Lieutenant Robert K. Weir became the evening-watch supervisor. Weir had been on the Rock for two and a half years. He had received high marks at McNeil Island and had been promoted to lieutenant in 1960 and transferred to Alcatraz as a new supervisor. Reserved, perceived by some as arrogant, he was said to have dismissed suggestions from subordinate but longer-term Alcatraz officers. Although he was a good officer, he was not perceived as a go-getter. And he was no Ordway.

Sometime after Herman's 8:00 P.M. count, Lieutenant Weir reentered the cell house to continue his rounds. Herman looked up and asked the gun gallery officer, A.V. Young, for the D block key. Young lowered the key on the lanyard. Herman unhooked it, and he and Weir walked to the segregation door, which Herman unlocked, allowing the lieutenant inside to check on the officer and inmates in there. Minutes later, Herman unlocked the lieutenant out of segregation. He then exchanged that key for the hospital door key, unlocked the hospital door and Lieutenant Weir walked up a flight of stairs, where he was met by Officer Irving "Levy" Levinson, a plump, engaging long-term officer with an infectious sense of humor. Weir checked on AZ 1444, Contreras. who was still in a coma from his beating on May 22.

OVER ON THE outside of B, Morris told West to keep a look out for him. He crawled out of his cell and climbed the pipes. He loosened the duct screws, quickly retrieved the bag of masks and lowered them down the chase, one each for himself, Clarence and John. Oink was laid outside of West's cell.

Morris entered his cell and rolled up two blankets, placing them under a top blanket. He folded them carefully right where the knees would be. He gently indented the pillow and placed Oscar on it, pulling the blankets up to the chin line. He stood back to see how real it looked, then ruffled the blankets a little more for effect.

Morris gathered up a pack of cigarettes and some matches. He grabbed his pea coat. He looked around his house one more time. Then he quickly opened his vent, closed it and disappeared into the pipe chase.

Clarence and John were waiting for him, grinning broadly.

It must have taken about forty-five minutes for them to retrieve the concertina, the life jackets, several long strands of electrical wire, the paddles and the raft from the blower, because Morris returned to the flats at about 8:45, appearing outside of West's vent. He asked for a glass of water. He told West he'd probably get the roof vent off by about 9:30. He also said that some work still needed to be done on the raft. West handed out the last life jacket and the last paddle, and he said he'd probably have his wall out by then. Morris nodded. He returned up the pipes.

BY 9:00 P.M., the wind had picked up. On the playground, our shrieks and taunts were taking on an hysterical edge. *Strike three!* someone yelled, *you're out!* and there was gleeful, revengeful clapping. We were really playing ball now; the kids who were serious were out yelling the ones who were just fooling around. The pale sky had turned darker, the sea had grown from cerulean to indigo. It was becoming difficult to distinguish sky from bay, now all melting into a dark deep blue defined only by the twinkling lights that marked the shoreline. We could no longer see the ball cross the home plate. Soon the winds freshened. Off in the distance, bell buoys swayed and rang, and overhead one or two seagulls glided by.

AT 9:05 P.M. HERMAN started another count. It took fifteen minutes for him to climb all the tiers and count heads. He finished at 9:20, filled out the count slip and called it in. In his memo he stated that he felt sure the Anglins "were there when I made my 9:30 count." But later he would see something that would change his mind.

Lieutenant Weir returned downstairs from the hospital and

Without knowing it, the officer had counted a dummy head.

Herman unhooked the key from the lanyard and unlocked the hospital gate, allowing Weir back into the cell house. He told the lieutenant about the Anglin's complaint, he wrote in his memo, and together they strolled down Broadway to the main gate, where they retrieved a key from Officer Gronzo. They went to A block and switched off a light.

If one of the Anglins was out of his cell by then, the two officers didn't notice. But the next day when Herman arrived at work, he saw that a razor blade was still on the bars of one of the Anglin's cell. He suddenly understood that the brother had never picked it up when Herman had exhanged it the night before. He had already left his cell.

And it was true. Clarence had already crawled out, and at 9:22 he appeared at the back of West's cell, rappped on the fake vent and whispered, "We can see the moon!"

DARKNESS HAD DESCENDED on our ball game. Somebody's mother had yelled out the apartment for her child to come in. A few shrieks later and the game had ended. We gathered up the mitts and the bats and dispersed slowly, like bit players meandering off a darkened stage.

But the evening was not yet over. I was wildly anticipating a CBS special that would show at 10:00 P.M. that night: "Julie and Carol at Carnegie Hall."

It's funny to think back on it now. I never associated that show with that evening. Carol Burnett was at the beginning of her career, continuing in the bawdy, physical comedy tradition of Lucille Ball. Julie Andrews, having become famous playing Eliza Doolittle in the Broadway musical of *My Fair Lady*, was a light-hearted proper British lady of no small comic talent. Theirs was a perfect comedic combination.

My mother probably fixed herself a cream and Kuhlua; I made hot chocolate. Once, a long time ago, my mother had been a dancer. Not a real dancer, she'd say; her large, poor, Irish family had no money for lessons. But she'd been transported in a limousine once and taken to a beautiful mansion where she danced for someone's birthday party. And I was a starstruck kid, desperately wanting to grow up and *be* somebody. My brother, Phil, was gone, probably out on a date. It was just the three of us. My father was already settled in, thinking he was going to read his library book, until the animation on the television would cause him at first to look at the television set over the top of his glasses, then to abandon his glasses altogether as the singing and dancing became too compelling. During the special Burnett would sing a poignant song entitled "Meantime," about the significance of what you do between the day you are born and the day you die. In scriptwriting, it's called the arc: it's the moment you change to become who you are at the end of the story.

It never occurred to us, as we excitedly waited for the special to begin, that events were arcing just up the hill that would have an immediate effect on all our lives.

5

IN THE MEANTIME something was wrong; Clarence could see it in West's face.

West had waited until this moment to try to break open the rest of his wall. But now he couldn't budge it. He'd tried everything without making noise. He was beginning to panic. *Your friggin' brother did this!* he said to Clarence.

You shoulda thought of this before! Clarence hissed, looking around, aware that cons on Broadway could hear them. He tried pulling on the concrete. A few small pieces crumbled off. Clarence braced his shoulders against the wall and tried to push it out.

That won't do nothin', West said. *I already tried that.* He was frantically digging holes in the piece, trying to weaken it enough so that it would crumble out.

Whaddaya want me to do? Clarence whispered hurriedly.

I don't know, find a pipe or something, West ordered, *maybe we can pry it out.*

It'll make too much noise!

Well, go get Morris then, West said frantically, *you don't fuckin' have to ask me!* West always wore a natural sneer, now his lips were taut, his eyes accusing. *Hurry!* he said as Clarence turned back to go up. *And tell him to bring somethin' down we can use.*

At 9:30 P.M., the main cell house lights were dimmed. Suddenly, the entire cell house settled into a tomblike silence.

Minutes later, Morris appeared at West's vent with a length of pipe. West looked awful. His face was red and pinched with fear. He had given up trying to bore holes through the piece, and now was using his pea coat to muffle the sounds of his kicking. Nothing was working. *This is all the Anglins' fault,* he whispered hoarsely, his eyes flashing.

Morris raised his hand in a show of caution. He handed over the pipe. West attempted to brace it against the wall and angle out the piece. But the pipe wasn't long enough. He handed it back to Morris and urged him to try. But Morris was becoming anxious with the Anglins up there, alone. He wanted to go.

You can't leave me! West whispered desperately.

They'll go without us! Morris said. *They'll take everything.* He tried prying the concrete. *We won't have a chance!*

West tried to regain his composure. He had to think clearly. *Go up top,* he ordered, *get Clarence. If all three of us try, we can get this thing open!*

Morris turned to go.

You've got to help me! West pleaded out the vent. His fear was palpable. *The whole thing was my idea!*

Keep trying, Morris murmured. *I'll be back.*

Morris left West about six or seven minutes after the lights had been turned down. And every step of the way he was probably weighing his options.

It's unknown what transpired between the Anglins and Morris once he arrived up top; whether they debated about returning to help West, whether the Anglins were angry at the delays and too anxious to go, whether anyone saw this as an opportunity to stick it to West, or whether Morris even put up a fight to help West. But it's obvious that at some point, the three men considered that returning to help him was no longer to their advantage.

Years later Carnes would say that West had set his own trap. West had believed that the '39 escape attempt had been doomed because McCain had lied about swimming, and in believing it, West had hammered the point that everyone had to be responsible for himself: there would be no going back to help anyone who couldn't pull his weight.

Morris stood, his hand on his hips, his eyes on the ceiling vent. He looked back at the Anglins. He knew he couldn't trust them now that they were so close. He looked back at the vent. In an instant he reached his decision. He climbed up the blower, wedged his arms between the rods and the grate and began loosening the roof vent screws.

Three stories below, West was still feverishly attempting to break out the chunk of concrete between him and freedom. He was engulfed in fear; panic was sweeping through his veins.

There would be many, many comments later about his real motives. But it's likely that at this moment West was in agony.

MORRIS, HOWEVER, WAS a realist. He may have told himself that it was West's fault. Not *his* responsibility. *You're in prison now—* the old saying went—*tough fuckin' luck.*

It was now between 10:00 and 10:30. After he loosened the last screw, Morris reached up with both hands, grabbed the struts and began to rock the vent hood back and forth. It was a huge, awkward thing. He wasn't sure how much it weighed. At first he could hardly move it. Then, suddenly, a gust of wind jerked it out of his hands, flinging it through the air, where it crashed on to the roof with a deep, resonating thunder.

Officer Young, in the west gun gallery, looked up sharply. "It sounded like a person hitting the end of an empty fifty-gallon oil drum with the heel of his hand," he wrote later.

"I heard [that] drop," Juelich said. "And when it hit, it shook every cell in the building. I thought, my gosh, they're not going to get away with this."

"Have you ever dropped a plate and seen it roll around and rattle and rumble until it falls?" said Bill Long, who heard about the noise the next day. "It was heard all through the cell house."

Dozens of panicked seagulls flushed from their nests, honking and squealing. Had the road tower been manned, the officer would have immediately flipped on his radio, called the dock tower or the control center. But it was empty.

Instead, Young was the only man to telephone it in.

The control room officer, his face registering concern, told Lieutenant Weir, who was in there with him.

Weir switched on a cell house paging station and listened. He heard nothing. He switched it off and flipped on another.

It's likely that after the vent banged on the roof, Morris quickly pushed the grate through the opening, and jumped up first, emerging onto the roof. It was black and cold and he could feel the wind rushing his face. It must have been a moment of complete triumph.

Then he looked up. Birds, flying overhead, calling out in distress, were illuminated by the lighthouse beam as it circled the roof.

Ignoring their cries, Morris reached back and grabbed a coat from John, then the life vests, the bag of photos, the paddles, the concertina, the wire and the raft. John squeezed through the bars and came up. He turned and reached back for Clarence's hand. *Let's go!* he said.

Clarence was the biggest of all three. He got his shoulders through with difficulty, grabbed the edge of the roof and tried to pull his hips through. For one panicky moment, his hips stuck, until, with a surge of adrenaline, he pulled himself through and onto the roof.

Later shoe prints around the vent would look like mouse droppings around food.

They grabbed their stuff and ran. Prints later pointed out their direction. In their hurry, a paddle flipped out of Clarence's hands and skidded under a catwalk.

Leave it! J-Dub shouted.

A con on the third tier later claimed he heard someone run directly over his cell.

Still down in the control

Tennis shoe prints on the roof showed their direction.

The pipe banged against the west wall.

room, Weir was switching from toggle to toggle, listening for sounds all around the institution. Nothing.

Within seconds the three were standing at the west edge of the roof. More and more birds had been startled and were now arching in a wider circle, alerting others on the west end of the island.

Morris climbed up the parapet. He looked down and reeled. He grabbed the bakery exhaust pipe, swung himself over and began shimmying down the side of the building. It was forty-five feet to the bottom. He was down in less than a minute. While Clarence tied electrical wire around their equipment and lowered it down, John climbed up on the pipe. It was about twelve inches in diameter and was held to the building by two rods of angle iron. In his haste, he bent one of the rods, and the big pipe banged against the wall.

Young, in the gun gallery, heard that noise. He estimated it came about five minutes after the first noise. Herman heard it too. He reported that it was between 10:30 and 10:45 P.M. It sounded like it was coming from the hospital. Young called the control center and reported a second sound, up near the hospital.

When Weir heard that, he was let out of the control room. He turned toward the cell house as the control room officer electronically activated the first barred door, opening it. Officer Gronzo, at the main gate, turned around. A second, loud, electronic click was heard, and the metal shield covering the key hole

They crawled around the water tower along the north. The hill tower, left center, was only manned during the daylight hours.

slid back, allowing Gronzo to use his key to open the massive steel door. Weir passed into the sally port and stood by while Gronzo shut the door, locked it, then slid another key into the last barred door, opening it onto the cell house. The lieutenant hurried up Broadway as rows of silent eyes on both sides of the aisle followed him. Three stories above him—like the ghosts they were to become—the blankets gently swayed with the breeze.

The lieutenant collected Herman, who had gotten the hospital door key from Young. Herman unlocked the hospital door and Weir disappeared upstairs.

A BLACK POWDERY soot lay around the bakery exhaust pipe, and later, a riot of powdery shoe prints landed where the three men picked up their homemade items and fled. They had to work fast. The roof down to the sidewalk was bathed in light. Gulls continued circling overhead, calling out their whereabouts. Two of the men climbed a fourteen-foot fence topped with barbed wire. One climbed over the other side and jumped down to the ground; the other remained at the top as a relay. The third man tossed up the packages one by one.

Within seconds they were adjacent to the prison yard, along a little catwalk that guards used to walk around the yard wall. They'd been told that the wall was only manned when cons were in the yard. Creeping along the catwalk, one of them cut a single strand of barbed wire, slipped under, and dropped down about ten feet to a grassy knoll near where the old morgue was. More birds flew up. The other two relayed the raft and the life jackets and quickly jumped from the catwalk. The three ran along the base of the water tower, then crawled, slipped and fell down a steep, rocky cliff—with twigs crackling all around them—as they attempted to hold on. More birds flushed, squawking and circling.

Relaying their equipment forward, stopping to search for guards, they crossed over a paved road and swept behind the old Officer's Club House. If they hit this checkpoint at the right time, they might have heard the thud of a bowling ball as it hit, then rolled down the lane, crackling apart ten bowling pins.

They passed a level, grassy area stacked with wooden planks and construction material, which they may never have seen, and found themselves on another steep incline, running, slipping, falling down, leaving a clearly marked trail of bent and broken tall grass.

6

ACCORDING TO HIS incident report, as well as his interview with FBI agents later, while this was going on, Lieutenant Weir remained in the hospital either "thirty" or "forty-five minutes," waiting to hear another sound that would give him some direction.

By remaining in the hospital for two or three quarters of an hour, Weir forced the main gate officer to also stay inside. The main gate man, who also acted as patrol, had to remain at his post as long as the lieutenant was inside. Thus, not a single man patrolled outside the building during the time when the noises were heard.

Speculation has continued to this day as to why the lieutenant remained in the hospital for so long rather than patrol outside the building.

"The prison is full of noise at night and we investigate every sound," Warden Blackwell assured a skeptical group of reporters eight days later on June 19. The reporters groaned. Blackwell's voice cut through the din, "If the wind blows over a bucket and it sounds like a bucket, we still investigate."

But that had not been completely true. In the *best of all* security arrangements, the lieutenant would have called for back up, patrolled outside, or demanded a prison-wide stand-up count. "With any suspicion," Levinson said, "a stand up count." The lieutenant's reports outlined no further plan of action. Either thirty or forty-five minutes later, he returned downstairs, having heard no further sounds.

Along with allowing West to work alone on top of the block, and allowing the blankets to be hung around the ceiling vent, this lack of surveillance outside the prison building when strange, unidentifiable noises were heard, would constitute the third major blunder to aid the escape attempt.

7

BY 11:00 P.M., MORRIS and the Anglins were probably down at the shoreline, out of breath, sucking in the smell of seaweed and salt water. Adrenaline rushed through their veins, heightening everything. The was it!—the moment they had waited for. They stood just in the shadow, and rolled out the raft. Morris dropped the musical instrument, slipped his foot into the strap while John fit it to a valve.

Looking out at the bay, all Morris could see were the waves breaking up against the boulders. Beyond even twenty feet, it was black on black. He could not see Angel Island, there were no lights along its shore to distinguish it from the bay. To the north, Sausalito was all lit up. John fixed the valve and Morris began pumping. Slowly the pontoon began to come to life. *Christ!* Morris may have thought excitedly, *I can't believe this!*

IT'S NOT KNOWN how big the raft was, nor how well it survived being flung over barbed wire and down the hills, nor how many inches in diameter the air baffles were, nor how tightly sealed the seams were. It's unknown how long it took to inflate it, using a little seven-by-seven-inch musical instrument made into a bellows. It's unknown if, later, one of the three men quickly threw a paddle into it, puncturing a pontoon with a long, skinny paddle screw. It's unknown if it held together while being beaten by the waves as they climbed aboard. All three men would have to wade out through a rough collection of boulders, ocean-polished porcelain and colored glass, old masonry and slabs of concrete—all slippery with a sleek brown moss. It's unknown if they swamped it, if they kept their shoes on while getting in. It's not known if the Anglins ganged up on Morris and pushed him out of the raft. Or if the three men drifted away quickly, using a flashlight to signal a waiting boat, and successfully escaped from Alcatraz.

It is only known that there was a swift tide the night of June 11, and they were entering a freeway—a cold, vast, choppy freeway that was rushing towards the Golden Gate Bridge and the Pacific Ocean.

8

BY MIDNIGHT, OFFICER Herman had left his shift without making his final count. It would be an honest admission to Captain Bradley for which he would later be penalized, although his count would have made no difference. Procedure called for the evening-watch cell house OIC to make his last count at 11:30 P.M., which would then match the count made by his replacement, the morning-watch cell house officer, Lawrence T. "Sarge" Bartlett.

"It was a busy night," Herman explained years later. He said the prisoners were "controlling the cell house." There were sick men in segregation, and Contreras, in the hospital, required attention. Some men along the west end of the cell house "were controlling the whereabouts of the lieutenant," and keeping him hopping, he said. Unfortunately, neither he nor Lieutenant Weir detailed that in their incident reports.

Instead, Bartlett made his count when he came on and both he and Herman signed the count slip. Unknowingly, Bartlett had counted three dummies.

At 11:55 P.M., Bill Long reported to captain's office as the morning-watch acting lieutenant. He spoke briefly to Lieutenant Weir.

"There wasn't a word said when I came on the watch that night," Long said. "I checked in and he says, 'Okay,' and down the hill he went. . . . I didn't know anything about all this until after the whole thing was over. . . .There wasn't *one* word in the log. I know. I read the log. There wasn't anything in the log."

It will never be determined if anything had been written in the watch log on the evening watch that night, because two pages of the ledger—comments dating from May 29 until June 21—were neatly, almost surgically, excised.

BY THE TIME the morning-watch officers were racked into the cell house, West knew they'd gone.

He continued working on his vent until around 1:45 A.M. on June 12. At that time, he said, he broke through his wall and went into the pipe chase. Later photographs of his cell show a large piece of concrete lying on his floor. He saw Oink laying there and climbed back to put it in his bed. He took his blue dungarees and his blue pea coat to the top of the block. But he moved without urgency.

He found the life jacket they had left for him. He removed his pea coat, climbed atop the blower and hoisted himself onto the roof. He put his coat on, picked up his life jacket and went to the edge of the roof where the bakery pipe led to the ground. Looking out at the bay, he could see nothing but blackness and a few lights sprinkled here and there. Later he would describe to investigators and prisoners what he had seen. But his descriptions were suspicious.

It's incalcuable what West may have felt at this moment. Standing on the windy roof of the prison, he may have felt hot, bitter tears streaming down his face. His stomach probably tightened with the feeling of loss and regret. But quite possibly, as he turned back to the vent, sobbing and wiping his face with his sleeve, a tingling of relief may have settled around his eyes.

He returned through the vent, leaving it the way he found it. Others reported that he climbed back into his cell crying audibly to his immediate neighbors that they had gone and left him.

The bastards had left him behind.

〜〜〜

Part 7

Discovery

BY 7:00 A.M., when the bell rang with a loud, angry peel, West had his story down. He dressed and waited.

Acting Lieutenant Bill Long blew the count whistle and guards climbed the tiers and rounded the flats. Eyes followed "Sarge" Bartlett down Broadway as he counted the flats then rounded the corner to the back side of B block, where he immediately encountered a "sleeping" Clarence Anglin. Startled, he knelt down and tried to wake the prisoner, but couldn't rouse him. Bartlett ran back up Broadway, shouting, "Bill, Bill, I got one I can't wake up."

Long looked up sharply, "Well, Hell, I'll get 'im awake," he said, as he rushed down the corridor and pulled in front of Clarence's cell. Several officers also rounded up behind him. "Anglin," Long yelled, "Anglin!" Puzzled, he moved closer to John's cell. John appeared to be sound asleep. Long reached through the bars and slapped the face, shouting, *ANGLIN!!* Suddenly, the face jumped off the pillow—as the lieutenant recoiled in horror—and crashed to the floor.

There was stunned silence, then pandemonium. "I got one here too!" an officer called out, standing in front of Morris' cell.

Then West said, "No shakedown could ever discover this!" Officers turned to him openmouthed. Holding up his fake grill and beating it with his fist, he said, "You may as well lock me up too. I planned the entire escape!"

Officer Long recovered, ran back up Broadway and called the control center. It was approximately 7:15 A.M. Mr. Burrows, the control room officer, called Acting Warden Art Dollison, whose immediate reaction spiked his heart rate. As he walked out of our apartment seconds later, the escape siren sounded, alerting everyone on Alcatraz.

By then officers had opened the three cells, had uncovered

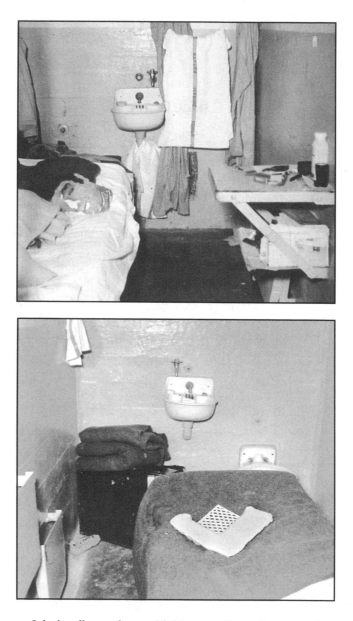

John's cell, top photo, with his camouflage of towels and raincoats, and West's cell, with his fake grill front on the bed and a piece of concrete on the floor at left.

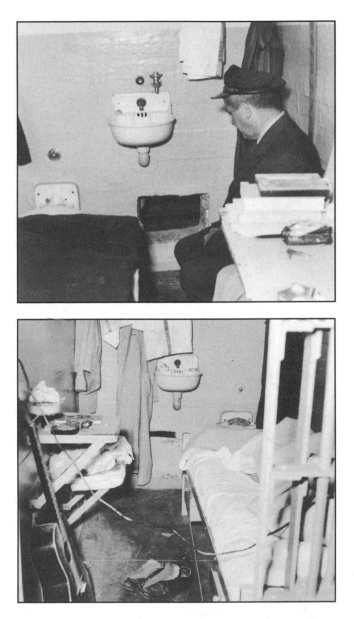

Morris' cell, top photo, with its precise opening usually
covered by a fake grill hidden behind an accordian
case. Clarence's cell still contained the wire with
which he could signal John.

the third tier, unlocked the utility corridor, which led to the
cloaked workshop at the top of the block, and a gaping hole in
the ceiling where the ductwork should have been attached.

Within minutes they found a small plastic container of "Rem-
Weld" book repair glue, the handmade periscope, large, cut pieces
of raincoat material, a long length of white knotted cord, a five
gallon bucket of hardened cement paint, and West's remaining
life jacket, all on the top of the block. The discovery of West's life
jacket told them that this was no ordinary escape attempt.

Others quickly unlocked the roof door where they found shoe
prints leading from the vent near the lighthouse to the west edge
of the roof where they found about a hundred feet of extension
cord. They also found the paddle under a walkway. At the bottom
of the bakery exhaust stack they saw the soot-rich foot prints leading to the fence, then the snipped strand of barbed wire along
the yard wall catwalk. Bloodhounds, brought over from San
Quentin, confirmed their trail. From the bakery exhaust pipe
(appearing left of the water tower running down the building), the three men circled the water tower, climbed down
the cliff, crossed the road, and climbed down the last cliff
where the broken and bent grass trail could be seen with the

naked eye. At the northern edge of the island, officers found another coil of extension cord.

Atop of B they looked inside the blower and located the discarded pontoon.

Within a day, Acting Captain Fred Mahan used a pry bar to crack apart the cement paint in the five-gallon can. Like archeologists digging for fossils, he and others quickly uncovered the electric motor from the vacuum cleaner, strands of electrical wire, bar spreaders, the handmade penlight, four pieces of strap steel etched with teeth, an iron rod, an icepick fitted with a handle and six sharpened spoon and ladle handles. That same day, another five-gallon cement paint can was found in A block. It was cracked open and inside were seven more utensil handles, nine pieces of heavy metal from two to twelve inches long, four pieces of heavy wire, two other metal pieces from five to seven inches

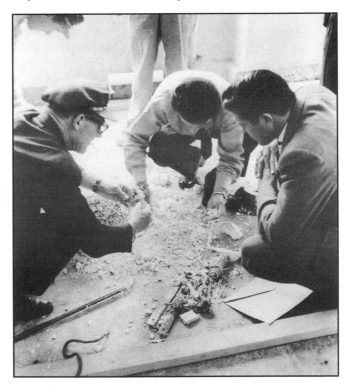

Lt. Mahan, left, officers and agents sort through cement paint.

long, and four-inch long screw bolts.

Eventually officers uncovered a score of brass screws, wrenches, a stapler, a handmade wrench, a barber clipper, a file wrapped on one end, ten drill bits hidden in a George Washington tobacco bag and another bar spreader.

But the paddle and the life jacket were the most important discoveries. Within days those two items would match similar items found in the San Francisco Bay.

Officers went about their search quietly, but their silence spoke volumes. Soon they would erupt into what Senior Officer Moore called a "seething turmoil." Heads were going to roll. Among the ranks, accusations flew as officers, lieutenants and administrators began pointing fingers at one another. Everyone felt duped by prisoners and betrayed by each other, and it was not a good feeling. Many of them were so embarrassed they never explained the details to their wives. Some still won't talk of it. Others who had worked there in earlier years were equally as shocked. A reporter called former Warden Paul J. Madigan who was at McNeil Island, Washington. "I miss San Francisco at times," he would tell a *San Francisco Examiner* reporter on June 17, "This is not one of those times."

One thing was immediately apparent. The motor from the vacuum cleaner, the lengths of electrical cord, the handmade penlight, and later, the revelation that the masks were constructed using electrical wire, all pointed to Glenn May.

But the most damning evidence was the least discussed: the scores of blankets that hung around the top of the block. Virgil Cullen said, "As soon as they hollered for men I run up there and told Bradley, 'What happened, did they go out the top?' and he said, 'Yeah, how did you know?' And I said, 'Them damn mattress covers!' and he just looked at me and kind of grinned." Although the blankets were not pulled down immediately, it was known among the officers not to talk about them. Reports from officers and lieutenants detailing their actions, summary statements from Bradley, Dollison, Blackwell, as well as the Assistant Director of the Bureau of Prisons, Fred T. Wilkinson, who flew in from Washington, D.C., all neglected to mention the blankets—even though they were *key* to the escape attempt.

There was evidence of their existence. They appear in two FBI photographs with a note on one saying that they, "covered an area approximately thirty to thirty-five feet from the end of the cell block and extended on both sides, giving perfect concealment." (See page 165 for a view of the blankets.) And mention of them was made in a July 17 *San Francisco Examiner* article on a tip, no doubt, from a disgruntled guard. But among everyone on the staff, it was known not to discuss them. The blankets were ripped down, perhaps as early as June 12, possibly before Assistant Director Fred Wilkinson even arrived on the scene.

ALLEN WEST WAS escorted to A block out of earshot of other cons, where he was interviewed by Dollison and Bradley. Shaky with excitement, he "bubbled over" with information, Dollison said. He also expressed bitterness over being left behind.

"I started thinking about escaping when I got out of D block on May 5, 1961," he said.

His story, even after repeated tellings, remained mostly consistent. He planned it, he made the life jackets and the paddles, the Anglins made the masks, John got most of the raincoats and made the raft. West couldn't remember where he got the other items—the electrical stuff, the nuts and bolts, the glues. He was stand-up; he never implicated anyone. The four men did it all. Even the FBI later thought West's story hung true. "He was glib. Kind of weasel-like," Special Agent Don Eberle called him. "But things he said kind of added up."

West's major discrepancy was the raft. He first described it as a six-by-fourteen-foot rectangular-shaped raft with fifteen-inch pontoons. There was some confusion about the fifteen inches, whether he meant circumference or diameter. It made a difference, but only a minor one. If the pontoons were fifteen inches in circumference, that meant they were only about four and three-quarter inches in diameter. If the diameter was fifteen inches— that is, if the measurement across the baffle was fifteen inches— it would mean much larger pontoons were built, almost forty-eight inches in circumference. It was "generally agreed" in both Dollison's and Bradley's reports that West meant fifteen inches in diameter. But since West never saw the finished raft, no one will ever know how big the air baffles really were.

West also told Dollison and Bradley that the Anglins left off a pontoon on one side, turning it into a triangular shape, either because they were in a hurry or because he never made the last pontoon. It became more or less a triangular shape, he told them. Then he told them that the raft was never finished.

In subsequent interviews with FBI agents, however, West neglected to mention the change in raft size or his possible part in its design change. He called it a six-by-fourteen- foot rectangular-shaped raft.

The discarded pontoon, possibly the side that was left off, actually measured twenty-one by seventy-two inches (six feet and two inches). A twenty-one-inch circumference would yield a six-and-three-quarter-inch diameter air baffle. Given that, it's unlikely that West's estimate of a fifteen-inch diameter pontoon is accurate.

AFTER WEST SAT nervous, edgy, emotional, enjoying the attention, a huge net of rescue services was put into effect. Dollison immediately called James V. Bennett, the director of the Bureau of Prisons in Washington, D.C. Bennett dictated a short press release to the warden's secretary, Walter J. Bertrand. Bertrand notified the U.S. Coast Guard, the California Highway Patrol, the U.S. Army, the State Harbor Police, as well as the San Francisco, Oakland, Berkeley, Tiburon, Sausalito and San Rafael police departments.

Dollison made a second call to Lake Berryessa, where Blackwell was fishing. When the two men talked, my father would have been the picture of calm, his "bullets" delivered as efficiently as that of a paramedic rolling a patient into a hospital. Inside, however, his blood pressure was high and he felt a tightness in his chest. Although he didn't feel responsible, he may have felt shame—in many ways, a more dangerous response. Initially, Blackwell was also calm. But he would have to pack and drive for an hour and a half, and his anxiety would increase with each mile. I have a picture in my mind of him standing at the stern of the boat as it rounded the island near our apartment, surrounded by officers, with his hand in his back hip pocket. He's puffing on a cigarette. I don't know if it's a real memory or an imagined one. But Blackwell would land on Alcatraz by noon that day, take charge, and blame, among others, Officer Herman for " 'costing me my job.' "

FBI Special Agent, Don Eberle, having heard about the escape on the radio, had arrived within the first hour. For the first two weeks the island was crawling with agents photographing evidence, checking files and interviewing prisoners and officers.

The Coast Guard deployed a helicopter and four patrol boats. The U.S. Army soon dispatched thirty-five military police and more than a hundred men from the 561st Engineering Company from Fort Baker to search Angel Island. Within hours FBI offices in Kansas City, Missouri; Mobile, Alabama; Tampa, Florida; Milwaukee, Wisconsin; and New Orleans, Louisiana were notified and given instructions on whom to contact. FBI agents in eight power cruisers searched the Marin County shoreline from Belvadere to the Golden Gate Bridges for several days, while other agents contacted boat owners in the area and people working along the shore. A door-to-door search by agents in Sausalito and Tiburon, especially houses with bay views, was begun by June 14. Professional and amateur divers searched around Alcatraz.

Jurisdictional challenges began to arise. Alcatraz officials had something to hide; the FBI was investigating the escape. The blankets were photographed, but mostly ignored as a factor. The job of FBI agents was to locate the missing prisoners, not to investigate the staff. Memos were telexed to Washington, with top FBI officials there often writing derogatory comments on them. The FBI immediately recognized the lapse in security at Alcatraz, and hollered vehemently about the mistake, in their opinion, of Blackwell's and Wilkinson's decision to hold a press conference on June 19. The director of the FBI, J. Edgar Hoover, notorious for his imperial disposition, watched from on high, as did other top FBI officials in Washington. They clearly felt that BOP director, Bennett, assistant director Wilkinson and Warden Blackwell were all "magpies" who "won't shut up" about the investigation. When the press conference went badly, because Blackwell and Wilkinson were "contradictory and evasive," they gloated.

Glenn May, Homer Clinton, Gates and Stones were among the first thirty-eight men interviewed. All denied involvement.

May said that West had asked him a couple of questions about the vacuum cleaner and he may have obtained electircal wire for West, but he didn't know for what reason. Nonetheless his activities, especially his work on electrical equipment in the prison kitchen, were more closely watched. As officers became more suspicious, May became more nervous.

The others who celled near, behind or above the four men were escorted to A block one by one and interviewed. The African-Americans were the most remarkably consistent. They barely knew West, Morris or the Anglins, never heard any digging, knew nothing about any escape plan, were playing musical instruments or listening to their radios that night, heard nothing, and knew nothing about it until the three were found missing the next day.

Files were scrutinized to see who had visited the four men. None of them had had outside visitors. A list of recently released prisoners were contacted.

West was interviewed numerous times. Then he was placed in segregation. Officer Fred Freeman was dispatched to the utility corridor behind D block, where he listened to West's description to other cons. "Is everybody on the telephone?" West asked—checking to see if they had emptied their toilet bowls of water and were ready to listen—because he was only going to tell his story once. "If this didn't do anything else," he bragged, "it ruined Alcatraz' thirty-year reputation."

2

THAT NIGHT, JUNE 12, at about 10:15 P.M., a homemade paddle matching the one found on top of the roof, was found floating off the northwest side of Angel Island. It was sent to Alcatraz and identified. Given the location of its discovery, near the escapees intended destination, FBI agents immediately suspected that they trio might have made it to land.

Two days later, on Thursday, June 14, the double-wrapped bags made of raincoat material was plucked out of water halfway between Alcatraz and Angel Island by the U.S. Corps of Engineer debris boat, the *Coyote*. It still contained nine sheets of paper with names and addresses of contact persons, seventy-eight photographs of the Anglin family and friends, the prison receipt and the letter addressed to Clarence.

On Friday, June 15, at about 3:30 P.M., a handmade life jacket, similar to one found on top of B block, was seen floating in the ocean just off Fort Cronkhite Beach. Known locally as Rodeo Beach in the Marin headlands, Fort Cronkhite Beach, is popular with surfers, bicyclists and hikers. It's located about three miles north of the Golden Gate Bridge near an area where bodies and debris frequently wash up. The life jacket's path was almost predictable: it had traveled outside the Gate for several miles, then returned to that beach on an incoming tide. Within ten minutes of spotting the jacket, a local couple picked it up and turned it into the Sausalito police, who turned it over to the FBI and Alcatraz administrators. There was a tear in a seam and its binder clip stopper was missing.

A week later, on Friday, June 22—eleven days after the three men pushed off in the homemade raft—another life jacket inexplicably popped up fifty or a hundred yards off the east side of Alcatraz. It was spotted by officers, who were still searching the bay for bodies, on one of the scheduled island boat trips to the city. It had brown stains on it, which were tested for, and eliminated as, blood stains; its binder clip stopper was missing and teeth marks were clearly indicated on the dipstick inflation tube. Agents speculated that the wearer had attempted to keep the jacket inflated by squeezing the dipstick with his teeth. Curiously, when it was picked up, this jacket's canvas ties were still knotted at the back.

The FBI labs tested the life jackets. Both jackets found in the ocean and the bay had to be repaired. In one, three punctures had to be sealed before the test. They were inflated until firm, the report stated, and then weights were placed on them. Both life preservers lost air within an hour. "However," the report stated, "the rate of deflation was slow, and pressure could no doubt be maintained by mouth." Ironically, the life jacket found on top of B block—which would have been West's had he chosen to go— tested as being completely air tight, remaining inflated for several hours.

THE RAFT WAS never found. In fact, no other physical evidence, directly linked to the three men, ever surfaced on land or sea again. While West and the escapees had turned their attempt into one of the most fantastic in U.S. history, Morris' and the Anglins' disappearance turned it into one of the biggest mysteries of the twentieth century. Aiding the mystery is the fact that escape from a federal prison is a criminal offense. Had any one of the trio ever been located, he would have immediately returned to prison.

A DIZZY ARRAY of "eyewitness" accounts, speculation, lies and fanciful stories began floating up immediately.

On Tuesday, June 13, a telephone call came into a San Francisco attorney's office. A woman answered and a man claiming to be John Anglin taunted her then hung up.

The same day a women in San Rafael, California claimed to have seen three men on a raft. While she was watching, the raft floated behind Marin Island—a small island about ten miles north of Alcatraz. She claimed that about a half hour later a speedboat also crept up to the island, then sped away with the three men on it. The story made headlines. Despite that it would have been impossible for men in a rudderless raft to have paddled against the current for six miles, reporters treated the story as gospel. FBI agents, circling overhead in a helicopter, also saw the "raft"—

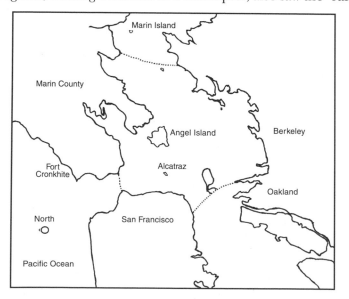

The tide was going out toward the Pacific Ocean.

which was in fact a fishing boat. Other agents contacted the men in the boat, who were in fact fishing.

That afternoon, Associate Warden Dollison picked up a telephone call from a man identifying himself as Frank Morris. He had called collect. When Dollison refused to accept the charges, the man reversed the charges, then said, "I guess you're glad to know I'm alive." Dollison was skeptical; he knew Morris both from industries and classification meetings. This was not his voice. When Dollison asked several qualifying questions, the man's answers became vague and indefinite. When asked where they landed, he said, "over where the boats come in." After several other questions, the stranger hung up.

On June 18, a con tipped off officials that Gates and Stones had also been involved. Knowing that he would be targeted by other cons if he were revealed, prison authorities arranged to have the walls scraped around the vents of all B block cells. Gate's and Stone's tampered walls were uncovered. Gates had dug eight

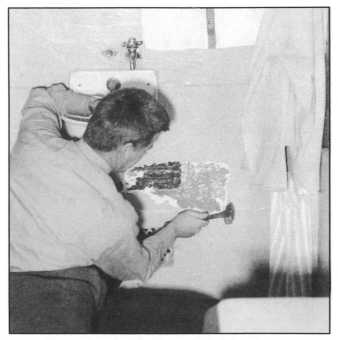

Officers scraped all B block cells and found two more
with holes around their vents.

holes; Stones, thirty-six. Both claimed others who had lived in their cells prior to them had dug the holes. But both men had used cement paint to fill the holes, a substance that reportedly had not been ordered on Alcatraz before October, 1961. It was this discovery that led to another understanding: the holes in Stone's cell, which were cemented over, but still can be discerned today in cell B-346, started at the top left corner moving right, then down, just as West described how he had worked (see page 94). Stones clearly never had access to a star drill, and it's probable that West and the others never had one either.

Also on June 18, Warden Blackwell received a postcard addressed to him. On the back, in pencil, was written, "Ha! Ha! Ha!, We made it," signed "Frank, John and Clarence." FBI lab would find no latent prints on the card. Handwriting analysis would determine that Clarence did not write it, but would be unable to determine if Frank or John did. Blackwell dismissed it as having the wrong address.

On June 19, an Alcatraz apartment was burglarized and a glass piggy bank violated. With tongue clearly in cheek, FBI agents investigated, dusted the window for latent prints, the scattered coins and the broken piggy bank pieces. There were small, child-size partials on the window. There were no latents on the piggy.

On June 20, BOP Assistant Director Wilkinson, speculated for reporters that the raft may have sunk, and if it did, "I'd know who'd go overboard first." He named Morris, who would have been outsized and out numbered by the Anglins. This was the origin of rumors that have continued until today, that the Anglins killed Morris and escaped without him.

Also on June 20, a tiki-god wood-carver found a bundle of planks along the Sausalito shore, lashed together with a three-quarter inch rope. The newspapers landed on the story with both feet, even picturing the man with his "mystery planks." The newspapers hinted that the discovery was an important clue. In FBI interviews later, however, the wood-carver's story quickly unraveled. He admitted having tied the planks together himself, dragging them down to the shore and calling the newspapers seeking publicity.

On June 26, a letter arrived on Alcatraz from a seventy-three-year-old woman who lived alone on a farm in Lincoln, Nebraska.

She claimed that a man who said he had escaped from Alcatraz tied her up and held her captive all night on June 18, taking her gold watches, her diamond ring and $75 in cash. The man had told her that if he went back to Alcatraz he'd be on the "Number One" diet. Blackwell chuckled; no one knew what the "Number One" diet was. It wasn't an Alcatraz expression. Other statements the woman made to FBI agents were inconsistent.

In July, one prisoner claimed that two officers had been bribed by Morris, and that Morris was in Chicago with his girlfriend. He said that if Lieutenant Mahan and another officer would only take him to Chicago, he would find Morris within sixty days. Blackwell was amused. On July 27, another claimed that another officer had been bribed and he could prove it "when the time comes." The time never came. Both leads were followed up and discounted.

None of the three men had any money with which to bargain. Morris had about $195 in his account, the Anglins, less than $25 each. Bank robberies by all three had netted them nothing. By then, of course, Morris' collection of coins had no doubt been dropped into coin-operated washing machines.

More than a month after the attempt, on July 17, 1962, a Norwegian ship named the *S.S. Noreffell*, sponsored by the Furness, Withy and Company, left Pier 38 in the port of San Francisco. At 5:45 P.M., about twenty miles west-northwest beyond the Golden Gate Bridge, John Rotick, the seaman on watch, saw a body floating in the ocean. He immediately thought of the escape from Alcatraz. He alerted Peter Igness, chief officer aboard the ship, who also sighted the body. Given that they would have to recover the body—which after four weeks would have been horribly disfigured—and return it to San Francisco, it was decided to do neither. Agent Eberle later described the ship as "bare of the essentials . . . with no radio contact with the coast guard." They notified no one.

That fall, the seamen returned to San Francisco and related the story to the San Francisco bar pilot. The bar pilot gave Agent Eberle the names of the men who had sighted the body. Eberle interviewed both Rotick and Igness separately on October 18, 1962. Both described seeing the body, clothed in "dirty white" trousers. White trousers may actually have been blue dungarees that had faded to white in the sun. That body, of course, was never recovered.

The most amusing sighting came at the end of that year after a December 19, CBS "Armstrong Circle Theater" program depicted the escape attempt. In a letter, dated December 31, a man claimed that he had his septic tank cleaned in 1956 or '57 and one of the men who cleaned it resembled one of the actors in the television show.

By July 2, the FBI's investigation had included exhaustive air, land and sea searches, interviews with all known associates and contacts—including families, and friends both inside and outside of prison—wanted posters, rewards and extensive media coverage. No one "broke" under questioning. No one acted suspicious. It was clear to agents that no one had seen or heard from Morris or the Anglins. They had vanished without a trace.

Two years later, in July 1964, agents reported that they had "vigorously pursued" all leads, rumors, innuendo, suspects, contacts, finding "nothing to indicate that the subjects made a successful escape from Alcatraz."

Yet sightings continued throughout the 1960s.

On February 16, 1967, a man claimed that while driving his truck in Silver Spring, Maryland, at the intersection of Georgia Avenue and Kennedy Street he saw Frank Morris. He claimed he had known Morris for thirty years. It wasn't clear if he meant he had served time in the same eight prisons as had Morris all those years, or if he had known Morris thirty years before. The story went nowhere.

For years, rumors would persist that Morris had been seen in the Midwest, in New Orleans, in Mexico or in Canada. But he was always here "last night," or acting suspicious in the bar "yesterday," or living in the room down the hall, but gone now. Most of these sightings evaporated under questioning.

In 1970, Rachel Anglin, the brothers' mother, sought a lawyer to begin proceedings to have the boys declared dead.

In 1979, Clint Eastwood's *Escape from Alcatraz* was released. In it, Patrick McGoohan, portrayed the warden who finds a flower on Angel Island—a tip-off that Morris made it. The flower is often cited as "evidence" that the trio made it. Yet the scene is fictional. Nothing was ever found on Angel Island.

In 1996, a man identifying himself as a grandson of Clarence Anglin, serving time in a Wyoming state prison for bank robbery, claimed that his grandfather made it. An Anglin sister later said that he was not related to the family.

Various Anglin family members have claimed that from time to time that heavily made-up, veiled "women" have shown up at family funerals, distraught and mysterious. Were they the brothers, made up as women, come to mourn? Were they FBI agents? Were they practical jokers, showing disrespect for the family?

Fanciful stories were not limited to floozies, deadbeats and hopeful family members. As late as 1997, a former Alcatraz employee told me that on June 12, he rode the Alcatraz boat to Angel island, where he found a "bloody raft." He claimed to have towed it to Alcatraz that day where *everyone* saw it. He definitely had my attention. Since I lived on the island during the escape and never saw nor heard about it, and since, in twenty-five years of interviewing officers and prisoners, I had never run across this story, I was skeptical. Nor had FBI agents heard of it. "We would have been tickled to death to find that," Agent Eberle said in 1997, chuckling. "We would have tested it for blood and everything else. *Never* saw it." In subsequent interviews with this officer, neither of us mentioned the "bloody raft."

A flurry of "evidence" surfaced during a 1993 "America's Most Wanted" television show, all of which vaporized under scrutiny. In connection to the television program, the Red & White boat fleet, owned at the time by Crowley Maritime, which for years ferried visitors to the national park on Alcatraz, issued a $1 million reward for the recovery of information leading to the arrest and conviction of Morris and the Anglin brothers. The reward lapsed in a year with no further clues and no arrests.

3

THE FACT THAT no bodies were retrieved from San Francisco Bay is not significant. Cold water can sometimes inhibit buoyancy by retarding the formation of body gasses. Clothes and shoes can drag a body down, as well as "snag factors" such as debris, vegetation and rocks. Eventually, marine life closes in and the body cavity is ruptured.

According to FBI investigation at the time, between 1960–62,

there were forty-seven suicides and probable suicides off the
Golden Gate Bridge (probable suicides are those witnessed by
only one person). Five hit land and their bodies were recovered.
Of the other forty-two, seventeen were recovered and twenty-five
were not. Today, the U.S. Coast Guard in San Francisco is more
efficient in searching for bodies falling off the Golden Gate
Bridge. A flag on a stanchion is dropped where the body landed,
on the theory that the flag will travel in the approximate direction
as the body. In about half the cases, the bodies are never recovered.

On June 11, 1962, the same day the three Alcatraz cons went
missing, witnesses observed thirty-three year old Seymour Webb
jump from the Golden Gate Bridge. In their search for Morris
and the Anglins, the coast guard also never found Webb.

On June 19, 1962, eighteen-year-old Robert Paris drowned near
Half Moon Bay, about twenty miles south of San Francisco. Although a helicopter observed his body, it sunk and disappeared
before a boat could recover it.

THE FACT THAT no evidence was found on land, is more significant. Escapees immediately need food, water, transportation
and money. That means contacting someone or stealing, which
leaves a trail. There were no missing boats, no stolen cars, no gas
station holdups, no burglaries, no stickups, and no verifiable
sightings. Although "sightings" occurred, they were too scattered
around the nation to fit a pattern of travel you would expect.
Escapees, especially in extremely high profile cases like this one,
find it difficult to disappear with no money and no resources,
and then remain anonymous for the rest of their lives.

Sadly, none of the three men had personality characteristics
or histories that would allow them to melt into society without a
trace. They would have reoffended within hours. And the Anglins
had proven to be big mouths.

ALTHOUGH NO BODIES were recovered nor any evidence
found on land, there were clues that told a story much like a
clearly marked trail.

Crime scenes, like archeology digs, tell stories. It's often apparent whether a murder was a crime of passion, or a random

act. Forced entries, or lack thereof, often tell a homicide detective where to start looking for the suspect. Murder weapons used, the transfers of blood, semen or fabric, blood spatters and prints can all point to the personality of a suspect, if the victim put up a fight, if there was a sexual encounter, and even, who the criminal might be. A logical, sequential story often emerges.

In the same way, archeologists see stories in human detritus. Slag heaps are full of broken pieces of pottery, seeds, grains and discarded flecks of stone tools. Enough pieces of pottery will yield an entire pot. Similar pottery found hundreds of miles away may indicate trading between two cultures, or show how far a culture wandered for food or water. Bones also tell a story—of violence, of diseases, such as arthritis, of age, nutrition, height and gender. Teeth are often the only identifiable remains, and sometimes even they tell a story about disease, food consumption, gender or age.

Few clues exist from the 1962 escape attempt, but they definitely tell a story.

It was a dark night on Monday, June 11, 1962. The moon rose at 2:15 in the afternoon. By 10:00 P.M—or about the time the three emerged onto the cell house roof—it was three-quarters across the sky and dipping, setting at 2:15 A.M. on Tuesday. A full moon would not occur until June 17, six more days.

The air temperature was dipping to about forty-seven degrees Fahrenheit, or eight degrees Celsius. The three men probably kept their dark coats on.

West, and others, said they were headed toward Angel Island. Shoe prints and clues in the foliage, as well as the bloodhound trail, showed them going to the north end of Alcatraz in the direction of Angel Island.

According to the Verified Hourly Water Level Data, as measured by the U.S. Coast Guard in San Francisco and sent to the National Ocean Service, the tide was going out. Very fast.

Tides sweep in and out of San Francisco Bay every five to six hours, with approximately four tides every twenty-four hours. In each twenty-four-hour period there occurs the lowest tide of the day, as measured by the hourly water level data. That's often followed by the high-high tide, or the highest tide of the day. In the hours after the high-high tide, the largest volume of water is departing the San Francisco Bay at the fastest velocity.

The low-low tide of 1.13 feet occurred at approximately 1:00 P.M. on June 11. The high-high tide, reaching a height of 5.23 feet, occurred at approximately 8:00 P.M. Within three hours— or at approximately the time when Morris and the Anglins put their handmade raft into the bay—the water level would drop almost two feet to 3.37, meaning that it was a very fast, outgoing tide. Between 11:00 P.M. and midnight, the water level dropped another half foot, to 2.73.

In other words, Morris and the Anglins entered the bay at *exactly* the worst moment of that twenty-four-hour period, when the biggest volume of water was going out to the ocean at the fastest velocity—a moment of what engineers call "extreme events."

Predictably, the only other escape attempt from Alcatraz, in which prisoners were never found, also occurred on a high-high tide.

On December 16, 1937, Ralph Roe, AZ 260, and Theodore Cole, AZ 258, escaped at 1:15 P.M. from the west end of the island—the Golden Gate Bridge side. The high-high tide that day occurred at 10:00 A.M. They, too, entered the bay at exactly the worst moment—hour number three of the high-high tide. It's no coincidence that they are also still missing.

Trying to cross a fast moving outgoing tide from Alcatraz is like crossing a river while swimming. You don't cross it—you go with it. Without a rudder to guide the boat, and using only paddles, experts say, Morris and the Anglins would have been in an extremely difficult position to travel north. The strong tendency would have been to float west toward the Pacific Ocean.

BUT THE SEQUENCE of items found in the bay adds a sad twist to this scenario. First the paddle was found, then a bag of names and addresses, then later, two life jackets, the last one mysteriously found next to Alcatraz.

If you are in a raft which is losing air or rapidly taking on water, a paddle becomes useless. Anything in your hands, in fact, or anything laying in the raft, that cannot help keep you afloat, becomes meaningless and drifts away without protest.

There is no way the Anglins would have let go of their double-wrapped bag of names and photographs if they had not been in some kind of trouble. They had no money, no food, no clothing and no transportation. Those contact names were their only lifeline. The photographs of family members were their most precious items.

Based on the evidence, the most likely scenario goes something like this: somewhere, maybe even close to the island, the raft began to sink. It's unknown if the three men had their shoes on, but if they did, their shoes would have immediately filled with water and pulled them down. It's unknown if they were wearing their navy pea coats, but if they were, the woolen jackets would have become lead weights. It's also unknown if they were forced to quickly put on their life jackets, fumbling to inflate them while thrashing around in extremely cold water, all while drifting in a direction that led to the ocean.

It is known that once they were bobbing around in water that was between forty-eight and fifty-four degrees Fahrenheit, that they could last only one to two hours before losing consciousness. The cold would have had an immediate numbing effect. Interestingly, thrashing around trying to build up body heat, a natural inclination, would have had the opposite effect of expending heat.

It's also known that a chaos of waves would have immediately come at them in every direction, making it hard to decide when to breathe without getting a mouth full of water.

All the planning, all the arranging and all the work would have come down to how well you could keep the panic and the cold bay water from overwhelming you toward an irreversible conclusion.

Morris, at five foot seven and a hundred and thirty-five pounds, may have been the first to succumb. His clothing would have pulled him down, he would have fought to remain afloat. But even his life jacket would have become an impediment for swimming.

The Anglins, heavier and better swimmers, might have had a better chance at drifting toward the Golden Gate Bridge. But had they survived, where would they go? How would they get money? How quickly would they be noticed? How far could they get, given the all-points bulletin that was issued by 8:00 A.M. on Tuesday, June 12?

San Francisco Bay Coast Guard Captain Larry Hall, says that as a general rule of thumb the coast guard will search eight hours with fifty-five degree water, "but that's being generous." In their case, by the time the search was mounted, Morris and the Anglins would have been drifting in the bay and the ocean for nine hours.

Few cons familiar with Morris or the Anglin brothers suffered any illusions that they made it, returned to normal lives and were never spotted again. All three were criminally hapless, mostly unemployable men, and the Anglins especially could have never maintained a life without bragging about their escape from Alcatraz.

4

THE 1962 MORRIS-ANGLIN escape attempt had an immediate impact on Alcatraz. Although the prison had already been designated for closure, the escape attempt accelerated that decision. That summer it was announced that Alcatraz would be phased out.

Prison officers who didn't want to leave San Francisco, began to quit. By September, Blackwell was concerned about the "marked letdown" of the staff, and fearful that other escape attempts were in the works. At custodial meetings, he urged officers to remain alert and asked the lieutenants and administrators to think of every possible escape idea. At one point they became concerned that cons would try to dig through the officers dining room on the second floor into the control center below it. Blackwell stated that he was "gripped with an unimaginable fear" whenever he thought of it.

But, like the months before the June escape, when officers were focused on the bars and not the concrete, Blackwell was once again focused on the wrong place, and unaware that decisions that he had put into motion would aid in the second escape attempt that year: the Scott–Parker attempt.

On September 14, the first salvo in that event made it into the watch log, when it was noted that a pair of hospital gloves were found in the kitchen basement. It was puzzling that a hospital garment from two floors up had been uncovered in the basement.

John Paul Scott, AZ 1403, and Darl Dee Parker, AZ 1413, among others, were kitchen workers. They frequently went into the basement to get supplies. Maybe they were down there only a few minutes at a time, but they were down there often, and, obviously, unattended. They had begun to saw through the basket bars that covered the windows and soon the window sashes themselves.

By October, the first airlift of prisoners—the least troublesome ones—departed Alcatraz, leaving the worst behind. By November, although Alcatraz was authorized for ninety-five officers, only eighty-nine were working there. It can be safely said that Blackwell was nervous.

And then it hit. On December 16, 1962, at about 5:47 P.M., Scott and Parker broke out of the basement window, climbed up a corner pipe to the roof, crossed the roof, and slipped down a length of electrical cord along the west side near the library. They scooted down the hill and behind apartment building A, then dropped down to the shore on an old sewage pipe. There, they inflated hospital rubber gloves and inserted them into shirtsleeves as floatation devices. The two men were gone before they were even missed.

"How the two bank robbers were able to slip out of the kitchen basement," one local newspaper wrote, "only a few paces from a sentry box and clamber over the top of the prison in full view of one of the principal guard towers has never been satisfactorily explained."

Never explained, nor understood, that is, until records were produced in March, 2000, that showed that Scott and Parker's route took full advantage of the fact that the road tower was closed and because of that, the "kitchen cage" officer—whose post was positioned to stop just such an escape attempt—was instead out patrolling the island. The two escapees had a clear path down to the shore—a path that put them right behind apartment buildings where island families lived.

Blackwell was said to have panicked when news of this second escape attempt reached him. He denied it years later. But he was so rattled that authorities in San Francisco were not notified until much later that maximum-security prisoners had escaped from Alcatraz.

Parker was soon caught up on a little island next to Alcatraz and returned unharmed.

But Scott drifted west to the Golden Gate Bridge on an outgoing tide and eventually drifted up on the rocks near Fort Point, under the base of the Golden Gate Bridge. Many thought that Scott's successful swim to the San Francisco shore lent support to the theory that Morris and the Anglins, too, might have made it.

Scott and Parker had a clear path behind the family quarters before
descending down a pipe and into the water.

And although he left on the low-low tide, only a subtle difference
of height occurred between the high and the low tides that winter day. More importantly, Scott departed Alcatraz at hour three
of the outgoing tide. He, too, had entered the bay at a critical
moment and was swept nearly out to sea. He washed up in what
was described as a "serious" condition, "unconscious and in a state
of shock." His temperature had dropped to ninety-four degrees.
Luckily for him, he was spotted and taken to a hospital. Paramed-
ics, who were initially unaware that he was an escapee from
Alcatraz, said he was "too convulsed to speak."

He was revived and returned on a gurney to Alcatraz the next day.
Alcatraz closed three months later, on March 21, 1963.

5

WARDEN BLACKWELL WAS not faulted for either escape attempt in 1962. And although he was not personally responsible
for "tickin' bars" and "eyeballin'" concrete, he had once told a
supervisory training class that "his employees will not enter into
the project with full support if they are doubtful of their

supervisor's ability . . . they will consciously or unconsciously restrict [their] activities—both mental[ly] and physical[ly]—if they have real or imaginary doubts and reservations about his ability." It was a telling statement. Unconsciously, Blackwell was projecting the truth while remaining in denial about his own responsibility in the breakdown.

Although he was well liked by his covey of friends and respected by my father as someone who was opening the institution with a new educational director, a new commissary, new recreational equipment and other amenities that had never been tried on Alcatraz before, he was also shutting down towers and taking risks about which his employees had serious reservations. In March, 1962, James V. Bennett wrote, "Dear Blackie, I really think you were born under pretty lucky stars." His luck, perhaps, was that he served under a benevolent director who liked him. And Blackwell—like a good gambler—also knew when to hold back his cards. He found "gross negligence" in the actions of two employees for counting dummy heads. He allowed that another officer, John Herring, on a "part of one day" had used "poor judgement" by allowing West to paint on top of the block. But then he wrote: "I can find no further evidence of personnel failure or negligence and would not recommend any further action be taken."

Blackwell remained on Alcatraz until May 1963, helping with the distribution of the island's equipment and was transferred as warden to the U.S. Penitentiary at Lewisburg, Pennsylvania.

In October 1965, he transferred as warden to Atlanta, where he retired in 1970. I interviewed him in 1982 at his home in Georgia. He remained there until he died of a heart attack in 1986 at age seventy-one.

My father was stricken with chest pains the summer of '62 and for three nights he paced the living room, unable to sleep laying down, until finally the pains disappeared. He was surprised later to discover he had had a "silent" heart attack. We were transferred on November 20, 1962, to the Federal Correctional Institution in Seagoville, Texas. It was a minimum-security, progressive institution—the opposite of Alcatraz. Within five months, he had a severe heart attack, had open heart surgery and was on leave for three months. Although he was never faulted for the '62 escape attempt, he was in effect "put to pasture" at Seagoville, and, realizing that he would never become warden, retired in 1965.

We had numerous telephone discussions about Alcatraz beginning in 1978, but it wasn't until several years later, when the blankets were disclosed by officers, that I began to ask him about them. By then he had had a stroke, which left his speech slightly impaired. I could neither hear nor understand his response to my question about the blankets. He seemed confused. I did understand, however, the emotional context surrounding his answer. He was reluctant to speak of it, perhaps embarrassed, or had pushed it from his memory. He died of a heart attack in 1983 at the age of seventy-three.

Captain Tom Bradley was cited by Assistant Director Wilkinson, for a "high degree of responsibility for the ineffectiveness of inspections, patrols and security measures." His promotion and transfer to Leavenworth was immediately revoked while he was still residing on Alcatraz. Instead, he was reassigned without promotion to the Federal Reformatory at Petersburg, Virginia, a minimum-security youth camp. A year later he received his promotion and was transferred to Lewisburg, where Blackwell was warden.

After Blackwell transferred to Atlanta in 1965, Bradley followed in 1966, as captain. In June 1968, Bradley was taken hostage in Atlanta along with twenty-four other employees, and released unharmed a day later. To some in the prison service, it was another bad mark on his record. Blackwell, however, included a glowing note in his file.

Six months later Bradley was transferred as camp superintendent at the federal prison camp at Maxwell Air Force Base in Alabama. He retired in 1972, and died four years later of a heart attack at the age of sixty-five.

No one was faulted or punished for allowing blankets to be hung around the top of the block for almost six weeks. Since the blankets were never revealed in official reports, no one could be blamed. Because it was reported that each of the cells had been shaken down in the months prior to the escape attempt, no cell house officer faced disciplinary actions. But it was clear, Wilkinson stated in his final report, "that there was acceptance by many officers over a long period of time that Alcatraz was so inviolable it was not necessary to recall fundamentals . . . [that] maximum-security shakedowns, where equipment and fixtures would be removed from the cell, were not made. Nor were critical, careful and suspicious inspections made of the utility corridor. . . . Many experienced officers and supervisors were duped. . ."

Although he cited the weakened concrete, he laid most of the blame to human error, never mentioning, of course, his and Bennett's complicity in the closing of the road tower and the reduction in force. And, he had agreed to the scapegoating of two officers, neither one of whom were responsible for the biggest blunders.

Alfred Anglin, who had been convicted along with his two brothers and was serving time in Atlanta, was transferred to serve his twenty-five year state time in Alabama concurrent with his federal time. On January 11, 1964, while trying to escape from Kilby state prison in Montgomery, he electrocuted himself. The funeral home notified FBI agents that the body showed no signs of mistreatment but two small burned areas in the upper back and burned areas above the eyes and on the bridge of the nose (possibly from eyeglasses). The family had suffered so much with two missing sons, a family member said, that they would probably never accept or understand the truth surrounding the death of Alfred.

Lieutenant Severson was transferred, in December 1962, to the Federal Detention Headquarters in New York City. In 1965, he transferred to Leavenworth and retired in 1968. He died at the age of seventy-four in 1979, interestingly, on May 5, the same day years before when West had walked out of segregation and set the escape attempt in motion.

Lieutenant Ordway returned to Alcatraz for one day on June 12 to aid in the hunt of the three missing men. He returned off annual leave in July and retired from Alcatraz when it closed in 1963. He died in 1988 at the age of eighty-three.

Lieutenant Weir transferred to the U.S. Penitentiary at Marion, Illinois. He retired at McNeil Island as a lieutenant in 1971 and died in July, 2000. He responded to only one of my numerous letters requesting interviews and declined to be interviewed.

Two officers were blamed and suspended, Officer Charles Herman was suspended for a month without pay for not making

his last count. He protested and then quit the federal prison service, went to work for the U.S. Post Office and retired in 1989.
Officer Lawrence Bartlett was suspended for one month without
pay for counting dummy heads; he remained in the prison service. Many officers I spoke with felt that both men received un-
fair disciplinary actions, and were, in fact, scapegoated. Many felt
that they, too, would have counted the dummies.

Officer John D. "Jerry" Herring was not disciplined for allowing West to work on top of the block without supervision, mostly
because he was deemed "lieutenant material." He went on to distinguished service until he retired in 1976 as captain, and died in
March 1990 at age fifty-six.

Whether Bumpy Johnson was ever enrolled to keep the other
black prisoners quiet, or used in any other way in this escape, was
only a matter of conjecture. It was Carnes who said in the late
1970s, that he'd seen Johnson nod to West almost imperceptibly
on the yard one day, and that had signified to him that Johnson
was a player. Others carried Carnes' theory forward, like a World
Series pitcher being hitched on the shoulders of his teammates
after the big win. They said Bumpy provided a boat. But there
was never any evidence of that; it was just a theory.

Although it might have been possible for a boat to have silently crept near Alcatraz at night without being seen, it would
have been much more difficult to arrange, requiring accomplices
who would need to be paid handsomely—and for a long time—
or be killed. Neither Morris nor the Anglins were so well heeled.

"Bumpy may have talked a good line," said a former prisoner
who wished to remain anonymous, "but if they were waiting for a
boat out there," he laughed, "don't hold your breath."

Nor was Ron Battles sure that "Bumpy" got involved with the
four men. If he did, Battles figured Morris was the only one who
would have even approached him.

Kent had a different theory. He figured West or the Anglins
scared Johnson, threatening to kill him. "He knew a dozen of us
white guys were pushing it," Kent said.

Johnson left Alcatraz on January 26, 1963, transferring to
Lewisburg, Pennsylvania. He was eventually released from federal
prison. In July 1968, while out on a $50,000 bail on indictment for

importing narcotics into Harlem, and while dining with friends in New York City, he was stricken with a heart attack, collapsed and died. He was sixty-two, and had spent at least twenty-five years in prisons. At his funeral, held in New York City later that week, twelve hundred people showed up, including a former Catholic priest from Alcatraz.

Bumpy's possible involvement was suggested by Clarence Carnes after Bumpy died. It's unlikely Carnes would have named him had he still been alive. It is also likely that Bumpy simply advised his black friends who celled near West, Morris and the Anglins to keep out of it.

Tom Kent actually thrived on Alcatraz and turned his life around there. He was considered "friendly, smiling, happy-go-lucky," his file calling him a "diligent, accurate clerk typist," and a "definite asset to the institution." He was transferred from Alcatraz on February 26, 1963, to Lewisburg, released from prison in 1966, and worked as a fireman in and around Boston, Massachusetts. He visited Alcatraz in 1995, entertaining visitors with his stories. We had several interviews. He died in June 1997 in his trailer home in Chula Vista, California of natural causes. He was seventy-one.

Larry Trumblay, who had thirty-six incidents of delinquency, assaults and robbery, strong-armed robbery, disorderly conduct, burglary, assault to murder and bank robbery, and had arrived in April 1954 with West, also turned his life around on Alcatraz. He became close to Father Bernie Bush, became an altar boy at Leavenworth where he had transferred in 1963, and was granted parole on May 19, 1965. On June 26, on the return drive from California after attending Father

Tom Kent visiting Alcatraz in 1995.

Bush's ordination, he was killed in a one-car accident. He was thirty-five.

William "Billy" Boggs, who admitted to using heroin when he was fifteen, and was at Alcatraz by the time he was twenty-one, was determined to have been "deeply involved" in the Morris-Anglin escape attempt. When the double-wrapped bag was fished from the bay and the lists of names and addresses were examined, several of his relatives' names popped up. His sentence expired and, because he had family in California, Boggs was released from Alcatraz in February 1963. He was in and out of prison after that, and died of pneumonia at age fifty-eight in March 1997.

Martin McNicholas was found to have a piece of raincoat material sewed and glued in his cell in July 1962. The list of mileages was also found, as well as a chemical explanation for nitroglycerin. He told the disciplinary board that he had "long ago given up on the idea" of escaping. He and the board agreed that he was only guilty of being stupid. He was transferred to Atlanta on February 8, 1963. Two years later, in April 1965, while changing planes during a transfer to Leavenworth, he tried to escape and was shot and killed. He was thirty years old.

Homer Clinton, the "Green Lizard," tried to steal a spoon from the Alcatraz dining room in July 1962. He died in Washington at age seventy-two in 1989.

The San Francisco Giants won the National League pennant in 1962—their best year—but lost the World Series in a heartbreaking seventh game to the New York Yankees.

Herbert "Lucky" Juelich paroled out of prison, got married and lived a normal life. He returned to Alcatraz several times to speak to visitors, and died in 1999 of complications due to diabetes.

Leon Thompson paroled out of prison, turned his life around after marrying a lovely British woman named Helen, wrote two books, and raises wolves on his ranch in California.

Clarence Carnes, who at age eighteen in 1945 had been one of the youngest prisoners ever sent to Alcatraz, remained there for eighteen years, until January 15, 1963. He was released from Leavenworth in 1976, returned briefly for a parole violation, then finally released in 1978. We met that same year in a fast-food restaurant in Kansas City, Missouri and began one of many conversations we held over the next eight years. In 1980, a television film was made about his life, entitled, *Alcatraz: The Whole Shocking Story.* That year he was also mugged and briefly hospitalized. It was the best and worst year of his life, he said.

Mr. Carnes returned to Kansas City, Missouri where for a time was involved with Habitat for Humanity. He contracted AIDS, broke parole and was returned to Springfield Medical Prison, where he died in 1988 of complications resulting from the disease. He was bur-

Carnes, in about 1979.

ied in the prison cemetery. James J. "Whitey" Bulger, a notorious Boston mobster who served on Alcatraz for bank robbery during the West-Morris-Anglin escape attempt, was said to have had Carnes' body disinterred and reburied in an Indian burial ground in Oklahoma, where Carnes had always wanted to be buried. In 1995, Bulger was indicted for racketeering, and, as of this writing, was still being sought as one of the FBI's "Ten Most Wanted" with a $1 million reward on his head.

Tom Kent expressed the opinion that Glenn May was murdered by the government for his participation in the escape attempt. It's a little dramatic, but it's easy to see why Kent thought that. That fall, perhaps because the suspicion that surrounded him became too much, Glenn May's health began to decline. He complained of various medical problems and was hospitalized three times. When he transferred to McNeil Island on November 28, 1962, he had lost a lot of weight. At McNeil, he continued to lose weight. Records show that he was diagnosed as being anorexic. This was confirmed by Juelich and others who knew him.

In May 1963, McNeil authorities transferred him to the U.S. Medical Center in Springfield, Missouri. He was too weak to be photographed standing up, and his mug shot was taken while he

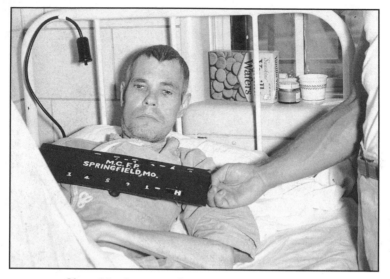

Glenn May in a mug shot taken while he lay in bed.

lay in bed. His file at Springfield contains page after page of doctors' and nurses' notes on his refusal to eat and his slow, steady decline. He died in Springfield on July 13, 1963 of starvation due to anorexia nervosa. He was forty-four years old.

ALLEN CLAYTON WEST left Alcatraz on February 6, 1963, transferring to McNeil Island, Washington. He was later transferred to Atlanta where he was released from federal prison on January 7, 1965 and sent to Georgia and then Florida to serve prison sentences in those states. Released in 1967, he remained free for about a year, and then was arrested in Florida on charges of grand larceny, robbery and attempted escape. He was sentenced to one commitment for five years, one for life, and one for three years to run concurrent, and on January 1969, he went to Florida state prison. On October 30, 1972, West fatally knifed another prisoner in what was probably a racial incident.

In December 1978, he was sent to the Shands Teaching Hospital for severe abdominal pains. He died on December 21, 1978 of peritonitis. He was forty-nine.

Few believed that West couldn't get out of his cell that night.

Officer Victor Mills, summed up many people's feelings when he observed that "underneath the tough convict exterior beat the heart of a coward." Many thought, as did former prisoner Clarence Carnes, that "he was scared of that water." In his final report, Wilkinson had written "the warden, the FBI agent and I believed that West 'chickened out'," adding, "He repeatedly evidenced his fear of the water."

West, when he departed Alcatraz.

"He made up some lame excuse," said officer Mills, "but those of us who knew him best knew that he had lost his nerve."

That may have been part of it. There's also evidence to support his contention that he could not get out in time. His cell, photographed by the FBI, showed a large chunk of concrete, possibly indicating that he was still trying to get out that night.

But there could have been a third reason. Because in the end, Allen West won the game. He *lived* to tell his story. And, more importantly, for the rest of his life, he got the bragging rights. If Morris or the Anglins had actually escaped, they could never admit it without getting caught and being returned to prison. The pint-sized Allen West could claim to be a giant, having engineered the most elaborate, the most fantastic, the most famous escape attempt in U.S. history—from the toughest prison of them all.

For the rest of his life he could claim that he had aided Morris and the Anglins in the most important ways. He conceived the plan, he made the life jackets, he got them to the roof. Without him, they were nothing.

His remaining behind could have been the ultimate double-cross. Because he had done what he had set out to do.

He had *broken* the Rock.

Source Notes

In the absence of accurate information about Alcatraz during the years that it operated, rumor, innuendo, trial "facts," error-filled newspaper accounts, sensational news reels and movies rushed in to fill the void. As I've shown here, even Frank Morris believed rumors of "Spanish dungeons" on Alcatraz, although Spain never occupied Alcatraz and the so-called dungeon—three cells and possibly six other storage rooms used as cells located in the cell house basement—had been dismantled by the Bureau of Prisons sometime around 1940. But the first thirty-two prisoners in 1934, who were holdovers from the U.S. Army prison, insured that rumors originating in the 1860s rolled over into the federal prison years and persist even today.

In the mid 1970s the BOP assembled most of the Alcatraz inmate and administrative files into a single collection, and in 1976, the boxes—comprising nearly four hundred cubic feet—were shipped to a university professor of sociology. He obtained a grant to study the consequences of long-term confinement under condition of maximum-security imprisonment and was also permitted by the BOP to write a popular history about Alcatraz.

The collection had already been compromised, however, because no list of its contents had been drawn up before its transfer. And since it was assumed that the sociologist's project would only take a few years, he initially sought to be allowed to restrict other researchers from seeing the records. But throughout the 1970s, the '80s and into the early '90s, most of the records were still under his jurisdiction, and there began to be reports of "missing" or "misplaced" records emanating from his office.

I began working on obtaining information about the 1962 escape attempt as early as 1978 as part of another book, *Eyewitness on Alcatraz,* interviewing officers whom I'd known in 1962. Most of my early interviews were tape-recorded, which is fortunate because many of those men have since died. My most extensive interviews were with my father, Arthur M. Dollison, and Philip R. Bergen, Benjamin Rayborn, James A. "Jack" Mitchell, Olin G. Blackwell, Bill Long, Tom Mahoney, Clarence Carnes, Fred Mahan, Lloyd Miller, Lew Meushaw. Leon Thompson and Bill Rogers. Fortunately, my father kept copies of many 1962 escape memorandums, which formed the basis of my early interview questions and much of this book, especially the moment-to-moment sequence in Part 6, Countdown.

In 1984, I filed a Freedom of Information/Privacy Act request pertaining to the tower shutdowns, comments about which I had begun hearing. The FOIA/PA request was denied based on the importance of the sociologist's still unfinished project.

In the early 1990s, pressure from several researchers compelled the Bureau of Prisons to request that the professor begin returning the records he no longer needed. Almost seventeen years after taking taken control of them, the professor returned many of the Alcatraz records to the BOP who then turned them over to the National Archives and Records Administration (NARA) in San Bruno, California. By 1995, he indicated he had returned them all. But there remained an alarming list of "missing" inmate files, many of which curiously happened to be those of the most famous inmates, or those involved in well-known events.

Finally, by 1999–2000, under pressure from numerous researchers, web and print publishers, as well as the BOP, the sociologist was compelled to return the files it was believed he still held. In March, 2000, approximately ten feet of files were returned to the BOP, and subsequently the NARA. Among the records returned were also files pertaining to the shutdown of the towers on May 5, 1962. They included a 1962 lieutenant's watch log, monthly captain's reports to the Bureau from 1962 and other important memos pertaining to the 1962 escape attempts. As of this writing, March, 2001, the professor's report to the Bureau, as well as his book, have not been released. Although I published statements about the tower shutdowns in my first book, I did know then the date, nor whether the shutdowns had a profound effect on the West–Morris–Anglin and the Scott–Parker escape attempts. Obviously, they did.

IN MY QUEST to get to the essence of an historical event which I did not witness, I felt it best to compare and contrast each man's statement against all the others. Inmate files can be notoriously misleading, given that the social and criminal history recorded by officers, clerks or psychology professionals is inmate self-reporting. Grandiose statements, outright lies, imprecise dates and repeated misinformation are constant. At times prisoners felt inclined to tell the reporter what they thought he wanted to hear. In other cases, recorders simply rewrote what had been written the previous year. In many cases FBI documentation of arrests did not coincide with the inmate's account or BOP records, making it difficult to decide exactly which one was accurate.

What follows is a list of people interviewed and records I reviewed solely for this book. All of these records will be eventually deposited with the Golden Gate National Recreation Area Park Archives and Records Center.

~~~~~

Author interviews:
Ron Battles, Philip R. Bergen, Walter J. Bertrand, Olin G. Blackwell, Kenneth Blair, Ben Blount, Rosemary Bones, Ira Bowden, Jerie Bremmeyer, Father Bernie Bush, Clarence Carnes, Jack Casey, Virgil Cullen, Arthur Davidson, Ed Deatherage, George DeVincenzi, Arthur M. Dollison, Evelyn E. Dollison, Donald V. Eberle, Clifford Fish, Fred and LuAnn Freeman, George Gregory, Charles Herman, John Hernan, Ruth Ann Herring, Herbert Juelich, Al Kaeppel, Bob Kelly, Thomas Kent, Melvin Kidney, Joseph Landers, Jim Langley, Irving Levinson, William Long, Jr., Fred Mahan, Don Martin, Pat Mahoney, Lewis Meushaw, Lloyd Miller, James A. Mitchell, Marvin Orr, Darrell Pickens, Don Pickins, James Quillen, Larry Quilligan, Benjamin Rayborn, Jr., Fred Richberger, John and Alma Ridlon, William Rogers, Tom Reeves, A.O. Severson, Frank Sprenz, Leon Thompson, Richard Waszak

Additional interviews:
Mike Mayo and Frank Silio, formerly of Airstream ventilation systems; Benny Wood, latex chemist and the president of Advance Adhesive Technology; George M. Rosen, director of quality control, Electrolux; Eric Muller, earth science teacher at the San Francisco Exloratorium; Dan Schaaf, hydrolic engineer, formerly of the San Francisco Bay Model; Captain Larry Hall, U.S. Coast Guard in San Francisco; Edwin Cook, insurance agent; Joseph Smith, deputy regional director of the Western Regional Office of the BOP; James Brandenburg, parole officer in Kansas City; retired Special Agent John Connolly, Boston FBI; J.L. Burnam, lawyer; Keith E. Inman, senior criminalist with the California Department of Justice, DNA Laboratory and Norah Rudin, Ph.D. Forensic DNA consultant, both excellent teachers and authors of *Principles and Practice of Criminalisitics, The Profession of Forensic Science;* Richard Phillips, retired executive assistant to the warden at the U.S. Penitentiary at Marion, Illinois; Jackie Heuman, sculpture conservator, Tate Gallery, London, who was one of the first persons to analyze the dummy masks when they were returned to the San Francisco Maritime National Historical Park in 1980; Leslie Bone, ethnographic conservator at the M.H. DeYoung Museum, San Francisco, and Philip Linhaure, chief curator of art, Oakland Museum.

Associate Warden Arthur M. Dollison's memos of the 1962 Alcatraz investigation:
June 12, 1962 memo from Charles Herman to Captain Bradley
June 12, 1962 memo from T.D. Bradley to A.M. Dollison
June 12, 1962 memo from Acting Captain F.D. Mahan to T.D. Bradley. "Out
   line of Activities and Procedures"
June 12, 1962 incident report from Officer Fred Freeman to A.M. Dollison
June 13, 1962 incident report from Lieutenant R. K. Weir to Warden
June 13, 1962 memo from Officer Lawrence D. Bartlett to Captain
June 1962 memo from A.M. Dollison to Warden Blackwell
June 14, 1962 incident report from A.O. Severson to T.D. Bradley
June 14, 1962 incident report from A.O. Severson to T.D. Bradley

June 14, 1959 memo from William H. Long, Jr. to Captain
June 18, 1962 incident report from A.V. Young to T.D. Bradley
June 18, 1962 memo for record by Olin G. Blackwell
June 19, 1962 memo from A.M. Dollison to Warden
June 19, 1962 memo from A.M. Dollison to Warden
June 19, 1962 memo "Escape from Alcatraz," by Fred T. Wilkinson
June 20, 1960 memo from T.D. Bradley to A.M. Dollison
June 26, 1962 memo from A.M. Dollison to Warden
June 26, 1962 memo from Olin G. Blackwell to James V. Bennett

Superintendent of Industries and Associate Warden Dollison's records:
Handwritten notes on Alcatraz prisoners
Copies of Alcatraz industries memos
"Supervisory Training Course, February 3, 1961 through April 26, 1961,"
     U.S. Penitentiary, Alcatraz

Federal Bureau of Prisons FOIA/PA requests:
Clarence Anglin, John Anglin, Olin G. Blackwell, Correspondence between
the BOP and David Ward, Ph.D., Thomas D. Bradley, Jr., Arthur M. Dollison,
John D. Herring, Glenn May, Frank Lee Morris, Maurice Ordway, A.O.
Severson, Robert K. Weir, Allen Clayton West

State prison records:
Allen Clayton West (Florida)
Frank Lee Morris (Louisiana)

Military records:
Allen Clayton West

FBI records:
"John Anglin, Clarence Anglin and Frank Lee Morris Escape From Alcatraz,"
File Number 76-26295, Volumes 1–17

Golden Gate National Recreation Area interviews:
Walter Bertrand, Clarence Carnes, Arthur M. Dollison, Donald Eberle, Frank
Hatfield, Herbert Juelich, Victor Mills,

*National Archives and Records Administration, Pacific Region, San Bruno,
California:Record Group 129, Records of the Bureau of Prisons, Comprehensive case
files of Alcatraz inmates, ca. 1924–1988:*
Anthony Accardo, Henry Armstrong, Thomas Austin, William Banks, Rob-
ert Barrett, John Battle, Leon Beardon, Walter Bearden, Billy Boggs, Joe
Boyes, B.J. Brous, Charles Burbank, William Cagle, Sherman Calloway, Walter
Campbell, Al Capone, Frankie Carbo, Clarence Carnes, Aubrey Carter, Rob-
ert Case, Homer Clinton, Mickey Cohen, Frank Coppola, Ralph Cozzolino,
William Dalton, Harold Davis, Frank De Ford, Roy Drake, William Duncan,

George Embry, Manuel Fernandex, LeRoy Fuller, Theodore Green, George Gilbert, James Grove, Chester Hamilton, W.C. Hamilton, Oliver Hanson, Nathanial Harris, Oliver Henson, Bernand House, Choyce Jackson, William James, Billy Jarrett, Jr., James Jenkins, Ellsworth "Bumpy" Johnson, William Johnston, Curtis Jones, Doyle Jones, James Jones, Alvin "Ol' Creepy" Karpis (Karpovitz), Spiro Karabelas. Arthur Kent, Thomas Kent, Abraham Levine, David Linkenaugher, Peter Macey, John Malone, Daniel Dwayne Maness, Berl McDonald, Martin McNicholas, Anthony "Stringbean" Marcella, Charles Marcum, Carlton Mathew, Lincoln Molless, Walter Mollet, Thomas Moon, Antonio and Gregory Nunez, Charles Oliver, Angel Padillo, Harry Payne, Willian Payne, Charles Peterson, Edward Pravato, Carl Price, Clifford Redden, Walter Sawyer, Lonnie Semiean, Robert Spears, Ernest Tatum, Courtney Townsend Taylor, Bruce Teetzel, Freddie Thomas, Harlan Tibbs, Larry Trumblay, Charles Stegall, Walter Splitt, Carl Wacher, Felix Williams.

NARA, RG 129: Alcatraz administrative files; Records of the U.S. Penitentiary, Alcatraz Island, California:
Buildings and Grounds, Launch, Supplies and Equipment, General Administration; Captain's Reports to the BOP, December 1961–December 1962; Captain's Watch Log, July 1961–November 1962; Custodial Staff meeting notes, December 1961–December 1962; Financial Budget and Planning 1952–63, Morning and Evening Watch Lieutenant's files, 1962 Morris–Anglin escape photographs; 1962 Scott–Parker escape photographs

Books, newspapers, manuscripts, web sites and other records:
Adams, Susan H., M.A.,"Statement Analysis: What Do Suspects' Words Really Reveal?" *FBI Bulletin,* October, 1996
Barron's Guide to Law Schools, 12th Edition, 1996
Bennett, James V., *I Chose Prison,* New York, Knopf, 1970
Carnes, Clarence, unpublished mss. National Maritime Museum Library
Cohen, Mickey, *In My Own Words, As Told to John Peer Nugent,* Prestice-Hall, 1975
Dolby, Alcatraz Officer Cuthbert U., "Notes on Alcatraz," a compilation of famous inmates and escape attempts
Johnston, James A., *Alcatraz Island Prison And the Men Who Live There,* Charles Scribners Sons, 1949
Karpis, Alvin, and Livesey, Robert, *On The Rock, Twenty-five Years in Alcatraz.* 1980, L.B.S., Paperback edition, 1998
Lehr, Dick and O'Neill, Gerald, *Black Mass, The Irish Mob, the FBI and a Devil's Deal,* Public Affairs, Perseus Books Group, 2000
Lightsey, Ed, "Escape from Alcatraz: Did These South Georgia Boys Make It?" *Albany* Magazine, October-November 1999
Martini, John and Babyak, Jolene, "Historic Structure Report Addendum: The Alcatraz Cellhouse Numbering System," May 1999
Thompson, Edwin N., *The Rock: A History of Alcatraz Island 1847-1972, An Historical Resource Study,* May 1979

Thompson, Leon "Whitey," *Last Train to Alcatraz*, Winter Books, 1988, 1995
San Francisco Chronicle, articles from June 12 to 30
San Francisco Examiner, articles from June 12 to 30
San Francisco News-Call-Bulletin, articles from June 12 to 30
www.co-ops.nos.noaa.gov/data_res.html (Verified Historical Water Level; sta-
    tion 9414290, San Francisco, CA, Local Standard Time; beginning date
    19620611 to ending date 19620614, (adjusting forward one hour for
    Daylight Savings Time); also date 19371216 for the Roe and Cole at-
    tempt and 19621216 for the Scott–Parker attempt.)
www.tntwebcraft.com/ccso/hypothermia.htm

Collections reviewed:
National Maritime Museum 1962 artifact collection, including examination of
four handmade masks, one life jacket, a piece of raft, two paddles, fake vents
with wall sections intact, vacuum cleaner motor, assorted wire, eating utensil
handles, handmade and professional wrenches, drill bits, handmade penlight, handmade periscope.
FBI, San Francisco, display of 1962 artifacts, including the barber clipper and
the post card allegedly mailed from those claiming to be Clarence, John and
Frank
Alcatraz building and grounds, including cell vent openings, cell wall concrete,
utility corridors, top of the block, roof vent hoods, comparison of the route
with historic photographs.

Notes
Part 1   The Man

page 16-18, 42-45: West's criminal statistics were culled from his Florida and
Georgia state prison files, his army court-martial records and federal prison
files. Many of his own accounts of arrests and escapes, as well as official accounts, are contradictory. His Florida Classification and Admission Summary,
taken on March 7, 1969, listed twenty arrests. In nearly every prison he was
described as a "racial agitator."

page 10: Carnes was the library orderly on Alcatraz from at least 1958 until
July 1962.

page 14-15: Industries information was gleaned from a letter from my father
to me about the changes he made as well as the July 1959 *Foghorn*, issue
which stated, "net profit of the last ten months of $69,558.32 as compared to
the same period last year of $3,525.02."

page 37: Edwin Cook, retired insurance agent, interview on June 22, 2000

page 28: Hal Weston wrote a wonderful op-ed article appearing in the July

15, 1999 *San Francisco Examiner* about the lovely foghorns around the bay in those days. He wrote: "The most interesting foghorn is Alcatraz South, which sounds like an Andrew Lloyd Webber chord. You'll hear it as a C, but it's probably an A."

pages 25-27, 62: Alcatraz escape details from Officer Cuthbert U. Dolby's "Notes on Alcatraz"

page 30: Larry Kirkland, as far as I know, is the author of the phrase "like living in a cow's mouth."

page 31: Facts about the saltwater cell house plumbing system were gleaned from Thompson's *Historical Resource Study, May 1979*, who wrote, "January, 1911, Salt water and fresh water services pipes have been placed in the cell room[s]."

page 36: Blackwell was assigned associate warden of Alcatraz on March 22, 1959 and arrived in April.

page 39: According to the *Dothan (Alabama) Eagle,* January 23, 1958, "Armed robbery carries the death penalty as a maximum in Alabama."

page 41: West's May 1960 annual review listed six disciplinary reports, and his April 20, 1961 annual review listed three more for a total of nine reports in eighteen months.

page 45: The associate warden was chairman of the Work Programming Subcommittee at each monthly meeting. Strangely, when Blackwell was associate warden he held meetings down at the CMS's office near the island's powerhouse. When Dollison was AW, he appropriately chaired the meetings in his office in the prison's administration section.

page 48: Alcatraz was on lease from the U.S. Army, at least for one year, so federal administrators could not initially make alterations without the Army's approval, necessitating paperwork and long delays. Many of the electric fans no longer worked properly and were eventually dismantled. This one, atop "B" block, may have never been removed because it was heavy and would require taking maintenance men away from some other project.

page 48: According to the FBI, it was "general knowledge among the inmates that above the cell blocks there were about eight ventilator holes to the roof." Actually, the remains of eight vents can be seen in the library and above A, B and C blocks. One newer vent behind D block also exists.

page 49: Willard "Red" Winhoven, AZ 772, on Alcatraz from 1947 until 1959, had been out on federal parole in 1962 when he was quoted in the *San*

Francisco News-Call-Bulletin. Later, he was sentenced in California for murder and died in San Quentin. Both he and Carnes said he had been an inmate electrician working up on top of the block and had thought of escaping from there.

page 49: Tom Kent was the first to say that Morris moved to cell B-356. This was confirmed in Morris' Alcatraz file.

page 52: In a short, informal biography written in the Alcatraz *Foghorn,* it was stated that Bradley graduated from high school, however his high school record, military record and federal prison record all indicate that he did not. John Marshal Law School in Atlanta, Georgia was listed as an American Bar Association non-approved school in *Barron's Guide to Law Schools,* 1996 edition.

Part 2 - The Plan

page 57: Alcatraz has 336 cells in B and C blocks. However, it also has 42 D-block cells for a total number of 378 cells. Additionally, it has a number of ward and individual cells located in the hospital. From 1934 to about 1940, it also used other cells as punishment in A block as well as the three cells and possibly six other storage rooms as cells in the prison's basement (the old citadel basement), before the bars were dismantled and discarded. Nonetheless, it's capacity during the federal prison years remained at 336.

page 60: One of the most enduring myths about Alcatraz is that cons showered in warm water in order to keep them from conditioning themselves for swimming in the cold bay. The origin of this myth may date back to the nineteenth-century army accommodations in which officers, as well as prisoners, often took cold saltwater baths. From 1912 until 1960 cells had cold water faucets only. The showers in the basement were always hot or, depending on which position you were in line, at least, warm.

page 61: The 1949 Butterworth Memo to the BOP, cited in Part 1, stated that number one on Butterworth's priority list of improvements was to replace the "entire plumbing system in the cell blocks B and C." That suggestion was ignored.

page 69: According to Warden Blackwell, Gates said in his interview that John Anglin had told him that Morris "was a good helicopter pilot and would fly the entire group to . . . the California desert where they would hide for a few days . . . then . . . steal two or more large house trailers, pull them into a remote area in the desert and stay there for four or five months until all the 'heat' was off."

page 70: The Capone anecdote, "wop with the mop," has a little history. Wop, an offensive slang used earlier in the century to identify Italians, is thought to have come from Ellis Island immigration documents denoting "With Out Papers." James V. Bennett repeated the Alcatraz cons' slur of the Italian-American mobster in his book, but he couldn't bring himself to use the word "wop" so substituted the word "Italian," which of course made the anecdote pointless.

page 71: Theodore "Teddy" Green, AZ 1180, on Alcatraz from 1955 until 1963, died in February, 1998. His obituary in an *Associated Press* story stated that "he tried to escape 12 times" from Alcatraz, which was a stretch. He had been discovered once assembling potential escape tools with Larry Trumblay in 1957. Green and Trumblay had collected, among other items, a bar spreader, several wrenches, a hammer, two hand drills, a screwdriver, a pipe wrench, numerous drill bits, and an oil funnel. It's informative to point out that other cons over the years had also assembled numerous tools. Photographs in Warden Johnston's 1949 book actually showed two crude hand-made guns uncovered during his period. One famous photograph, date unknown but sometimes erroneously identified as one taken of tools found from the West–Morris–Anglin escape attempt, is anchored by a large heavy-duty bolt cutter, underwater goggles, handmade flotation devices or paddles and pieces of plastic and rubber.

page 78: In 1960, monthly budget meeting notes showed that Alcatraz was so short of officers and money that they considered delaying or canceling annual leaves which they knew would result in a "serious morale problem," as well as a "tremendous backlog" of purchase requests for the mechanical service. But by 1961, notes about excess salaries began to take on a new meaning, allowing the remodeling of facilities and of the purchase of furnishings. Yet staff shortfalls had not changed. Future historians would be aided simply by seeking information from monthly "Notes from the Office of the Captain," notes from budget meetings, the Lieutenant's Watch Log and notes from staff meetings in order to discover how poorly Alcatraz was funded, how seemingly inconsequential incidents like prisoner trials and transfers could affect the monthly finances and how adeptly administrators managed funds.

page 84: On eating utensil handles, please see note in Part 7.

Part 3 - Breaking Rock

page 105: Wings, Bull Durham and other roll-your-own cigarettes were dispensed on Alcatraz freely to keep bartering down. Additionally, other packaged cigarettes, like Camels, were passed out about twice a week.

page 104-105: Leon Thompson said that boxes departing the industries were stenciled USPAZ and he speculated that they could be stenciled twice, or the stenciling could be smeared, which might cue the dock workers to pry them open and pull out what contraband might be concealed.

page 112-113: Examination of the fake wall artifacts shows great ingenuity using found items. The fact that canvas art board had been ordered by Morris and the Anglins that fall indicated they had decided how to camouflage the walls even before beginning to drill holes.

Part 4 - April Fools

page 134-138: The institution-wide shakedown, occurring on April 11, may have been a precautionary move prior to the shutdown of the two tower.

page 139-140: No rubber cement–type glue was found among the items left behind, and it appears that the FBI did not test the glue on the life jackets or the remaining raft piece, although they described it up as a "rubber adhesive," a description that Benny Wood, latex chemist and the president of Advance Adhesive Technology, easily identified as a waterproof adhesive similar to superglue today. The FBI lab did determine that the glue used on the life jackets, as well as the remaining raft piece, was not the same as that used on the periscope, which was a white glue that can easily be observed today. At one point, West told agents that he used glue for the life jackets which he had obtained from the Alcatraz glove factory.

page 140-141: Glove shop and clothing shop employees numbered about 35–45 men, at least in 1960.

page 143-144: Given that Alcatraz had been transferred during the Great Depression, Warden Johnston had written, "Money was scarce, appropriations were hard to get at that time."

page 144: It's possible that the OIC allowed West on top of the block without an officer because he had no officers to spare, nor were there extra maintenance officers available.

pages 141, 151-153, 169-170: It's not clear if tests were conducted on the dummy masks by the FBI or later by the National Park Service. They have never been x-rayed to see if "rope" was used in one mask, as NPS conservator Jackie Heuman called it, or electrical wire as reported by the FBI (although some electrical wire can be observed in places where the surface has been disturbed). It's not clear if three of them were made of concrete, as West and the FBI reported, or plaster, as Jackie Heuman reported. The strange color underneath the hair lines could be the result of aging and resultant discoloration of the glues, or of ink or oil paints applied by one person and handed to another for proper placement of the hair. Those colors would also need to be tested.

page 150: Although West and several others claimed Angel Island was the escapees' ultimate destination, the statements could have been intended to mislead investigators. The trail, however, did lead to the Angel Island side of the island, despite the vacancy in the road tower on the opposite side.

page 150: West told the FBI that the Anglins had cemented up his wall after he had inadvertently cracked it during his excavation.

page 151: Lieutenant A.O. Severson, in his memo on June 13, 1962, had determined that many cell walls from the utility corridor side, including fourteen cells along the flats of B and C blocks were in a weakened conditioned, about what you would expect if the pipes were leaking and the salt water was corroding the concrete. Sixteen second-story cells were also weakened and only eight were deemed weak around the vents on the third tier. He theorized that at one time during the army years the vents had been larger and were made smaller, possibly using a poor grade of concrete. Further examination by Alcatraz historian and NPS Ranger John Martini and me did not confirm that in 1998. Severson also stated that there were obviously additional concrete pours in cells B-156, 154, 152, 150, 144, 140 and 138. Cells 152, 150, 140 and 138 were, of course, the cells of the Anglins, West and Morris. But, if Severson could recognize the additional concrete on June 13, why were they not discovered by officers before that?

Part 5 - Under Cover

page 159: Carnes thought there were eighty to eighty-five blankets hung; Officer Virgil Cullen said thirty to forty. Fred Freeman thought there might have been a half dozen to a dozen. B block east measured seventy-five feet by twenty-five feet wide. If each army blanket was about five feet wide, as Cullen estimated, that would amount to forty blankets. Although Carnes may have overestimated how many blankets were hung, his story of how they were hung remained the same after repeated interviews. We had numerous formal interviews, some taped, over an ten-year period. He was interviewed by National Park Service rangers, and wrote his own memoirs, which are located in the National Maritime Museum Library. Although he used different names in his written account, the story remained essentially the same.

page 167: West called them "tapins," as reported by the FBI. Blackwell and BOP Assistant Director Wilkinson used the word "tampions." Of these, tampions is the only word which exists and it is described as a plug or a cover on the muzzle of a cannon to keep out dust and moisture. That surely is not what West meant. But rivets are tapped into metal and West may have picked up the expression "tap-ins" from his work in the Savannah shipyards.

page 176-177: Stories vary as to when the tool clambered down from B block, whether West dropped it one day when he was on top of B block, as Calloway, AZ 1219, had claimed, or whether it had been dropped the night of the escape, as Leon Thompson, AZ 1465, has said on the Alcatraz Audio tour. Calloway worked in industries during weekdays and would not have heard it during the day, but he also worked around the cell house on weekends when West may have been on top of the block. Calloway was on furlough in the cell house one week beginning May 21 and may have heard it then. This noise may have also been confused over time, with noises that were heard the night of the escape. The scene, as described, is the only one which couldn't be verified as to its time and is included in this chapter at this time for dramatic effect.

page 180-181: According to Captain Bradley's memo, West had said in his first hasty interview that he had tried the barber clipper and the vacuum cleaner motor while drilling out of his cell. However, in his far more thorough interview with FBI agents, he clearly stated that both motors were used up top on the ceiling vent and not in the digging of their cells. He also stated that the morning an inmate was hit over the head in the kitchen was the moment when he was able to smuggle out the vacuum cleaner—an attack that other administrative reports date as the May 22 attack of Contreras, AZ 1444. For several years, the vacuum cleaner motor and the barber clipper appeared in one of the Alcatraz exit cells although its placement there seems to be historically inaccurate.

Part 6 - Countdown

page 189-190: With soap chips and ponytails of hair found near Clarence Anglin's toilet, it appears likely that he made this mask, and it was done in his last days on the island. The FBI described the mask's interior as a "bundle of white cotton rags."

page 193: It was noted on the back of an FBI photograph that the two wooden planks "may have been used when 'vulcanizing' the seams on the raft and 'Mae West' jacket." Agents turned in the raft piece and jacket to FBI labs but did not ask them to check if the glue had been heated, and they were not tested to ascertain that.

page 203: Captain Bradley's memo differed slightly from OIC Herman's in that he wrote that Herman did his 8:00 P.M. count and at that time the Anglin's asked about turning off the A block light.

page 207: In his FBI interview, West stated that Clarence Anglins had used the phrase "We can see the moon," as a signal. Carnes also said the phrase was a signal and undoubtedly got the information from West.

page 208: West had three interviews, a first brief interrogation with Dollison and Bradley, then two more in-depth interviews with the FBI. His last interview was by far the most chronological and detailed. In it he stated that John was the first out of his cell by about April 25, that Oink and Oscar were named by the Anglins; that "Oscar was given to Frank." Later West told cons in D block that he was the first one out of his cell, but sealed up the back because he wouldn't need to get out except the night of the escape. He also told cons that Frank was out of his cell by May 11.

page 217: The watch log was among the items not returned to NARA until March, 2000. Because of privacy issues, I was initially able to see only a copy, however NARA staff graciously allowed me to view the original log where the two pages were missing. You practically needed a microscope to see that the pages had been removed.

Part 7 - Discovery

page 223: Two different documents in FBI files show that two five-gallon cans of cement paint were discovered and broken open on June 13, each containing different items. In the one can, found on the top of B block, six eating utensil handles, six or seven metal pieces made into saw blades, the electric vacuum cleaner motor, a file, the penlight, an ice pick wrapped in tape and assorted electrical cords were uncovered. The other can, found in the A block painting area, contained seven utensil handles, nine pieces of metal ranging from two to twelve inches in length (similar to those in the cell vent framework), four pieces of heavy wire (similar to those in the cell vent grill), two pieces of miscellaneous metal and one 3/8 inch screw bolt. If accurate, that means thirteen eating utensil handles were found.

page 225: According to Eric Muller, an earth science instructor at the San Francisco Exploratorium, even four-and-a-half-inch-diameter pontoons on four sides could hold up three men weighing a combined four hundred fifty pounds, assuming that the glue was insoluble and the seals were airtight. The seals, however, would have been the weak link.

page 239: The U.S. Coast Guard has what is loosely known as the Fifty-fifty rule: "Fifty degrees, fifty minutes, fifty-fifty chance."

page 240: By July, 1962, it was publicly announced that Alcatraz would be closed.

page 247: Although "Bumpy" Johnson's *New York Times* obituary said he was sixty-two when he died, his BOP files cited his birthday as 1908, which would have made him sixty at his death.

page 249: In a 1997 telephone conversation with retired FBI Special Agent John Connolly, later indicted over the Bulger affair, Connolly recounted the Bulger–Carnes story.

Illustration Credits

Federal Bureau of Investigation: 40 (lower two), 113, 139, 147, 153, 165, 170, 171, 173, 181, 188, 190, 192, 213
Bureau of Prisons: 6, 18, 19, 28, 35, 37, 40 (top two), 41, 47, 50, 53, 65,
San Francisco Maritime National Historic Park: 126, 135, 148, (Fischetti Collection), 172 (FBI Collection), 186 (Fischetti Collection), 206 (Charles P. McKinnon Collection), 211 (FBI Collection), 212, 218, 220 McKinnon Collection)
National Archives and Records Center: 10, 44, 93, 97, 223, 231, 242, 249, 251, back cover
Phil Dollison Collection: 12, 64, 67, 77(top), 81, 110 (top), 141, 222,
Jolene Babyak: xi, 55, 59, 61, 198, 247, 249
Bill Long: 58, 66, 77 (lower), 101, 105, 110 (lower), 160
Fred Straley: 80, 109, 128, 132,
David Gehringer: iv, v, 203,
National Park Service Collection: 72, 73, 85
George De Vincenzi: 124, 191
Benny Batom: 230
Ira Bowden: Front cover
Don Bowden Collection: 70
John Brunner: 14
Corinne Dollison Edwards: 21
Jim Hudson: 162
United Press International: 29

Acknowledgments

ALLEN WEST WAS the first, but by no means the only, informant. Many others have shared their time and expertise. First among the long list is Anne Diestel, archivist, Federal Bureau of Prisons, who was instrumental in tracking files for my numerous Freedom of Information Act (FOIA) requests, in compiling the list of known Alcatraz dead, in sharing anecdotes, in nailing down facts, and for working to bring the Alcatraz records back to the National Archives.

Mike Rowbar, Freedom of Information Act/Privacy Act Section, BOP; John M. Kelso, chief, FOIA/PA, Federal Bureau of Investigation; Linda Kloss, FOIA/PA, FBI, and George Grotz, Special Agent, San Francisco FBI were all generous in responding to my requests.

Special thanks are also extended to Dan Nealand, director of archival operations, Claude Hopkins, archives technician, Rose Mary Kennedy, archive technician and reference coordinator, Kathy O'Connor, archivist, and especially Lisa Miller, senior archivist, and Joseph Sanchez, archive technician, all with the National Archives and Records Administration, in San Bruno, California, who screened and retrieved files so that I could study them.

Judith M. Hitzeman, supervisory museum specialist; Mary Gentry, Leigh Newcomb, and Karen Sherwood, of the San Francisco Maritime National Historical Park, where many of the artifacts are housed; and Susan Ewing Haley, park archivist of the Golden Gate National Recreation Area Park Archives and Army Records Center, which houses early interview materials, were always gracious and allowed me considerable access.

Jackie Heuman, sculpture conservator, Tate Gallery, London; Leslie Bone, ethnographic conservator, M.H. DeYoung Museum, San Francisco, California, as well as Philip Linhaure, chief curator of art, Oakland Museum, also were helpful in understanding the artistry involved in the making of the masks.

Since West never saw the work being done on the ceiling vent and used slang words rather than proper names, I had the additional help of Paul Eames and his sister, Barbara Eames Gapoff, who jointly operate Ellis Ace Hardware (the *best* hardware store in Oakland, California) to identify photographs of tools, wire gauges, and the sizes and composition of nuts and bolts.

Others, who were an enormous aid in understanding the ventilation system at Alcatraz, include Ira Bowden, general foreman on Alcatraz from 1958 to 1960; Clifford Fish, an officer and welder on Alcatraz from 1938 until 1962; and Ray Katsanes, maintenance worker, National Park Service, Alcatraz, who helped compare current structures with old photographs. Truly, I could not have understood the progress of this escape attempt without these men.

Pat Bergan Rothschild, the Alcatraz Alumni Association historian, deserves mention for her continuous aid and support for my projects.

A number of Alcatraz officers, or their wives, provided me with never-before-published photographs, among them Ira Bowden who provided the stunning night shot of Alcatraz on the cover taken when he lived there and courtesy of his son, Don Bowden, who along with his wife, Catherine, have always been enormously generous with their knowledge, photos, warmth and good humor. George DeVincenzi, Alcatraz officer from 1950 until 1957, and Bill Long, officer on Alcatraz from 1954 until 1963 both took beautiful shots of Alcatraz. Jim Hudson, an officer on Alcatraz from 1951 to 1955 provided a shot of himself in the kitchen cage. Virginia Straley, provided numerous color slides that her husband, Fred Straley, general foreman, Alcatraz, 1960–63, took in 1962; John Brunner, a resident on Alcatraz from 1950 to 1963 has always been generous with his photographs in my numerous projects. Benny Batom, NPS ranger, drew the map. Evelyn E. Dollison, my mother, Philip F. Dollison, my brother and Corinne Dollison Edwards have always been generous with their photo collections and to whom I owe a lot. Mike West of Image Communications Professionals answered my every call for copies, and Chuck Stucker who has an amazing collection from the 1930s and '40s was also helpful. Jim Albright, Irene Stachura, and Bill Kooinan were also generous with their time and expertise.

National Park Alcatraz Supervisory Park Ranger Craig Glassner deserves mention for quickly alerting me to the seventeen volumes of FBI material on their web page. Joel GAZis-SAxe, an internet author of one of the better Alcatraz sites, deserves a high five for his help in retrieving files.

I'm grateful for the permission from the Hal Leonard Corporation to quote from Jailhouse Rock, words and music by Jerry Leiber and Mike Stoller ©1957 (Renewed) Jerry Leiber Music and Mike Stoller Music. All right reserved.

Other important supporters are National Park Rangers Lori Brosnan, Libby Schaaf, John Cantwell, Benny Batom, Jim McDonald, Brett Carré, Mark and Mike Combs, Roger Goldberg and Nancy Goodman, as well Edith Modie, Donna Middlemist, Stan Cordes and Joe Weber of the volunteer staff. Chris Powell, NPS Public Information Officer, has broadened my media horizons. Also, the Golden Gate National Park Association Evening Tours staff including Kate Kennelly, manager; Sonja Williams, assistant manager; John Moran, Jim Nelson, Curtis Greenhaw, Yesenia Nyland, Dan Cooke, James Sword and Mary McClure. Rangers Dan Unger and Jayeson Vance have also been supporters.

Golden Gate National Park Association staff who have always been supportive are Porsche Westfall, Edwin Sera, Summer Isabel, John Jamison, Robert Blackiston, Jorg Jorgensen, Louise Bradley from the Antenna Audio staff, Dinilo Prado, Vic Balauat, and Imelda Chen and Celeste Ferris, and especially Eddie Krause, Mr. Shaggie himself, my detail and chocolate guru.

Most important for their humor, warmth and good nature are Stan Zbikowski, retail manager; Chris Warren, assistant manager, merchandizing; Milagros (LaLa) Macapagal, assistant manager of operations; as well as Maggie Rosario, Alvin Rebaja, Angelita Cecilio, Lourdes (LuLu) Antonio, Mark Brown, Lizeth Espinoza and Grace Viray, all of whom have sold my ideas and supported me in times of reckoning.

A number of people have helped my career and deserve special mention, among them, Michael Hoff, Sarah Kass and Lydia Rheinfrank of the Michael Hoff Film Productions, who have, by their numerous television videos often appearing on the Discovery Channel have raised the bar of accurate knowledge about Alcatraz. Not only have they called upon me for information, but they have always shared their knowledge and expertise, some of which aided me in the telling of this story.

I would also like to acknowledge Glenn Allison, David Mana, Ann Meagher, Helen Adler and Diana Lambert for their dear friendship and generous support all these years.

George Mattingly carefully and artfully designed the cover, while David Bullen provided consultation. Alice B. Acheson was an enormous help in marketing decisions and generously supplied important names and address. I would never hesitate to recommend her classes to those wishing to write and market a book. Laurie Harper, agent provocateur, has always been a close source of information and advice, and Taz Tally, whose expertise in preflight helped me get off the ground,

Moreover, I wish to thank those whose help in the conception, writing and editing of the book were enormous—namely, Nicki Phelps, who seldom failed to listen and respond to all my thoughts and kept me laughing; Susan Tasaki, whose thoughtful comments highlighted and deepened my understanding; Jay Wurts, a genius, whose developmental suggestions turned the book around; John Martini who is an especially knowledgable, thoughtful Alcatraz historian and who keeps my memory synapsis sharpened just to keep up with him; and Katherine J. Hoggard, my dearest and longest friend, who consistently brought me out of the throes of chaos by suggesting yet another book title, which forced me to think in new ways, and to whom I credit with some of the brighter insights in this story. Roxane Buck-Eczcurra gently corrected all of my typos and made me see the error of my ways.

And, finally, both my father, Arthur M. Dollison, who had the foresight to retain copies of his notes and documents and who endured endless hours of impertinent questions about his conduct and activities, and Tess Eisley, collaborator, editor and conscientious objector who has the right touch in all matters personal, are my heroes. Of course, Madames and Messieurs R., C., C., and the two Mr. B's were a constant source of diversion, which is always a welcome respite for an author in prison.

❧❧❧❧

Index

photos in italics.

Order these Jolene Babyak books through your bookstores or by calling 1-800-597-9550 (10 A.M. to 8 P.M. Pacific Standard Time)

Eyewitness on Alcatraz
Life on The Rock as told by the Guards, Families & Prisoners

– 128 pages; 76 photographs –

A lively, anecdotal history of Alcatraz, including life among the families, famous prisoners and escape attempts, as told by someone who lived there.
$12.95   **OUT OF PRINT**

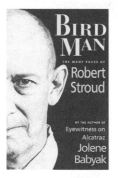

Birdman, The Many Faces of Robert Stroud

- 328 pages; 24 photographs -

A psychological profile of a sociopathic personality once portrayed by actor Burt Lancaster. Gritty, fast paced, well-written, with never-before-published prison reports and Stroud's own writings, with quotes from prisoners, officers, psychologists and avian pathologists, *Birdman* explodes the myths surrounding Robert Stroud.
$13.95

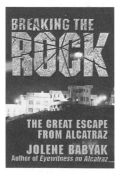

Breaking the Rock: The Great Escape from Alcatraz

-288 pages, 96 photographs -

After months of digging with common tools, four men placed dummy masks in their beds in June 1962 and broke "the Rock." Jolene Babyak reveals in her fast-paced, ground-breaking book how they did it, who aided them, and how it caused the infamous prison to close nine months later.
$14.95